T0295577

Things Worth
Keeping

Things Worth Keeping

The Value of Attachment in a Disposable World

Christine Harold

UNIVERSITY OF MINNESOTA PRESS
MINNEAPOLIS
LONDON

The University of Minnesota Press gratefully acknowledges the generous assistance provided for the publication of this book by the Margaret S. Harding Memorial Endowment, honoring the first director of the University of Minnesota Press.

Portions of chapter 2 were originally published as "On Target: Aura, Affect, and the Rhetoric of 'Design Democracy,'" *Public Culture* 21, no. 3 (2009): 599–618.

Published by the University of Minnesota Press
111 Third Avenue South, Suite 290
Minneapolis, MN 55401-2520
http://www.upress.umn.edu

LIBRARY OF CONGRESS CATALOGING-IN-PUBLICATION DATA
Harold, Christine, author.
Things worth keeping : the value of attachment in a disposable world / Christine Harold.
Description: Minneapolis : University of Minnesota Press, [2020] | Includes bibliographical references and index.
Identifiers: LCCN 2019053569 (print) | ISBN 978-0-8166-7723-8 (hc) | ISBN 978-0-8166-7724-5 (pb)
Subjects: LCSH: Attachment behavior. | Consumption (Economics) | Waste (Economics)
Classification: LCC BF575.A86 H37 2020 (print) | DDC 306.3—dc23
LC record available at https://lccn.loc.gov/2019053569

For Lainie, Josephine, and Liam
Loves of my life

Contents

Acknowledgments

Buddhists have a practice known as "sharing the merit," which provides an opportunity to pause and acknowledge all the teachers, friends, and fellow travelers who have contributed to the cultivation of one's own wisdom. Sharing the merit also affords one the chance to recognize past mistakes, to take stock of one's present place on the path, and to offer whatever fruits have been harvested thus far for the benefit and well-being of all. This is not a book that claims to have figured out, once and for all, a solution to the challenging issues it addresses. But as an offering to the larger conversation about possible steps forward, I hope it is of some value. To the degree that it is, I share that merit with the many teachers, friends, and fellow travelers who have helped me along the way. Because writing this book was a slow process for me, I have undoubtedly overlooked some names, which I regret. Any oversights or errors in its content are wholly my own.

My sincerest thanks to the hundreds of students at University of Georgia and University of Washington with whom I thought through some of the ideas expressed in these pages. A deep thank-you to my teachers and friends at Willamette University and Penn State for enlivening in me a love for the study of rhetoric and the scholarly life. Thank you to my colleagues at University of Washington for providing me a cherished intellectual home for the past decade. In particular, thank you to Leah Ceccarelli, LeiLani Nishime, and Ralina Joseph, who gave insightful feedback on various iterations of these chapters. UW's Royalty Research Fund provided much-needed financial resources. UW's Whiteley Center, a beautiful retreat space on San Juan Island, provided a quiet place to work and the company of the local deer as I finished the book. David Domke and the communication department at UW offered additional research support, for which I'm grateful.

Many graduate students have provided valuable assistance, including Lisa Slawter, Brian Cozen, Elodie Fichet, Sam Woolley, Luyue Ma, K. C. Lynch, and Josh Losoya. Thank you to Dominic Muren for conversations that inspired me greatly during the early stages of this project. Thank you to artists Andy Singer, Jeff Carter, Bethan Laura Wood, and Hyerim Shin, who all graciously permitted me to use their work, and to the Duke University Press, which permitted me to include portions of an article I wrote on Target published in *Public Culture*. Thank you to Kevin DeLuca, Scott Palmer, and Maria Klots for their enduring friendship. Thank you to Jason Weidemann, editorial director at the University of Minnesota Press, who has seen me through two books now, always with kindness, patience, and rigor.

Finally, and above all, thank you to Ken Rufo. He encouraged me when I was ready to chuck the whole thing. He helped untangle the stickiest knots in my argument. He showed me new conceptual lenses that brought things into focus. My whole-hearted gratitude to Ken for these and so many other things.

This book is dedicated to my children, Lainie, Josephine, and Liam. A person couldn't ask for better fellow travelers on the path.

Turning toward Things

Accumulation, Attachment, and Agency

The route to lower impact does not require putting on a hair shirt. Nor does it entail making consumption less important. . . . We don't need to be less materialist, as the standard formulation would have it, but more so. For it is only when we take the materiality of the world seriously that we can appreciate and preserve the resources on which spending depends.

—Juliet B. Schor, Plentitude: The New Economics of True Wealth

A young Japanese organizing consultant seems an unlikely avatar for our current cultural moment. Nevertheless, Marie Kondo has achieved global decluttering superstardom, ridiculous as such a label may sound to those who haven't heard of her. That population is rapidly dwindling after the launch of her wildly popular Netflix series, *Tidying Up with Marie Kondo* (2019–).[1] Kondo has inspired countless headlines, analytical think pieces, and millions of posts and pictures shared on social media as disciples follow her trademarked KonMari Method to clean out their closets, garages, and bookcases, shedding the unused and unloved objects cluttering their homes.

Kondo's celebrity bona fides were on full display when she walked the red carpet at the 2019 Oscars, generating nearly as much buzz as the nominees as she obliged Hollywood A-listers seeking selfies with her. That week she even cracked the top ten in a global TV Personalities ranking based on analytics from Facebook, Instagram, Twitter, You-Tube, and Google Plus.[2] As celebrated as Kondo is in the West, she is more so in her home country: "She's so famous in Japan that she can no more ride the Tokyo subway than Beyoncé could."[3] It all started with Kondo's book, *The Life-Changing Magic of Tidying Up: The Japanese Art of Decluttering and Organizing* (2014), which to date has sold more than eight million copies in over thirty countries and was on the *New York Times* bestseller list over three years. Kondo has struck a resounding chord in the cultural zeitgeist. She is at the center a global tidying frenzy as people search for a more meaningful relationship to their stuff.

Kondo's popularity has much to teach us about the present state of consumer capitalism. What is it about her eccentric approach to ti-dying one's home that has so captured the imagination of consumers, two decades into the twenty-first century? Netflix's decision to drop all eight episodes of *Tidying Up* on New Year's Day, just in time for reso-lution season, offers a clue. "Americans woke up on New Year's Day, bloated in body and soul," writes one *Washington Post* commentator, "and stumbled out of bed to survey their overstuffed post-holiday homes."[4] To our consumption disorder, a collective hangover that people seem desperate to remedy—KonMari offers a bracing antidote to such overindulgence, inviting people to consider that maybe, just maybe, they don't need All. That. Stuff.

Perhaps the answer to "why Kondo now?" is because after decades of bingeing, of stuffing ourselves to excess with all the goodies and doodads that industrial capitalism can supply, Kondo offers a gentle, aesthetically pleasing, even charming way to purge. She prescribes a method for letting go—a purification ritual of sorts, a regimen of ti-dying as self-care. Kondo "has combined letting us throw stuff out with the very appealing idea of living a more simplistic life," says Carl Cederström, a Swedish scholar who studies the wellness and self-help industries. "She has arrived during a time when life can feel overbearing. People want a simpler, cleaner life—a detox. . . . Kondo gives us a moral license to throw things away without guilt."[5]

I will explore Kondo's method for curating our possessions in depth in the following chapter. In short, she invites us to hold each object in our hands and ask ourselves the question, "Does it spark joy?" This deceptively simple formula contains within it an implicit confession: despite the best efforts of generations of advertisers, product designers, and increasingly sophisticated algorithms intended to persuade us otherwise, our emotional return on investment, consumerism's ability to satisfy people's quest for happiness, has failed to deliver. Despite the bingeing, despite the decades of promiscuous consumption, consumer capitalism's promise of "better living through buying" seems to be saturated by false starts and failed efforts.

It's not for lack of trying. We tried. We updated our phones every eleven months. We converted sneakers into a luxury good. We pursued lamps that were inexpensive facsimiles of the high-end styles featured in some shelter magazine or design blog or influencer's Instagram post. We took these coveted objects home in convenient layers of cardboard, polymers, and supposedly disposable plastics. We built hills, then mountains, then entire floating continents of debris amassed through our efforts to satiate that hunger to belong and connect, to make a home in this world, with clothes, gadgets, and decor that expressed ourselves, one credit card swipe at a time.

Although the central thesis of the KonMari Method is about the importance of tuning into things that delight us, the emphasis is palpably more on letting go of things that don't. This emphasis on disposal is demonstrated in her books and every episode of her show; Kondo's pupils assemble mountains of trash bags filled with unwanted stuff as evidence of their self-discipline. This purge is repeated on Instagram and Twitter feeds (#konmari, #kondo, #tidyingup, #sparkjoy) across the globe as followers document piles of clothes and other discarded objects—piles that act as badges of honor as they clear their clutter. Although after decades of bingeing the purge was inevitable, I cannot help but wonder where all those piles ultimately end up after they have been deemed unworthy of lasting commitment.

Waste More, Want More

Today's consumer culture has been propelled by our ability to produce and acquire objects more quickly and cheaply than ever before, as well as by a seemingly insatiable desire for more. All economies, capitalist or otherwise, produce waste. But perhaps no system has become so adept at hiding the magnitude of its waste generation as our contemporary mode of global capitalism. In the industrialized West, waste disappears into landfills, a world physically and cognitively apart from the hustle and bustle of urban life, and usually far removed from suburbia. It gets shipped out on barges, transported to lesser developed regions for processing, or dumped into an ocean to float miles and miles away from crowded human shores.

This may be about to change. At the close of 2017, China announced it would refuse imports of most forms of foreign waste. Its own growing middle class is now discarding quite enough to keep its factories stocked with adequate supplies of plastics, textiles, and mixed paper. Although the impacts of the ban are only beginning to emerge, they are predicted to be huge because many industrialized countries have relied on exporting their waste to developing regions without creating the necessary infrastructure to deal with it. In 2016, Chinese manufacturers imported "7.3m metric tonnes of waste plastics from developed countries including the U.K., the E.U., the U.S. and Japan."[6] Without China to process Western waste, where will it all go?

"Waste" is really just a pejorative term for excess, and excess is something capitalism generates in abundance. Georges Bataille dubs it "the accursed share," a remainder to be addressed, managed, and processed through cultural rituals—a phenomenon I will discuss in the following chapter by way of an examination of hoarding narratives and a deeper exploration of the KonMari Method. Climate change may generate headlines, but the inconceivable amount of consumer waste generated daily is a driver of the environmental crisis we now find ourselves in. Perhaps this is because until now, the industrialized world has so shrewdly outsourced its waste management to developing countries, so the problem has remained in the shadows of our awareness, out of sight and out of mind. In the decades to come, however, the limits of our ability to handle the waste products of consumer culture will be increasingly harder to ignore. A study by the World Bank projects a 70 percent global increase in urban solid waste, "from 1.3 billion tonnes per year [in 2012] to 2.2 billion tonnes per year by 2025."[7] And we likely won't reach peak garbage until about 2100. Until then, the volumes are expected to escalate daily.

Daniel Hoornweg, one of the researchers who authored the World Bank report, says he is less concerned about the environmental impacts of solid waste than he is about the larger consumer lifestyle it represents—the number of new products we regularly buy and the resources spent and the pollution created by their manufacture and distribution. "It shows how much of an impact we're having globally, as a species, on the planet as a whole," he observes.[8] As a symptom of a larger global malady, consumer waste is certainly among the most striking. That said, waste is undeniably a devastating environmental harm in its own right. One obvious cause for alarm is that we humans largely aren't dealing with all this waste properly. Much of the world's waste doesn't make it to a recycling facility at all. A "whopping percent" of plastic, for example, isn't recycled—a fact that Great Britain's Royal Statistical Society cited as its 2018 Statistic of the Year.[9] Much of this debris ends up in the world's oceans. You are likely familiar with the so-called Great Pacific Garbage Patch, a giant mass of plastic waste discovered in the 1990s floating in the North Pacific. Although difficult to measure, scientists estimate it spans nearly a million square miles, three times the size of France.[10] In summer 2017, it was confirmed that another patch, approximately one and a half times the size of Texas, is floating in a remote area of the South Pacific.

In 2015, a team of researchers set out to quantify for the first time how much plastic has been produced globally and where it is now. (Plastic takes more than four hundred years to disintegrate.) The researchers were shocked by what their analysis revealed: "Of the 8.3 billion metric tons that has been produced, 6.3 billion metric tons has become plastic waste. Of that, only nine percent has been recycled. The vast majority—79 percent—is accumulating in landfills or sloughing off in the natural environment as litter. Meaning: at some point, much of it ends up in the oceans, the final sink."[11] These garbage patches are like tumors spreading across the Pacific, plastic dead zones increasingly inhospitable to marine life. A 2016 report from the World Economic Forum predicts that by 2050, there will be more plastic in the ocean, pound for pound, than fish.[12]

Sense and Sensibility: Raising Consciousness

The central rhetorical move performed by those hoping to mobilize people to address the environmental impacts of consumer culture has been to raise awareness—to urge us to foster an environmental consciousness, to see the error of our greedy, wasteful ways, to course correct before it's too late. Since 1970, for example, the world has celebrated Earth Day on April 22. Earth Day was inspired in part by the first photographic image of Earth, an image now known as "Earthrise," which was taken by Apollo 8 astronauts as they entered the moon's orbit on Christmas Eve 1968. The big blue marble floats, vulnerable and alone, driving home the reality that we're all in this together, and that at least for the foreseeable future, this is the only home we've got. As command module pilot Jim Lovell notes in a live broadcast, "The vast loneliness is awe-inspiring and it makes you realize just what you have back there on Earth."[13] Earth Day activities include demonstrations, educational programs, and major global initiatives. The recycling campaigns of Earth Day 1990 contributed to huge increases in recycling efforts, for example, and Earth Day 2016 was the day 174 countries and the European Union signed the United Nations' Paris Agreement to reduce carbon emissions.[14] For all the successes we've seen in educating the larger public about the dangers of climate change, deforestation, pollution, and overpopulation, when it comes to our consumption practices—arguably the most significant contributor to the problem of waste—mere consciousness raising feels terribly inadequate.

Part of the reason for this is that we in the West have become so damned good at rendering our waste invisible, or at least artfully contained, an issue I'll take up in chapter 1. But I suggest that a more powerful reason that the effort to mitigate consumer waste remains such a conundrum is the nature of what it's up against: the interconnected industries whose sole raison d'être is to sell us more things. The design industry creates countless objects that seduce the eye and excite the senses. The advertising industry delights us with fantasy worlds that we are invited to inhabit, or it threatens us with nightmares to be avoided; the price of entry or security is our acquisition of this or that product. Social media influencers and their corporate sponsors ensure that brands are constantly streaming through our various feeds, creating the sense that everybody is using, wearing, or watching them—and so should we. The sheer magnitude of commercial images and messages that the average American is exposed to is widely documented and widely varying—anywhere between 2,000 and 10,000 ad and brand exposures a day, depending on whom you ask. The nature of these images and stories is largely emotional; they play on our fears and capitalize on our desires. They comfort, soothe, tantalize, and stimulate. In such a world, conspicuous consumption is built in part on inconspicuous waste.

In the face of the wily seductions and titillations produced by those tasked with getting us to buy stuff, a sober, reasoned call to consciousness is a tough sell. Most consciousness-raising campaigns use the cold-shower approach, which is based on the assumption that if we only knew the facts about the issue at hand, we would wake up and, with clear eyes, change our behavior accordingly. But this is a problematic assumption. As Peter Sloterdijk observes, we may know perfectly well, for example, that our consumption practices are not sustainable, yet we keep consuming anyway.[15] We know, but perhaps we don't care—at least not enough.

Many visual artists are attempting to change that. Vik Muñiz, for example, an artist based in Brooklyn, returned to his native Brazil to develop an art project featuring local waste pickers, known as *catadores*, who collect valuable recyclables in the world's largest garbage dump, which is located outside Rio de Janeiro. As documented in Lucy Walker's 2010 Oscar-nominated film about the project, *Waste Land*, Muñiz took photographs of the *catadores* and then collaborated with them to create large-scale collages of the portraits on the floor of a nearby warehouse, using the recyclable materials they collected as their medium. The resulting photographs of the trash portraits were sold at auction, garnering over $250,000, all of which Muñiz gave to the *catadores'* co-op, along with the prize monies *Waste Land* earned at multiple film festivals.

An exchange in the film captures well Muñiz's mission of inviting people to see both trash and those who work with it in a new way. Speaking to the group of *catadores* who will become his subjects and collaborators, Muñiz describes the tendency of museumgoers to lean in and out, moving closer and farther from a work of art, modifying their gaze as they take it in. "Have you seen this? Everyone does it. . . . They go like this, and then they go back, then maybe take a little step back, and then they see the image. Imagine it's a beautiful landscape with a lake and a man fishing. They look and they see the man fishing, and then they lean and everything vanishes and becomes paint. They see the material. They move away and see the image. Then they get closer and see the material. They move away and they see the idea. They get closer and see just the *material*." One of the *catadores* laughs, responding, "I bet you get people staying longer at your exhibits than anyone does. They will spend so much time looking at the image, because then they will see the leather, the piano, they will look at everything. They will spend hours looking at the same picture." Muñiz agrees: "The moment when one thing turns into another is the most beautiful moment . . . a combination of sound transforms into music . . . and that applies to everything. That moment is really magical."[16] The transformative moment that Muñiz describes, a moment when our perspective shifts ever so slightly, allows us to see the material world in a different way; in this case, we can see the interconnectedness between garbage and the people whom society often treats as garbage. This transformation of perspective is key if we are to find and cultivate new ways of knowing and new ways of making meaning.

Seattle-based artist Chris Jordan's work is another attempt to shift our collective perspective about consumer practices. Jordan made a name for himself making art out of the data indicators of consumer waste. His series of photomontages, *Running the Numbers: An American Self-Portrait*, is intended to impress upon viewers the sheer scale of our waste production—a difficult task given the fact that so many of us have no sense of how much waste we produce, let alone where it goes. For this series, Jordan assembles smaller photographs of everyday objects such as plastic bottles, Barbie dolls, telephones, cigarette butts, and aluminum cans, which he then multiplies and compiles into larger composite prints to quantify graphically, even beautifully, the otherwise dry statistics of terrible realities.

For Jordan, the problem with much environmentalist rhetoric is that it doesn't adequately move the collective will. "There is a broken aspect to the world of activism and environmentalism," he explains. "The typical approach of activists is to say 'Here is the problem and here is the solution.' Then they say, 'You should all go do the solution,' with their fingers wagging." The tendency of environmentalists to repeatedly barrage people with statistics in the hopes they may change their behavior misses the point, says Jordan:

> We can't make meaning out of these enormous statistics. And so that's what I'm trying to do with my work, is to take these numbers, these statistics from the raw language of data and to translate them into a more universal visual language that can be felt. Because my belief is that if we can feel these issues, if we can feel these things more deeply then they'll matter to us more than they do now." [Only then can we answer the question,] "How do we change?"[17]

Zooming in on waste. Chris Jordan, *Cell Phones*, from *Running the Numbers: An American Self-Portrait*, 2007. Copyright Chris Jordan.

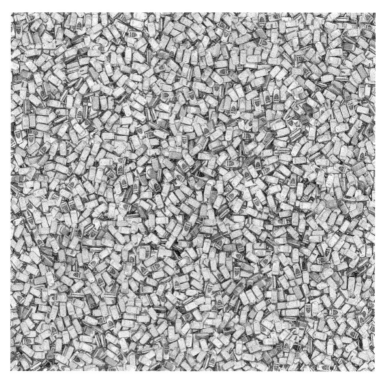

Detail of *Cell Phones.* Copyright Chris Jordan.

If *Running the Numbers* is about learning to see the sheer scale of environmental waste differently, Jordan's 2017 project, *Albatross*, is an intimate and repugnant close-up of the devastation wrought by human consumption. Over a number of years, Jordan and a film crew visited Midway Island in a remote part of the Pacific, nearly 2,000 miles from any continent, and roughly halfway between North America and Asia. The beaches of the island are awash in debris from the Great Pacific Garbage Patch—a reported twenty tons a year. It is also home to nearly 1.5 million Laysan albatross (*Phoebastria immutabilis*), who are dying in huge numbers from ingesting the waste. Nearly a third of albatross chicks die before reaching maturity. Jordan's heartbreaking images focus on the starved corpses of these once beautiful birds, their bellies full of cigarette lighters, bottle caps, and drinking straws.

The literary symbolism of the albatross isn't lost on Jordan, who opens his documentary with a quote from Coleridge's "Rime of the Ancient Mariner." In the poem, after bearing the burden of the dead albatross around his neck as punishment, the mariner discovers a love for all creatures, even the "slimy things" of the sea that previously revolted him. As for Coleridge, it is love and a sense of compassion that brings Jordan to a deeper sense of the connectedness of all things: "I had the experience of falling deeply in love with the sentience and brilliance of the albatross," he says.[18]

Sadly, although certainly a step in the right direction, kindling compassion for all the creatures of the earth is likely insufficient. In a world where waste exists at a level beyond the scale of human comprehension, the connection between the immediate enjoyment that comes from any individual act of acquisition and the consequences of the collective aggregation of waste can feel thin, even nonexistent. Awareness of the macro doesn't necessarily imply an intensity of conviction at the level of the micro.

As Jordan's work attests, we humans are bad at making personal meaning out of abstract statistics. Scientific evidence documenting environmental degradation, such as that offered by Al Gore in his Inconvenient Truth films, is crucial to our understanding of the

Image from Chris Jordan's film *Albatross* (2017), depicting the plastic-filled bodies of Laysan albatross. Copyright Chris Jordan.

problems we face. We cannot change what we do not measure. Yet as a basis for moving our collective will, facts alone are often inadequate. To be moved, we must care. We must feel the visceral, intimate connections between ourselves and the world around us. As I will argue in this book, an important but often overlooked piece of the "environment versus consumer culture" puzzle is that we need to care not just about the oceans, albatross, forests, and factory workers, but also about the vast network of human-made objects that share our world. Jordan, in his shift from visualizing data to visualizing waste, tends to focus on the object at one stage of its life cycle—the terminal stage of disposal. Although his work will undoubtedly move many by revealing what happens to a device that was once an integral part of daily activity, it does less to demonstrate why this new device was coveted enough to justify discarding the old. One art critic, commenting on

Jordan's work, notes, "Although Warhol's soup cans confronted us with the 'on the shelf' stage of our obsession with consumption, that confrontation camouflaged the final stage of products, the disposal stage documented so vividly by Chris Jordan."[19] Jordan's insistence on the motivating power of emotion is a crucial step in the right direction. However, this focus alone—exposing the devastating end result of the commodity fetishism that so fascinated Warhol—may be too narrow. Although it steers our attention from one stage in the life cycle of an object to another, what we need is to open up the object in all its complexity, which may call for a broader perspective still.

The work of artists such as Muñiz and Jordan offer important provocations, disruptive chinks in the gleaming veneer of consumer culture, alerting viewers to the human and environmental realities our practices beget. As Magna de França Santos, one of the *catadores* featured in *Waste Land*, puts it, "It's easy for you to be sitting there at home in front of the television consuming whatever you want and tossing everything in the trash and leaving it out on the street for the garbage truck to take it away, but where does that garbage go?"[20] As crucial as it is to consider what happens after we throw things away, I will argue throughout this book that if we are to open up new paths and possibilities, new forms of agency in relation to the material world we have constructed, then we need to imagine and amplify the myriad of moments in the lives of objects—inception, production, use, disposal, and all points in between. These moments each offer opportunities for new connections, new configurations, and perhaps new choices.

Toward an Opening Up of Objects

Objects do not merely exist as something we either use or discard. Like us, objects have their own life cycle—extraction, design, production, initial consumption and point of purchase, continued consumption or use, discarding or repurposing, and eventually disposal. For those of us who engage these objects as consumers, rather than as designers or developers or recyclers or disposal operators, most of this life cycle is obscured through an almost willful blindness. We know objects come from somewhere; we know they don't disappear when we toss them into a nearby trash bin. But we often don't need to think about these stages or care about them, unless we are motivated to become sufficiently aware, or more fundamentally if the object itself prompts us to value those other stages of the cycle, be they antecedent to the moment of acquisition or subsequent to it.

Indeed, when it comes to addressing the problems of consumption, our current approach looks to marshal the powers of the human subject to restrain the excesses of the object. This is what awareness and consciousness raising purport to accomplish, after all; apply enough independent cognitive processing, toss in informed analysis, understand the full range of opportunity costs, and the individual will draw conclusions that favor modifying behavior. The individual subject in this model is powerful and active—at least potentially so. But we know from decades of academic research and philosophical meditations on the question of subjectivity that human beings are certainly not autonomous, and rarely ever sovereign. The term "subject," after all, comes from the Latin *subjectus*, "to place something under." Today messages run over and through us from new and noisy channels; objects pile up and define the basic boundaries of our lives, including devices we use to connect with each other, fast fashions, plastic widgets, and the constantly upgraded miracles of science that listen, speak, buzz, slice, and dice. But as etymology tells us, "subject" also means "to expose to," which reminds us we are also open and exposed—that is, inextricably and intimately connected—to the material world we are a part of. In that connection lies the possibility for a positive affective shift in how we relate to the world. As political philosopher Jane Bennett remarks, "Moments of sensuous enchantment with the everyday world—with nature but also with commodities and other cultural products—might augment the motivational energy needed to move selves from the endorsement of ethical principles to the actual practice of ethical behaviors."[21] Feelings are powerful rhetorical resources for inspiring new practices that recognize and account for our material vulnerabilities and ethical responsibilities.

If the attention that objects are receiving within the disparate worlds of academia, design studios, and policy think tanks is any indication, there is reason for hope that new paradigms are on the horizon. A primary sign that change is afoot is the sheer plethora of designers, scholars, makers, and consumers of various stripes who are attempting to articulate and put into practice new (and old!) approaches to how we engage objects. Fascinating and important conversations are emerging across our culture from people hailing from different backgrounds and skill sets, many with an eye toward how we might reimagine our lives with things.

In the academy, we've seen a promising materialist turn in a variety of fields—political theory, communication, philosophy, cultural studies, and literary studies, for example—each with differing but often related lines of thought. Anthropologists, for example, given their long-standing focus on artifacts as keys to understanding human collective life, were among the first to turn their attention to the cultural role of mass-produced objects. British anthropologist Daniel Miller, to cite a towering example, has contributed dozens of important studies of how we make meaning within material culture, beginning with *Material Culture and Mass Consumption* (1987), then more recent anthologies of his work in this area, *Stuff* (2009) and *Consumption and Its Consequences* (2012).

Actor–network theory, for its part, is an ongoing attempt to understand the social, manufactured, and natural world as an interconnected web of actants, based on the assumption that reality itself can only be understood through these multiple and shifting relationships in which, say, humans, smartphones, viruses, and mushrooms enjoy equal status as agents. The influential ANT, as it's often called, led by philosophers of science and technology Bruno Latour, Michel Callon, and John Law, continues to offer new methods for charting the relationships between the semiotic and the material structures in which we live and to offer a valuable approach to understanding the agency of objects.

Object-oriented ontology has pursued a similar goal, seeking to reorient philosophical thought toward objects and to afford them

a long overdue ontological status that is equal to that of humans—
and everything else for that matter. As Ian Bogost, a chief advocate
of the movement, puts it, "All things equally exist, *yet they do not exist
equally*."[22] This observation is a central tenet of fellow object-oriented
ontology proponent Levi Bryant's argument in his concept of onti-
cology, or a flat ontology in which all being is nothing but a dynamic
system of objects of which we merely are a part.[23]

In the humanities and social sciences, this materialist turn acts
as something of a corrective to the excesses of the linguistic turn
and the attendant social constructivist approaches that dominated
much of twentieth-century critical theory, and which continues
today. As Diana Coole and Samantha Frost note, "While we recognize that radical constructivism has contributed considerable insight
into the workings of power over recent years, we are also aware that
an allergy to 'the real' [. . .] has had the consequence of dissuading
critical inquirers from the more empirical kinds of investigation that
material processes and structures require."[24] The cost of critical
scholars' "allergy" to the material world, they suggest, is a "nonre-
flexive habituality" that "imbues objects with familiarity that makes
artifacts, commodities, and practices seem so natural that they are
not questioned. It is in this sense that ideology or power operate most
effectively when embedded in the material, practical horizons and
institutions of everyday life."[25] Their book, and the larger new materialisms movement of which it is a part, is an attempt to interrupt this
taken-for-grantedness of objects and to acknowledge that they have a
vitality all their own with which we must reckon.

An important influence on how many of us working in the area of
material culture think about human–object relationships is Bennett's
Vibrant Matter (2010). In many ways a follow-up to *The Enchantment
of Modern Life* (2001), in which Bennett promotes a reinvigoration of
a premodern sense of enchantment and wonder as a means to open
up new ethical possibilities, in *Vibrant Matter* Bennett turns her focus
from humans' experience of the world to the world itself. Bennett
theorizes what she calls a "vital materialism" through which she aims

to promote an ecological politics that attends more carefully to the powerful agency of nonhuman, even inanimate, beings. This "thing power," as she describes it, is "the curious ability of inanimate things to animate, to act, to produce effects dramatic and subtle."[26]

Bennett's innovative rethinking of matter provides a guiding posture from which I have attempted to think through, in a decidedly more practical way, what I will describe as an opening up of the life cycle of objects. As Bennett writes, "Why advocate for the vitality of matter? Because my hunch is that the image of dead and thoroughly instrumentalized matter feeds human hubris and our earth-destroying fantasies of conquest and consumption." She continues, "The figure of an intrinsically inanimate matter may be one of the impediments to the emergence of more ecological and more materially sustainable modes of production and consumption."[27] Indeed, our tendency to think of objects as lifeless, discrete, and existing only as instruments for our use or pleasure has produced one of the most challenging rhetorical obstacles to promoting practices that might reorient our engagements with them.

We know we shape and define objects, and we are increasingly recognizing the ways objects shape and define us. This moment of cocreation, the mutual definition between subjects and objects, can best be understood through the concept of attachment. Some of these attachments are strong, as when an object is sufficiently valuable, either emotionally or financially, that we are loath to part with it. Others are weaker, as with objects that are designed to be disposable, intended to become either functionally or aesthetically obsolete. But our capacity to think through those attachments, to cultivate a sense of agency among them, depends on our opening up space within the moment, event, or state of attachment itself, thereby creating opportunities for us to respond in new ways rather than merely reacting impulsively according to the well-worn paths of mass consumption.

When we attach to an object, we assign a value to it, and implicitly to our relationship with it. Sometimes assessing that value is simple and easily quantified. Other times it's harder because the value is more sentimental and the standards of measure more idiosyncratic. Nevertheless, these moments of attachment offer fertile ground for intervention. Any meaningful conversation about the possibilities within aesthetic capitalism must include our careful consideration of the various alternative modalities of attachment available. Today objects exert influence and offer opportunities for engagement from their design to their disposal. These influences affect all of us, and these opportunities are available to all of us. Toward that end, this book is aimed at consumers, scholars, designers, and makers; it intends to explore the various ways we might connect with and respond to objects in ways other than those that tend to be prescribed by mainstream commercial discourse. With this in mind, I draw from the important scholarship being conducted on the topics at hand, and my own interpretations are informed by my training as a scholar of rhetoric. But my goal has been to establish an idiom and vocabulary accessible to readers who may not be engaged in specific academic conversations about things, objects, and materiality. If we are to change course in terms of the political, ethical, and environmental effects of consumerism, we must find new points of entry into our fabricated world, new platforms and venues upon which we might ascribe meaning, foster connections, and change and be changed vis-à-vis our consumption practices. For that, we need all hands on deck.

The central question of this book is, how might we manage the material excesses of consumer capitalism by building on, rather than repudiating, our attraction and attachment to objects? How might we, in practical ways, deepen our "sensuous enchantment" with even those commodified objects that often appear utterly mundane, or alternatively seductively deceitful? This question cannot be addressed simply by marshaling ever more awareness, or by placing faith in our own cognitive resources, or by assessing the goodness of our motivations. These are all necessary parts of the puzzle, to be sure, but they are not enough. For, as Bennett suggests, "if a set of moral principles is actually to be lived out, the right mood or landscape of affect has to be in place."[28] We must complement our intellectual awareness by cultivating a new affective landscape, in part through a thorough understanding of attachment, the process and mechanism by which a subject and object come together for any given period of time. Attachment is simultaneously a psychological process and a phenomenological one in that we project an assessment of value onto an object, and the object defines the nature and contours of our sense of value. In other words, attachment is the subject acting on and being acted upon by the objects that surround and define it.

Attachment, of course, is rarely permanent. Sometimes it's most potent at the moment of attraction, when a connection feels alive with possibility. Inspiring attraction is the goal of most advertising and product design. *Attachment* is merely the word we give the act of connection itself, even if (as with many human relationships) that sense of connection doesn't last forever. Although some moments of attachment are fleeting, others are far more durable. One of these isn't inherently better than the other for identifying strategies and solutions for the problem of waste, but we need to understand instantiations of both to see how the process of attachment works in general so that we can promote design, objects, discourses, and consumption practices that facilitate an environmentally and psychologically healthier relationship between human beings and the ecosystem of objects in which we find ourselves. Attachment is one register on which we can create practices that open up—expose—both subjects and objects such that their mutual connectivity is felt more viscerally. As Bennett writes, "Our trash is not 'away' in landfills but generating lively streams of chemicals and volatile winds of methane as we speak."[29] We have too long allowed this reality to be obscured by the aesthetic rhetorics of the commercial persuasion industry, which is invested in focusing our attention on some aspects of our relationship to objects at the expense of others.

We are living in what Jeffrey Nealon has dubbed postpostmodernism.[30] Updating Fredric Jameson's famous analysis of postmodernism as the cultural logic of late capitalism, Nealon observes that we now live in an age defined by an intensified version of postmodernism, in which capitalism has so permeated every aspect of cultural life that rhetorics of liberation somewhat miss the point. There is no longer an outside to which we can escape. Gernot Böhme highlights a different dimension of the same contemporary scene: aesthetic capitalism.[31] Cultural critic Steven Shaviro describes our current moment as an "age of aesthetics,"[32] a phrase that describes the incredible sense that our just-in-time reality is increasingly designed and delivered to emphasize aesthetic potentials that prompt and define how we enjoy and negotiate the world around us. Today, most products are designed to produce a "right here, right now" form of attachment unconcerned with enduring commitment.

Every object that comes into existence is part of a larger and more granular and intricate network of communications. Saussure noted in his theory of signification that any signifier works in part by its not being any of the other signifiers in the larger available lexicon (a dog, in other words, is defined in part by its not being a cat).[33] Objects today operate the same way. A particular phone, shirt, or car derives its value in part by what it is not (all those other phones, shirts, and vehicles that occupy their various market segments). At the same time, every object communicates directly with its user or consumer. Every object speaks in the languages of branding, industrial design, and material science. They carry within them a dialect and an accent composed of feel and footprint, form factor and function. Attachment, in other words, is an object-driven act of influence and persuasion.

This is why the perspective and practice of rhetoric, my primary discipline, provides such fertile ground from which to understand the nature and language of attachment. Rhetoric is the study of how humans think, feel, and do things, as well as how we interpret, identify with, and place value on messages, images, and objects. It is, among other things, a collaborative art of meaning making. Sherry Turkle notes that "we find it familiar to consider objects as useful or aesthetic, as necessities or vain indulgences. We are on less familiar ground when we consider objects as companions to our emotional lives or as provocations to thought. The notion of evocative objects

brings together these two less familiar ideas, underscoring the insep-
arability of thought and feeling in our relationship to things. We think
with the objects we love; we love the objects we think with."[34] Because
attachment is both a psychological and phenomenological act (as well
as intellectual, physical, and emotional), we need to better understand how we talk about and frame our interactions with objects, as
well as the way these objects themselves speak to us through their own
affects and languages—languages in which we could all afford to become more fluent.

A Brief History of Commodity Fetishism

The object hasn't always communicated in the same way across the
historical evolution of capitalism. In many ways, we can look at the
major theoretical engagements with capitalism as attempts to track
the ways the object communicates particular social and cultural formations to its users. Karl Marx, for example, notes, "A commodity
appears at first sight an extremely obvious, trivial thing. But its analysis brings out that it is a very strange thing, abounding in metaphysical
subtleties and theological niceties."[35] As we think about the political
and social life of objects, it makes sense to start with Marx, the thinker
who first theorized objects as commodities. In *Capital*, Marx examines a phenomenon, unique to industrial capitalism, that he describes
as "the fetishism of the commodity and its secret."[36] This famous
concept—commodity fetishism—is central to Marx's economic theory and remains among the most salient for the many scholars working
in the ever-evolving Marxist tradition—a mode of analysis known as
political economics or, more broadly, critical theory. Marx argues
that under capitalism, commodities take on a mystical quality that
obscures the social relations endemic to their production. For Marx,
this obfuscation lends an undue magic to commodities, which leads
to confusion over the abstract system of exploitation that determines
their value. Under capitalism, objects garner their power not as a result of their use value but from their exchange value—that is, the place
they hold in a larger economy.

For example, the use value of my new boots might be that they keep my feet warm and dry, or even that I like their style. Their exchange value, however, relates to what equivalent value the boots might fetch on an open market. They might be comparable in value to, say, a handbag, or a lamp. The boots might even, in the language of money—that "pure" commodity that has no use value except as a unit of exchange— "equal" ninety dollars. For most of us, the most valuable commodity we possess is our own labor, which we exchange for a wage that we then translate into other commodities that are valuable to us primarily for their usefulness. The burrito satisfies my hunger, the boots keep my feet warm and dry, the computer allows me to type this sentence.

The social dynamic that is obscured by exchange value, or the commodity form, for Marx, is this: when workers sell their labor, they turn their very life into a commodity, or a unit of exchange. This transaction—selling quantified chunks of their lives to the capitalist— alienates workers from their own self-determined engagement with and transformation of the material world. For Marx, this capacity to change the form of natural materials to satisfy one's own needs is the essence of what it is to be human—what Marx calls *Gattungswesen*, "species-being." However, under capitalism, the products of our own work become alien to us, mere commodities lining the pockets of the capitalist who controls the means of production. For Marx, this alienation from the things we make amounts to a fundamental separation from our very humanity.

From the consumer's perspective, however, this sad tale of alienation—the clandestine secret that Marx claims is central to but concealed within the commodity form—is hidden from view. Although in reality the commodity is a physical product of material processes wrought by human hands within a larger political hierarchy, it is instead understood as a magical talisman, a totem imbued with meaning by those who see only its dazzling surfaces yet remain blind to the conditions of its emergence. "To find an analogy," Marx writes, "we must take flight into the misty realm of religion. There the products of the human brain appear as autonomous figures endowed with a life of their own, which enter into relations both with each other and with the human race. So it is in the world of the commodities with the products of men's hands. I call this the fetishism which attaches itself to the products of labor as soon as they are produced as commodities, and is therefore inseparable from the production of commodities."[37] For Marx, exchange value perverts and overwhelms use value—the traditional, precapitalist mode of the human–object relationship. Further, labor becomes increasingly mechanized and segmented as the capitalist strives to shave ever-more labor hours off the manufacturing process, a trend that further alienates workers from both the process and product of their work. In two short decades after Marx's death, Henry Ford's assembly line mode of production would evolve this mechanization and segmentation well beyond what Marx described. Nonetheless, for Marx, the factory is the stage upon which labor and the social relations that enable it are themselves objectified—that is, made into things to which we have increasingly limited access. All the while, commodity fetishism perpetuates a sense that the objects of our labor appear as if by magic, devoid of process or history.

Although he did not express it as such, commodity fetishism was essentially, and by necessity, a theorizing of attachment, a way of describing the character of the connection between humans and objects in Marx's time. Fetishization is a form of attachment that operates through a kind of attention blindness. So attached and enthralled are we by the commodity form that the early life-cycle stage of production is glossed over in the process of exchange. This is a central part of Marx's larger exploration into how value is established. Marxist theorists writing in the early decades of the twentieth century begin to develop Marx's conception of the commodity form and to foreground its contribution to the cultural domination of the elite classes. Russian scholar I. I. Rubin declares, for example, "the theory of fetishism is, *per se*" to be "the basis of Marx's entire economic system, and in particular of his theory of value."[38] Along with Rubin, the most notable of Marx's early commentators are Antonio Gramsci and his critique of cultural hegemony, as well as (particularly relevant for our purposes here) Georg Lukács's analysis of the reification of human society under capitalism. In *History and Class Consciousness*, published just months before Rubin's essays on Marx's theory of value, Lukács develops Marx's concept of commodity fetishism to suggest that the commodity form is not confined only to the realm of production but that it now permeates "every expression of life" and "remould[s] it in its own image."[39] Reification, literally the thing-making (from the Latin word *res*) of human society, according to Lukács, is a direct outgrowth of the emergence of the commodity form:

> The commodity can only be understood in its undistorted essence when it becomes the universal category of society as a whole. Only in this context does the reificiation produced by commodity relations assume decisive importance both for the objective evolution of society and for the stance adopted by men towards it. Only then does the commodity become crucial for the subjugation of men's consciousness to the forms in which this reification finds expression and for their attempts to comprehend the process or to rebel against its disastrous effects and liberate themselves from servitude to the "second nature" so created.[40]

This "second nature," like "ideology" or "hegemony" for Gramsci and those working in the critical tradition he inspired, refers to a phantom reality that, although a product of social hierarchies, is taken as a naturally occurring, objective phenomenon. Martin Jay suggests that for Lukács, reification means "the petrification of living processes into dead things, which appeared as an alien 'second nature.'"[41] In Lukács's analysis, capitalism is an objectifying, thing-making machine. For Marx, the fetishization of commodities amounts to a veil or a mask (terms used often by both writers), concealing this reality. Revolution, then, calls for the "secret" of the commodity's illusory sway to be revealed. Revolutions aside, what Lukács adds to the equation is important and more influential than his limited name recognition might reveal. Lukács's analysis points to the fact that as capitalism evolves, all our attachments—our romantic relationships, our bodies, our spiritual life—become subject to commodification, to becoming objects from which we are increasingly alienated. In other words, the object, in its commodity form, mediates even subjective attachment.

From Production to Consumption

For all his exhaustive analyses of labor, commodities, economic value, and capital, Marx has little to say about consumers, the agents most contemporary students of capitalism understand to be the engine driving the global economy. In Marx's era, capitalism is largely understood through the prism of production. Not until the 1960s would theorists focus their collective eye on what Jean Baudrillard terms the consumer society,[42] in all its various manifestations. Intellectuals influenced by Marx—Baudrillard, Guy Debord, Pierre Bordieu, Roland Barthes, and Zygmunt Bauman, among others—develop ways of understanding consumerism from their varied Marxist-inflected perspectives. But as many ruefully observe, the revolution was not to come. What Debord terms "the society of the spectacle" proves too seductive.[43]

Debord, writing in 1967, stands at the precipice of the image-saturated, commercial-dominated world we live in today. Stridently in the Marxist "false consciousness" camp, Debord's mission is to reveal to readers the mystifying role of mere representations shilling for corporate interests, which has come to stand in for authentic human interaction. Debord and his comrades are responding to an important shift in the logic of capitalism. As production processes become more efficient in the early decades of the twentieth century, manufacturers begin to seek new ways to distinguish their products from the rest through new designs and clever ad campaigns. Legions of psychoanalysts are brought in to help marketers figure out how to best align their products with consumers' deepest desires. Here we begin to see attraction and attachment as central objects of the capitalist enterprise. Now that we could make so much stuff so quickly and so affordably, the question becomes how to mobilize desire for all that the marketplace has to offer.

For Debord, the resulting spectacle still smacks of a fundamental alienation. Desires are manufactured by those producing the goods—desires often dressed up as needs—and the act of consuming those goods only accelerates and intensifies the spectacle. The subject becomes a desiring machine, and individual consumers are further separated from the awareness they would need to combat or contest the evolution of capitalism.

But alienation, we should recall, is a term that emerged out of a much earlier understanding of attachment, one in which we fetishize the commodity so much that we forget the labor and human relations that produced it—so much so that we commoditize the totality of our social interactions. We are, for Marx and others, trapped within a logic of exchange, such that good old-fashioned use value, which would more closely tie us to the work inherent in the production of any product, is sublimated. In a world of spectacle, where desire is being manufactured as an additional value to shape and differentiate one product from another, we move beyond attachment as a simple fetishization of the object in its commodity form and toward something else—the object as a vehicle for motivation, or as a device for the consummation of desire. In such a world, the contours of alienation shift. What if, for example, the use value of the object is the satisfaction (or attempted satisfaction) of a given desire? What if the presence or ownership of the object is its own use?

Jean Baudrillard addresses this transformation in the commodity by suggesting the addition of a third dimension, outside of what Marx originally envisions in his analysis of the commodity form. In addition to exchange and use value, Baudrillard suggests the inclusion of sign value, a way to assess an object's value as a signifier within the larger system of objects. In chapter 2, I further address the nature of sign value and its use in understanding the impact of contemporary design and celebrity designers, particularly in consumer products. For now, however, it is sufficient to note that Baudrillard offers the first formal, structural evolution of the commodity form beyond the original Marxist formulation. Although Lukács, Gramsci, and Debord add dimensions to the analysis of its consequences, Baudrillard suggests that the object Marx dubs the commodity has in fact become more structurally complicated since Marx's original analysis.

The inclusion of sign value is an early stage of Baudrillard's own career, which eventually evolves to an analytical structure that critiques Marx as wrong and insufficient. The problem for Baudrillard is Marx's own fetishization of use value as the proper, more natural part of the object or commodity form, with exchange value acting as both the dominant term and the perversion of use value. As such, Baudrillard argues, it becomes easy to speak of alienation, of a warping of the natural relationship between our labor and our work, and between our social relations and our objects. Most commodities do not really represent needs, so they do not have natural uses. They have, as Baudrillard notes earlier, a signifying function, a sign value, and this creates the impression, or mediates the reality, of any particular use case for an object. "All critical theory depends on the analysis of the object form," he argues, even as he suggests that Marx's analysis is insufficient, even problematic, for addressing the capitalist formations of the 1970s.[44]

Instead, Baudrillard argues, we must turn away from analyses of the subject and toward analyses of the object: "It is no longer the desire of the subject, but the destiny of the object, which is at the center of the world."[45] The overabundance of objects, the omnipresent pervasiveness of design, the larger ecosystem of signification that surrounds and situates these objects and our interactions with them—these all generate new systems of meaning, where everything, every desire, every possibility can be realized (that is to say, made real). In this world, attachment has to be understood and appreciated in a far more nuanced manner because different object forms, within different ecosystems of meaning, will produce different orders of reality, create new degrees and types of satisfaction, and define novel and more varied forms of subjectivity. But we can no longer begin that analysis from the comfortable stability of the subject. We need to do so by focusing on objects themselves because these objects generate logics of attachment. When it comes to these objects, there are far more of them than there are of us.

Object Overload

Thanks to technological and system innovations, today's global capitalism has become incredibly efficient at manufacturing and distributing durable goods. IKEA, which I will discuss in chapter 3, is just one of a number of global corporations contributing to and profiting from modern advances in factory production, data collection, and systems of distribution. Walmart, for example, uses big data analytics to optimize shipping routes, muscle down suppliers' prices, and calibrate its global inventory down to the last pair of cheap sunglasses in its Milwaukee supercenter. Amazon's use of KIVA robots to manage its warehouses allows it to stock more inventory and cut costs; the company's extensive use of algorithms permits it to home in on purchasing habits with ever-increasing detail. These vast systems undoubtedly allow more objects to travel the globe with unprecedented speed and efficiency, which in all kinds of ways is terribly convenient for consumers who have the means to participate.

But how many of us, even in the most vestigial way, really understand the processes—of material extraction, production, distribution—that enable the objects we buy to arrive on our doorstep, or on the shelves of our local big box store, so quickly and so cheaply? If Nealon is right, if in this era of postpostmodernism there is no longer an outside to which we can escape, then we must recalibrate our analysis and our politics accordingly. But if the sensibility that dominates much consumerist discourse is any indication, few of us seem to want to escape. It sometimes seems as if we have collectively adopted the entitled visage of Veruca Salt, that spoiled little girl from *Willy Wonka and the Chocolate Factory* (picture the 1971 film version for greatest effect), who demands that her factory-owning father immediately grant her every wish, shrieking, "Don't care how! I want it now!"

However, even if we don't care how the objects we use, wear, and live with got here, or even where they'll go when they no longer interest us, the residue of those systems and processes that brought them into being remains. Objects are imprinted with the legacy of their production. Consuming them amounts to an inheritance of sorts, and we do have some choice about what kinds of systems we want to inherit. Consumption is never an act of passive reception. Although it may be somewhat Pollyannaish to say so, and although it may ignore the realities of those who have less say in the objects they consume, the decisions we make as consumers are as consequential as the decisions we make as voters. When we choose, for example, to buy this pair of sneakers over that one, we inherit the entire political economy that makes the sneakers possible. What chemicals went into the glues and preservatives that hold them together? What were the working conditions of the young woman who stitched the uppers in a factory in some faraway land? How many fossil fuels were extracted and burned in order to get them from her hands to mine? There's nothing in the form of mass-produced objects per se that reveals this inheritance. By design, they bear no explicit marks of the labor that went into their manufacture. Indeed, industrial manufacturing still depends on a certain degree of uniformity, a universality of form, in the objects it produces so efficiently.

A Tale of Two Trends: Stockpiling and Downsizing

Consumption and accumulation sometimes seem to have a momentum of their own while we're just along for the ride. Members-only discount stores like Sam's Club and Costco, as well as practices like extreme couponing—a practice documented in five seasons of its own reality show on TLC—allow people to accumulate massive stockpiles of extra merchandise, their garages and basements becoming miniwarehouses, housing years' worth of nonperishable food and paper products, just in case. Consider too the meteoric rise of self-storage facilities, those clusters of windowless boxes that dot the American landscape. Self-storage is now a $24 billion a year industry.[46] According to one account, "the industry boasts more domestic locations than McDonald's, Subway and Jack in the Box combined."[47] Throughout most of its history, self-storage was intended as a short-term solution for people in the middle of a move who needed a temporary place to stash the things they would soon put in their new home. By 2007, however, according to a study by the Self Storage Association trade group, "fifty percent of renters were now simply storing what wouldn't fit in their homes—even though the size of the average American house had almost doubled in the previous 50 years, to 2,300 square feet."[48] Although houses may be getting bigger, it is estimated that "seventy percent of home-owning Americans cannot park cars in their garages because there's too much stuff," and approximately one in ten American households has essentially annexed their homes with self-storage units to hold their surplus belongings.[49] And either because of financial struggles or sheer indifference, thousands of these units are abandoned each year, creating a parasite market for those who compete for the contents at cash-only auctions. Perhaps not surprisingly, yet another popular reality show, A&E's *Storage Wars* (2010–), along with its many spin-offs, chronicles the adventures of those hoping to profit from what others have left behind.

The rise of self-storage does not mean that we are all hoarders, those suffering from an affliction that I will discuss at some length in chapter 1; but it does suggest that lots of people feel too guilty or too attached to their stuff to part with it completely—at least until it's been out of sight long enough to finally be out of mind. However, an episode of the popular ABC comedy *Modern Family* (2009–2020) highlights just how fraught this process of separation can be. A determined Claire enlists her family in a house-decluttering mission. Her three teenage children vehemently resist; her husband, Phil, protests, "All this stuff is packed with meaning!" before reluctantly donating some of their things to keep the domestic peace. By the episode's end, Claire has a change of heart and tearfully regrets her clean sweep of her family's mementos: "Years of stress cleaning has eradicated a lifetime of precious memories!" she cries.[50] In typical sitcom fashion, all turns out well in the end, when Claire is delighted to discover that Phil has secretly maintained a self-storage unit to house all the beloved things she has insisted on donating over the years. For the Pritchetts—and I suspect for many modern families—self-storage offers a liminal space where objects can be placed in abeyance while their owners' emotional ambivalence is resolved.

It's not only the self-storage industry and those scavenging its forsaken detritus who are cashing in on our seemingly insatiable appetite for consumption—or in some cases consumption of consumption. So-called haul videos in which (predominantly) young women, surrounded by shopping bags from popular mall staples like Forever 21 and Sephora, share their most recent acquisitions, and unboxing videos, in which people enthusiastically remove new tech gadgets from their packaging, have proven surprisingly lucrative for those who make them and upload them to YouTube. Similarly, what might be termed collection porn, on websites like the Things Organized Neatly Tumblr (now a book), invites viewers to admire the carefully curated collections of other people's stuff. Rob Walker explains the popularity of these sites: "It has become a cliché to talk of 'curation' as the great skill of the info-saturated online world, but probably what matters here is the overt display of that skill—the de facto announcement that someone is in charge. After too many years when stuff seemed to rule many lives, these things have been culled, sorted and mastered."[51] Tools for mastering stuff are themselves incredibly profitable, as evidenced by booming sales for retailers like Storables and the Container Store, which specialize in clutter management products, not to mention all the books, blogs, magazines, and reality TV shows devoted to how to effectively and stylishly corral one's possessions. Perhaps not surprisingly, Marie Kondo now has her own brand of boxes, which retail for $89 for a set of three. Meanwhile, the National Association of Professional Organizers has seen its membership multiply tenfold, jumping from 400 to 4,000 in the last two decades.[52] Modern consumers appear to be obsessed with buying, collecting, organizing, displaying, storing, and increasingly downsizing their belongings. It's not just those whose tales of excess are featured on basic cable reality shows who have a complicated relationship to their stuff. We all do.

The massive quantity and diversity of affordable, (relatively) well-made products available force consumers in the industrialized world to negotiate what psychologist Barry Schwartz calls the "paradox of choice" like never before.[53] Faced with advertising messages that are constantly telling us what products should mean, it has become increasingly difficult to determine what they might actually mean for ourselves. In response, another trend is afoot in consumer culture, one ostensibly all about uncomplicating one's relationship to things. It's no coincidence that stockpiling, haul videos, and the self-storage boom have arisen at the same cultural moment as the tiny house movement, capsule wardrobes, and other so-called voluntary simplicity practices. What anthropologist Katie Kilroy-Marac calls "consumption critical lifestyle movements" are on the rise as our awareness increases about the negative impacts of overconsumption on the environment and human rights, or simply our own sense of well-being. The popularity among Gen Xers and millennials of waste reduction trends such as "100 things" challenges illustrates our paradoxical relationship to the excesses of contemporary capitalism. "We've been asked to curtail our own consumption," says Kilroy-Marac, "and yet we are all consumers. . . . We consume every day in all sorts of ways."[54] These kinds of mindful minimalism movements promote abstinence, or at least restraint, often dressed in aesthetic or even spiritual garb.

Books, magazines, and blogs challenging readers to pare down their possessions are everywhere, and their popularity seems to be growing every day. Take, for example, the 100 Things trend that emerged in the early 2010s, in which people challenged themselves and others to "break free from the confining habits of excessive consumerism" and reduce their personal possessions to just a hundred items. As 100 Things founder Dave Bruno explains, "A lot of people around the world feel 'stuck in stuff.' They feel like their closets and garages are too full of things that do not really make their lives much better." Bruno's method for getting unstuck plays off the well-known 3 Rs of environmentalism. His version encourages readers to "Reduce (some stuff); Refuse (more new stuff); Rejigger (life priorities)."[55]

Bruno chronicled his experiments on his blog, which he later published as a book. Like the KonMari followers we'll meet in chapter 1, the #100TC community is still going strong, as people seek happiness by doing more with less. Similarly, Sheena Matheiken's uniform project, in which she wore the same little black dress every day for a full year, embellishing her look with only thrifted, handmade, or donated accessories, is an attempt to promote what she calls sustainable fashion. By the end of a year wearing the same dress and posting her daily ensembles on her website, Matheiken claims to have received over two million hits and raised over \$100,000 in donations for a foundation providing education to the children in India's slums (http://www.theuniformproject.com/).

The most prominent voices of this latest instantiation of minimalism are undoubtedly Joshua Fields Millburn and Ryan Nicodemus, who, in their blog, three books, TED talk, podcast, speaking engagements, and 2016 documentary film, are known as the Mimimalists. Feeling a sense of "lingering discontent," the two white thirtysomething friends gave up their lucrative tech industry jobs, big homes, and luxury cars and moved to a modest cabin in Missoula, Montana, in search of a simpler and more meaningful way of life.[56] Millburn came to minimalism a few years earlier, when his mother died and his marriage ended in the same month: "I sort of looked around at what had become my life's focus, and I realized I didn't know what was important anymore." After purging most of his possessions, he says, "I started to feel freer, happier and lighter."[57] Nicodemus, inspired by his friend, says that as an early experiment, he put all his belongings in boxes and, for twenty-one days, removed things only as he needed them. In the end, 80 percent of his things remained boxed up, proving to himself how little of his stuff he actually uses.

As a lifestyle brand, the Minimalists are impeccable. Across their various platforms, the aesthetic and attitude of the Minimalists are orchestrated with a degree of consistency that would make Steve Jobs proud. Their message is coherent as well; the *Boston Globe* aptly describes it as "like Henry David Thoreau, but with Wi-Fi."[58] Like Marie

Branding minimalism: the Minimalists' logo.

Kondo and *The Life-Changing Magic of Tidying Up*, the Minimalists emphasize the deep connection between our emotions and the degree of control we have over our possessions, pointing to the positive effects of downsizing on our sense of well-being: "Minimalists don't focus on having less, less, less; rather, we focus on making room for more: more time, more passion, more experiences, more growth, more contribution, more contentment. More freedom. Clearing the clutter from life's path helps us make that room."[59] Like Kondo, the Minimalists have amassed a huge and enthusiastic following. They regularly tour in the United States and abroad to promote their philosophy and various projects. More than 1,400 people RSVP'd to see them talk at a San Francisco bookstore, and their 2016 tour of ten cities to screen their documentary sold out months before its release. They claim that four million people read their blog, and their memoir, *Everything that Remains*, is a best seller. The breadth of the minimalism trend is too big to fully account for here. From the ongoing popularity of the midcentury modern design aesthetic, with its clean lines and less-is-more aesthetic, to the various experiments in simple living like Colin Beavan's *No Impact Man* (a blog, book, and film), to people intentionally downsizing their lifestyles in myriad ways, a desire for order and simplicity is clearly one outgrowth of the excesses of contemporary consumer culture.

For all its well-meaning intentions, minimalism's claim to be a path to the good life is not so simple; nor is it without its critics. Some find the minimalist movement oppressive, as they are simply too attached to their belongings and the memories they represent. Blogger Karen Bertelsen, inspired by the "virtuously clean-looking homes" that pervade certain regions of the Internet, says she made an ardent attempt at becoming a minimalist: "This is it," she thinks. "I am a minimalist.

This is how it's going to be, everything calm from now on." However, as Jacoba Urist reports, "Her venture into minimalism made her realize how much she enjoyed viewing the physical manifestations of memories, reliving moments through concrete reminders. 'I want to see the drumsticks from the last Ramones show I went to in 1994, or the rock I picked up climbing a mountain in Vancouver,' she said. 'I want to see the titles of all the books I've read.'"[60] This connection between our possessions and our memories is one I will explore throughout this book. Memories are one of the central reasons we decide to keep certain objects and not others. In chapter 4, I will look at the work of designers who are attempting to intensify the relationship between people and things, to write the capacity for meaning and sustainability into the very DNA of the object. Those promoting what Jonathan Chapman terms "emotionally durable design" are experimenting with ways to prolong the attachment we feel for objects, in the hope that we will be less inclined to discard them. Such an approach is not appropriate to all objects, of course, but as a mode of slowing down the effects of a fickle consumer culture, it's a valuable step in the right direction.

Other critics of minimalism note the utter presumptuousness of attaching a kind of moral superiority to a practice that is possible only for those who can afford to ditch their belongings and buy new ones when they need to. "It has become an ostentatious ritual of consumerist self-sacrifice," argues Kyle Chayka, pointing out that the most vocal proponents of minimalism tend to be well-to-do white guys in the tech industry. "People who have it all now seem to prefer having nothing at all." He concludes, "This new minimalist lifestyle always seems to end in enabling new modes of consumption, a veritable excess of less. It's not really minimal at all [. . .] The fetishized austerity and performative asceticism of minimalism is a kind of ongoing cultural sickness. We misinterpret material renunciation, austere aesthetics and blank, emptied spaces as symbols of capitalist absolution, when these trends really just provide us with further ways to serve our impulse to consume more, not less."[61] One need only peruse popular shelter blogs like Apartment Therapy or an issue of lifestyle magazines such as *Real Simple* or *Dwell* to see that Chayka has a point. The white walls, carefully curated collections, and austerely (but expensively) furnished homes they feature are often accessible only to those with ample disposable income. Joel Stillerman, author of *The Sociology of Consumption* (2015), suggests that minimalism is also a way for those in the upper socioeconomic classes to distinguish themselves from others, thereby demonstrating their refined taste and superior aesthetic literacy. "These people," he says, "are making the statement that 'I can afford to have less. I appreciate books and travel and good meals.'"[62] Often the minimalist ethic is subsumed by a minimalist aesthetic and an expensive one at that.

De-signing Discourse

This tension between ethics and aesthetics deserves careful attention as we try to assess the fate of the object in this era of aesthetic capitalism. The practices of consumers, designers, crafters, and makers of all sorts will be a central focus of the chapters that follow. We will look at design in its broadest sense—the art of creating objects that will prove to be useful, attractive, and potentially worthy of our attachment. The celebration of design is a central theme in contemporary commercial discourse. I will explore the relationship between industrial design, mass- and small-scale consumption, grassroots production such as crafting and making, and environmental sustainability. In doing so, I build on my work on the rhetoric and politics of consumerism, a theme that *OurSpace: Resisting the Corporate Control of Culture* (2007) explores in depth.

Whereas *OurSpace* is about the different types of political agency afforded in a marketplace defined by brands, the language and imagery of consumer culture, this book is about the agency afforded by the rhetorical character of things themselves. As prominent as the discourse of branding continues to be, what we now see in the foreground of contemporary commercial culture has increasingly less to do with branding products by way of hip or authoritative campaigns than with the poetic hybrid of form and function offered by the material objects themselves: their design. Design writer Steve Kroeter notes that whereas "branding was the most talked about business concept during the decade of the 1990s . . . design has evolved as the strategic initiative driving differentiation among brands."[63] As Kroeter suggests, to observe the rise of design in our current moment is certainly not to suggest that branding has gone away—far from it. But the focus of branding is shifting dramatically toward the formal components of products (their shape, texture, weight, footprint, etc.) more than the graphic and narrative discourses meant to create positive connotations with them. Tellingly, whereas marketers talk about brand identity, designers talk about the design DNA of objects themselves. Identity has to do with the stories we tell about things; DNA suggests something inherent to the thing itself.

With this in mind, in this book, I explore our relationship to the material objects we buy, collect, consume, and integrate into our daily lives, as well as the ways we make meaning, craft identities, inhabit lifestyles, and announce our politics through our relationships with and creative use of commodities. It is also a book about designers—a group who may be the most important, albeit underinvestigated, communicators of the contemporary age. Designers are material rhetoricians who conceive and plan everything, from automobiles to cities, from public spaces to commercial and political imagery. Ultimately this is an attempt to investigate the interfaces we confront in this material culture. Although the philosophical tradition has not always conceived it as such, questions of interfaces have governed much of rhetorical scholarship since the time of Plato. In contemporary parlance, an interface is a program that controls a display for a user; it is a sensory gateway that allows a user to interact with a system. If we live, as Baudrillard has suggested, within a system of objects, then design is the art of planning the way that users connect with those objects, and how we interface with this system.

An old folk saying notes that a fish would likely be the last to perceive water, as it is so ubiquitous to escape notice. In a similar vein, graphic designer Bruce Mau points out that although we live in a heavily designed world, for most of us, design is transparent. He writes, "The secret ambition of design is to become invisible, to be taken up into the culture, absorbed into the background. The highest order of success in design is to achieve ubiquity, to become banal."[64] Through investigating the discourse of design, it is my goal to make design visible by exploring the underlying strategies, politics, and aesthetics that produce our manufactured world. But it is also important to investigate, as I do in chapter 5, the ways that consumers are themselves redesigning the world of things.

The current apotheosis of design will play an important role in determining the fate of objects and the environment in which they, and we, exist. Two very different fates lie before us as we attempt to achieve some modicum of balance between our ecological and manufactured worlds. On one side of the scale is the assumption that design can continue to obscure, by promoting a frivolous mode of attachment, the larger life cycle of the object. It can continue to confine our attachment to those stages tied simply to the act of acquisition, that intoxicating but all too ephemeral moment of "I want it now!" exemplified by the voraciousness of *Willy Wonka*'s Veruca Salt. Here the object remains closed, discrete, fetishized, wholly other to ourselves. If this is our choice, then we can expect that our landfills and oceans, already teeming with the surfeit of our caprice, will increasingly suffer the burdens of excess.

On the other side of the scale, we can encourage modes of production, consumption, and use that allow objects to open up, thereby revealing their role in larger networks, systems, and ecologies. Here we can chart and coax an escalating dissolution of the object—from discrete and disposable to porous and hackable, to a node within a larger life span of which we are a part. On this side of things, we may come to better understand our own interconnectedness with the objects we encounter, such that we recognize our obligation to and responsibility for them, thereby becoming better stewards of the world we all inhabit. This side, as Juliet B. Schor suggests in the epigraph to this Introduction, asks us to be more materialist in our thinking rather than less so. This book is an attempt to understand these two options before us, to explore how they play out, and to place a thumb on the scale in favor of the latter.

ONE

The Dreams Stuff Is Made Of

Attaching to Inanimate Objects

Tables and chairs, beds, mirrors, a clock to remind the happy couple
of the passage of time, an armchair for an hour's pleasant daydream-
ing, carpets to help the housewife keep the floors clean, linen tied with
pretty ribbons in the cupboard and dresses of the latest fashion and
hats with artificial flowers, pictures on the wall, glasses for everyday
and others for wine and festive occasions. . . . Are we to hang our hearts
on such little things? Yes, and without hesitation.

— *Sigmund Freud in a letter to his fiancée, Martha*

In this chapter, I look closely at the ways we talk about our attachment
to inanimate objects. Among humans and other animals, attachment is
laden with emotion, is target specific, and is characterized by an affec-
tionate feeling of being connected to another.[1] "Attachment" emerges
etymologically from the old French *atachier*, to "fix" or "fasten,"[2] con-
noting a physical tethering of two things often expressed positively
as feeling bonded, connected, and coupled, or, negatively, as being
stuck, trapped, or tied down by a ball and chain. Attachment is crucial, of course, to the health of infants and children, who require the
feeling of safe belonging that strong familial and communal ties provide. Attachment is also important for parents; it fosters the sense of

responsibility and obligation to one's offspring that the survival of the species requires.

But humans do not only attach to other humans, of course. We attach to beloved pets, to familiar and sacred spaces, and to things. I'm certainly not unique, for example, in the deep attachment I feel for a sun-faded, lumpy assemblage of cotton and wool I've called Poohbear since he was given to me by a friend of my mom's over forty years ago. As a toddler, Poohbear was for me what psychoanalysts would call a transitional object, in that he provided the bridge I needed as I detached from mom and dad to become a more autonomous individual. With these objects, attachment has the potential to inspire a sense of obligation, a sense of responsibility for the well-being of the object of one's attachment. Poohbear, for example, is tucked safely away on a high shelf in my bedroom closet, his use value as a plaything usurped long ago by his current value as significant object.

How and why we attach to objects is a growing line of inquiry in industrial design scholarship. Ruth Mugge and her colleagues at the Delft University of Technology, for example, have conducted a number of studies attempting to understand why some products seem to endear themselves to us while others remain less significant, and hence are more easily replaced. On the basis of their findings, Mugge and colleagues propose four determinants of product attachment, as follows:

Pleasure: the product provides pleasure
Self-expression: the product expresses one's unique identity
Group affiliation: the product expresses one's belonging to a group
Memories: the product is a reminder of the past[3]

Designers working with an eye toward stimulating an emotional bond with the products they create are exploring a number of strategies to promote one or more of these qualities. Products provide pleasure, for instance, when they have aesthetic features above and beyond mere functionality. Fans of the iPhone, for example, cite its intuitive interface and its minimalist look as key reasons for their devotion. A plethora of customizable products allow consumers to tailor objects in ways they feel express their own personal identity, another main determinant of attachment. Following a concept popularized by Seth Godin in his 2008 book *Tribes*, brands like Nike and REI like to talk about their customer base as a brand tribe, in that they provide consumers a sense of belonging to something larger than themselves by way of affiliation with a particular company's message or aesthetic.[4] However, the final determinant, memory, appears to be the most powerful factor in product attachment, as a 2004 study by Schifferstein and Pelgrim shows.[5] They found that when subjects explained why they had kept some objects for twenty years or more, it was because those objects were closely connected to a meaningful personal memory. In another study, Kleine and Baker explain that "special possessions, such as clothing, are among the cues that evoke autobiographical memory rehearsal."[6] They go on to note, "Autobiographical rehearsal is self-comforting and presents opportunities for self-encouragement or confrontation and resolution of life issues, as numerous examples in literature and poetry portray."[7]

Although the autobiographical power of memory is clearly important in fostering emotional bonds to products, creating objects as meaningful as, say, Rosebud is to Charles Foster Kane in the 1941 film *Citizen Kane*, may be the hardest design nut to crack because "product-related memories usually develop independently from the product design and are difficult to influence by the designer."[8] However, as I will explore in chapter 4, many designers interested in promoting a more sustainable relationship to the objects in our lives are attempting to do just that: to create objects that encourage our commitment to care for, rather than discard them, over time. Such stewardship, I suspect, is possible only when we feel invested in an object to the degree that we care about its fate. We invest in objects all the time, of course, from the money we spend on them, to the time spent researching and acquiring them, to the space they take up in our homes. But in this current cultural moment, nearly everything is seen as disposable, yet nothing really is. Phones, coffee makers, clothes, and cars are subject to the incessant solicitation of the upgrade. In this environment, what inspires us to invest emotionally more in some objects than in others?

It's worth noting that attachment isn't always the most ethical response to objects. Some things, like consumer electronics, are necessarily transitory and should be designed with their safe disposal or repurposing in mind. However, as we know, so many of the objects that find themselves cast into dumpsters, landfills, and oceans are discarded not because they are no longer useful but because they are no longer *wanted*. As design scholar Jonathan Chapman puts it, "Waste is symptomatic of failed relationships."⁹

This chapter starts a conversation that will continue throughout this book. Here I explore a variety of ways we value and attach to the things in our lives. I begin with hoarders, those who attach either so indiscriminately or so intensely that attachment has devolved into affliction. Like many of us, hoarders often cling to objects because they evoke memories from the past. However, testimonials from hoarders demonstrate that attachment can also be inspired by an object's promise of a better future. The broken clock will again tell time, once we get around to fixing it. One day we'll finally get those cobweb-covered skis out of the garage and slalom down the slopes. Those favorite jeans will surely fit again, once we dust off that treadmill in the basement. Potential—the notion that an object has latent capacities for future usefulness or beauty—is, like memory, intimately linked to identity, and it is therefore a powerful cause of attachment. If memory helps us create a coherent sense of self by providing fodder for our personal narrative, then potential allows us to envision an idealized version of ourselves yet to come. Whereas some objects are valuable because they remind us of what was, others are so because they inspire us to imagine what may be.

To further explore the role of memory and potential in our relationship to things, I look at the KonMari Method, a wildly popular approach to curating possessions that sees things as having a vitality that waxes and wanes in response to care or neglect. Hoarders cling to objects that either remind them of the past or help them imagine a better future. The KonMari Method, in contrast, is more focused on the present. It characterizes both memory and potential as psychological traps—deceitful distractions from the joyful here and now that threaten to drain our very life energy. Followers of the KonMari Method are encouraged to tune in mindfully to the objects they possess to see if they still inspire joy. If not, their owners must free themselves from this dead energy and discard them. Memories and future hopes are mere delusions that keep us mired in stagnant stuff we no longer want.

In both hoarding and the KonMari Method, an object's role in either memorializing one's past or animating one's future is the standard for measuring its worth. However, that worth is assessed differently. For hoarders, objects are so meaningful that to discard them is unthinkable. The KonMari Method holds that any object's value is necessarily ephemeral, and clinging to memories or fantasies stymies the dynamic process of letting go and living in the moment. The examples of relationships between people and their things described in this chapter may be extreme, even polar opposites. But their coinciding prevalence in the popular imagination is instructive. As different but related responses to the overabundance of consumer goods, they offer important insights to the power of memory and the potential to imbue our material world with a sense of vitality and meaning that demands an ethical response of us.

On Packrats and Clutterbugs

People exhibit myriad responses to the massive deluge of consumer products available across the industrialized world. Negotiating this seeming world of plenty is a challenge for some more than others. In recent years, so-called hoarders have been thrust into the national spotlight, most prominently by way of no fewer than four documentary series airing on North American basic cable networks. *Hoarders* (2009–) aired for six seasons on A&E before moving to Lifetime. A&E reports that the series premiere of *Hoarders* was watched by 2.5 million viewers, and it was the most-watched premiere in the

network's history among the coveted demographic group of eighteen-
to forty-nine-year-olds. The TLC network began running its own
program on the subject, *Hoarding: Buried Alive* (2010–). The Discovery Life network has *Hoarding: Behind Closed Doors* (2015); Oprah
Winfrey's OWN network debuted *Extreme Clutter!* in 2011; and even
Animal Planet offers a show featuring animal hoarders. Anthropologist Susan Lepselter, in her study on hoarding narratives in popular
culture, argues that this "increasing collective fetish for the hoarder's fetishes" highlights economic anxieties in these early decades
of the twenty-first century: "In the manic depression surrounding
crashes, foreclosures, and the secular jeremiads on consumer folly
and greed, all occurring against years of confident neoliberalism and
globalization, the hoarder's monstrous accumulations loom with
an increasingly ambivalent fascination."[10] Anthropologist Katie
Kilroy-Marac puts it more simply: hoarding is "clearly having a moment of sorts."[11] Like much reality programming, these shows tend
to offer up hoarders as targets for us to gawk at, to pity, and to gape at
with appalled fascination at the obscene chaos of their homes.

Yet hoarding is a legitimate affliction. In 2013, when the American
Psychological Association released the fifth edition of the *Diagnostic
and Statistical Manual of Mental Disorders*, hoarding was for the first time
listed as a disorder in its own right, rather than merely a symptom or
subset of other disorders, such as schizophrenia or obsessive compulsive disorder (OCD). Hoarding disorder is defined as "the excessive
acquisition of and inability to discard objects, resulting in debilitating
clutter."[12] Although its inclusion in the DSM-5 makes hoarding official, this description tells us little that's not already out there in the
cultural ether. Those who study it acknowledge that we have a long way
to go in understanding the condition. Psychologist Randy Frost, who
published the first systematic studies of the phenomenon as recently
as the 1990s, describes hoarding as "a brand-new disorder, something
we didn't recognize before," acknowledging, "We know nothing about
it. And I've been doing this for 20 years. The field is wide open."[13]

It's estimated that 2 to 5 percent of the American population suffers from hoarding; that's six to fifteen million people in the United States alone.[14] These numbers could actually be much higher because the shame and secrecy associated with hoarding means that many hoarders do not seek treatment, thus making it difficult to diagnose. Further exacerbating the issue, hoarders are often reluctant or unable to identify themselves as such. Yale neuropsychologist David Tolin and his collaborators note that hoarders frequently exhibit "poor insight about the severity of their condition, leading to resistance of attempts by others to intervene."[15]

Hoarding is considered pathological when an uncontrollable compulsion to acquire and save objects begins to negatively impact one's family and work life, and one's living space becomes debilitating. Tolin and his team conducted brain scans of hoarders and found that they demonstrated inhibited decision-making abilities, especially in the face of uncertain outcomes (for example, the possibility that one might need a particular newspaper clipping for future reference). Hoarders' brain activity was compared to two control groups: those with OCD and neurotypical adult subjects. When asked to decide which from a collection of their possessions to discard, results of functional magnetic resonance imaging scans of hoarders showed that they were both slower and more reluctant to choose among the items than were control subjects. They appeared similarly attached to all of them.

Hoarders often also have OCD, anxiety disorders, and depression. However, unlike those syndromes, as Frost and Steketee note in *Stuff: Compulsive Hoarding and the Meaning of Things*, "In hoarding . . . we frequently see *positive* emotions propelling acquisition and saving."[16] When conducting their study, they found that despite the obvious negative effects of living among so much stuff, hoarders describe the genuine pleasure they take in being surrounded by their treasures. Frost and Steketee liken this pleasure to that of the safety and comfort of building a cocoon or bunker in which one ensconces oneself in a nest of one's own making.

Pleasure is also to be had in the thrill of acquisition. Home shopping networks are popular among hoarders, as are thrift shops. Irene, a central figure in *Stuff*, describes her compulsion to shop: "That's my thing. It's what gives me joy. I get a real high from finding a bargain."[17] Irene's belief that shopping gives her a high is echoed throughout scholarly and popular testimonials from hoarders. In a *Dateline NBC* special, for example, Phil describes being "in the zone" when buying a pair of left-handed golf clubs at a thrift shop, even though he already owns several sets of golf clubs and is right-handed.[18] Frost and Steketee say that the hoarding clients they work with "often describe dissociative-like states, periods of time where they are so focused on the item they want to buy that they forget about the context of their lives—such as whether they have the money, space, or need for the item. Some people may have a tendency to experience this 'flow state' more readily than others, making them vulnerable to becoming compulsive buyers or hoarders."[19] This sense of being "in the zone" or "high" while shopping can, like drugs, alcohol, and even gambling offer a momentary respite from the problems in one's life, as it focuses all one's energy in the present moment. The surge one receives when, say, discovering a designer dress offered at a discount, or a finding a rare LP to add to one's ever-expanding collection, puts a person squarely in the here and now of bodily and mental sensation. That state of presence allows one, however temporarily, to escape from a haunting past or the anxieties of an unknown future.

Hoarding behavior tends to fall on a spectrum. Some may be considered merely eccentric collectors, a shopaholic, packrat, or clutterbug. Others take hoarding to the painful extremes we see on cable television. But it goes without saying that difficulty exercising impulse control at the mall is not a challenge faced only by hoarders; nor are they the only ones among us who enjoy the thrill of hunting for and acquiring something new. Shopping for the fun of it or as a means of escape is a widely accepted, if derided, commonplace in modern consumer culture. Indeed, although it falls under the "humorous" category, "retail therapy" is an official entry in the *Oxford English Dictionary*, as is "shopaholic."

The joy of acquisition is certainly a component of hoarding, but emotional attachment to the things one already owns is its most pernicious characteristic, as it leads to the piles and squalor that inhibit a hoarder's everyday life. Hoarders seem unable to part with things even after the thrill is gone or the item has outlived its usefulness. Hoarding appears to be an excess of attachment, a compulsion to see all of one's possessions, however mundane, as significant. One group of psychologists suggests that the intense attachment to things that hoarders exhibit might best be characterized as "empathy in overdrive," in that hoarders care so much for things and the memories associated with them that they become unable to distinguish or prioritize their respective value.[20] For example, as part of their study, the researchers gifted small key chains to sixty-two subjects diagnosed with OCD, asking them to assess their attachment to the object at the time of receipt and then again one week later. They found that although most of the subjects grew somewhat attached to the key chain over the course of the week, those who tended to hoard described experiencing a kind of "love at first sight," and were significantly attached to theirs right away.[21]

In reality, hoarders tend to belie the traditional stereotype of the miserly recluse. Testimonials from hoarders offered in scholarly and popular accounts tend to emphasize the empathetic quality of objects, which they see as powerful links to other people and experiences. Irene says she usually saves things because they might be useful or interesting to people she knows. "Instead of replacing people with possessions," write Frost and Steketee, "Irene was using possessions to make connections between people and to the world at large."[22] In keeping with other research that finds hoarders to be exceptionally empathetic, Frost and Steketee point to the intuitive intelligence of hoarders, suggesting that even though hoarding is a painful mental disorder, "it may stem from an extraordinary ability. For hoarders, every object is rich in detail. We disregard the color and hue of a magazine cover as we search for the article inside. But if we paid attention, we might notice the soothing effect of the colors, and the meaning of the object would expand in the process. In this way, the physical world of hoarders is different and much more expansive than that of the rest of us."[23] For hoarders, the material world around them feels alive with meaning and promise, beginning with that feeling of love at first sight experienced at the moment of acquisition. That thrill inevitably passes, yet hoarders express an inability to let go of either the memory or the promise they attach to an object. Often hoarders attach to an object because they see it as a record of their relationship to a loved one who is now gone. One hoarder describes it as "keeping items that belong to dead loved ones to keep those persons around."[24] Another notes that she hoards "just to reminisce, just like listening to an old song brings back memories. Nostalgia."[25]

Similarly, some hoarders see themselves as archivists of their family or the era in which they live—a responsibility they take very seriously. Debra describes herself as someone who fears change and wants to freeze time: "I don't like forwards," she says. "I like backwards." Debra photographs things in order to preserve them: "Every second of my life I can document. If I want to remember it, I'll take a picture." She uses photography (up to thirty rolls of film in a month) as a way to capture the essence of things in order to cope with getting rid of things she cannot keep, like perishables. She even admits to photographing her trash.[26] Hoarders like Debra see their possessions as priceless documents of their past; they feel that discarding their possessions would be to lose a bit of themselves. Others express feelings of responsibility to the objects they own. As Linda tells researchers, "The idea of jettisoning something that's had long and faithful service and when it gets mucked up or a bit dottery, it seems cruel to throw it out." Linda admits that her position "may be personalizing the object a bit," but she nevertheless feels unable to separate from the objects at hand—in this case, a worn pair of shoes.[27]

In her memoir *Coming Clean*, Kimberly Rae Miller documents her childhood growing up with a father who hoarded. Like others, she observes the intense empathy and sense of connectedness that often underlies the affliction:

Many hoarders start hoarding as a form of connecting to other people. And so when they see something that reminds them of someone they love, they hold on to it. If it reminds them of a way they felt good, or a positive memory in their life, they hold on to it. A lot of hoarders are incredibly intelligent people, and they're able to see things in ordinary objects that we wouldn't necessarily see. And so, getting rid of those items is incredibly hard for them.[28]

Miller here captures a theme that repeatedly arises in interviews with people who hoard: that the objects serve as proxies; they represent emotions—toward loved ones, or experiences—that are simply too unbearable to discard. To get rid of something thus feels like committing a violent act to oneself and one's memories. A worried Irene remarks, "If I throw too much away, there'll be nothing left of me." When attempting to clean out her home, Irene struggles to discard a "decades-old history book" and starts to cry: "I just feel like I want to die," she says. "This is one of my treasure books. I know I haven't looked at it in thirty years, but it feels like a part of me." As Frost and Steketee explain, "Hoarded objects become part of the hoarder's identity or personal history. In a sense, they come to define his or her identity."[29]

If some treasured objects provide a link to the past, then others are valued for their promise of a better future. Lorraine describes the conflict she feels over her "clutterbug" tendencies, especially when it comes to her books: "To achieve my goal to get the house uncluttered, I have to get rid of some of them. But it's very difficult to pick which ones to get rid of."[30] Part of the difficulty is that many hoarders believe that one day, they will eventually read all those stacks of magazines, or make a meal from one of the cookbooks piled in the corner, or have occasion to use the gadgets accumulating in the garage. This is why so many hoarders continue to keep things they don't actually use. As one poster to an online hoarding website explains, "I truly believe that once I organize my house, I will finally be able to use all the items that have been 'hidden' or in piles or behind other things. So, I have blind faith that I will soon clean up, and that perpetuates the comforting and incorrect belief of future use."[31] Another fears squandering the latent value of her collection: "The Antiques Road Show is terrible for me. I hoard antiques, and fear selling them, because I might need the money some day."[32] A man named Ralph, interviewed by Frost and Steketee, holds onto everything he sees as having potential use to himself or other people, even a piece of an old broken venetian blind: "Most people would throw this out. Not me," he tells them proudly. Ralph also insists on keeping an old bucket despite its hole, because for him, anything he could imagine a use for, even a bucket that could not hold water, was worth saving.[33]

Squandering the potential of objects—perhaps especially for those raised in poverty—is nothing less than a sin. One hoarder claims to avoid neighbors seeing her bringing in the groceries or taking out the trash for fear of being judged by others: "[My behavior] seems to be predicated on the idea that if people see what I bring in, consume, and discard, they will assume that I'm spendthrift, selfish, wasteful. I know that one bag of trash a week isn't all that much, but I'm still petrified of being seen with it. As though I hadn't made full use of the things I purchased."[34] Of Irene, Frost and Steketee write, "It was not [the objects'] use that she found reinforcing, but the idea of having them. Their potential appealed to her."[35] If some objects are prized as bearers of one's history, then the insistence on an object's potential, or the opportunities it affords, is also a central theme in hoarding discourse. Even if it is perpetually deferred, the object is seen either as a vehicle to a better life for oneself or as latent value yet to be realized. It is that potential—for connection, success, happiness—that is the source of the unbreakable bond hoarders feel for many of the objects they save. To discard an object is to abandon or sacrifice a relationship with the past and the future.

Sparking Joy and the Rise of a Curated Life

After the overwhelming success of *The Life-Changing Magic of Tidying Up*, Kondo published a manga version, as well as an illustrated companion book, *Spark Joy: An Illustrated Master Class on the Art of Organizing and Tidying Up* (2012). *Time* magazine named Kondo one of 2015's most influential people, and the *New Yorker*, the *New York Times*, *Le Monde*, *Fast Company*, the *Atlantic*, the *Wall Street Journal*, and the *Economist* are among the many publications to have offered profiles and long-form analyses assessing the influence of the Kon-Mari Method for relating to one's possessions. The movement she has inspired has only intensified. "To kondo" has become a verb used to describe the act of curating one's possessions. Followers across the world, calling themselves "konverts," use a variety of hashtags to share their tidying trials and triumphs on social media sites like Instagram, Pinterest, YouTube, and Twitter. Popular television shows like *Younger* (2015–), *Transparent* (2014–19), and the Netflix *Gilmore Girls* reboot (2016) all make references to KonMari. NBC toyed with greenlighting a sitcom about a young woman attempting to get her life organized called—you guessed it—*The Life-Changing Magic of Tidying Up*.

In the end, Netflix won the right to capitalize on the Kondo craze, dropping eight episodes of *Tidying Up with Marie Kondo* on New Year's Day 2019. The format of the show features Kondo, along with her translator, visiting the homes of American families and guiding them in the process of assessing how they feel about the objects in their home. She gently works with them as they let go of those things that no longer delight them. The climax of each episode is less a big-reveal finale, with its familiar visual tropes of tidy closets and organized pantries so common to domestic makeover shows. Rather, the emotional engine of *Tidying Up* is the cathartic purge Kondo's clients engage in as they struggle to face their messy demons. They bravely make the hard choices, then ultimately purge the excess stuff holding them back. A central theme of the show is detachment. People struggle to part with mementos and to discard outdated collections, but eventually they commit to the purge and make space for new, better things to come. The show frames tidying up as a sort of wellness cleanse for one's home, a process of releasing the dead weight of objects lying dormant—or, worse, toxic and festering from lack of use.

Marie Kondo feels the spark of joy in *Tidying Up with Marie Kondo* (Netflix, 2019).

Although the show's families all live in the greater Los Angeles area, they are quite diverse: straight, gay, white, African American, Asian American, Latinx, young, middle-aged. One couple struggles with the clutter that comes from raising toddlers; another couple, empty nesters, face a house teeming with decades of memorabilia; twenty-something writers look to graduate into full-fledged adulthood; a recently widowed woman in her sixties takes a life-affirming step into an uncertain but hopeful future without her beloved husband, processing her grief by processing the possessions he left behind. Different as their life circumstances may be, the families in each episode represent important milestones, seasons of life that most of us face. With Kondo's guidance, they discover how organizing their homes and discarding unwanted things can help them lead the lives they want.

Kondo's surge has generated some controversies, most importantly around the perceived racism in white people's response to her massively popular show. Some have suggested her popularity is due in part to a fetishized orientalism; they suggest that people's fascination with her is the latest instantiation in an ongoing habit of Westerners to turn to Asian cultures for the earthy spirituality they find lacking.[36] Others have argued that the many critiques of Kondo (most vociferous were bibliophiles enraged by a mistaken belief that she mandates people keep only thirty books) fall back on retrograde "dragon lady" stereotypes that have long cast Asian women as possessing a mystical but severe power.[37] These debates notwithstanding, the KonMari Method does have a decidedly Japanese sensibility to it, reinvigorating in modern consumers across the globe a traditional reverence for objects. Kondo's method for streamlining one's home is straightforward, but not necessarily easy. Rather than tidying by looking for things to get rid of, she argues, we should focus on what it is we want to keep. And how to decide what's worth keeping? "Take each item in one's hand and ask: 'Does this spark joy?'" she writes. "If it does, keep it. If not, dispose of it. This is not only the simplest but also the most accurate yardstick by which to judge."[38] What follows this simple mandate is a systematic program in which readers are to go through their living space and, by category, not room, tackle their clothes, then books, then papers, then *komono* (miscellany), and finally mementos, in that order. Only once this first phase is complete, a process Kondo acknowledges may take several months, can one start deciding on appropriate places to store the joy-sparking possessions that made the cut.

The popularity of the KonMari Method is undoubtedly buoyed by the rising tide of interest in what I described earlier as meaningful minimalism. Kondo is a fellow traveler among the minimalism movement, to be sure. But what distinguishes her book as such a runaway hit with readers across the world is precisely that her approach doesn't call for self-denial, restriction, or even actually minimalism. Instead, it encourages readers to forge a more intimate relationship with the objects in their lives. Throughout her books, lectures, interviews, and television show, Kondo affords inanimate objects a magical quality, a vital energy that, when appropriately fostered, has the power to make us a bit more magical, too. The German translation of the book's title is *Magic Cleaning*, which captures its essence perfectly well, because

Kondo's liberal use of "magic" isn't metaphorical. She means it. Her "Does it spark joy?" metric echoes the well-known criterion offered by nineteenth-century designer William Morris, a founder of the Arts and Crafts movement: "Have nothing in your house that you do not know to be useful, or believe to be beautiful."[39] But Kondo is less influenced by European Marxist maker movements than she is the devotional practices of Shintoism, the ancient Japanese religion for which spirits live not only in people but also in inanimate objects, including rivers, trees, shoes, and chopsticks.

As it happens, Kondo worked for five years at a Shinto shrine, where she sold charms called *omamori*, believed to offer protection or good luck. She writes that she loved visiting shrines as a child, especially collecting the small charms that she understands to be imbued with magic. However, she explains, "Please keep in mind that charms are not something you buy but something with which you are entrusted. They are effective only for one year after you receive them, so those that are past their expiration dates should be returned as soon as possible."[40] This key Shinto observation—the waxing and waning of vitality in all things—infuses Kondo's approach to living with objects. Animism is one of its defining principles. Properly caring for the objects in our lives is important not only so they last longer but because they have feelings too. One should unpack one's bag at the end of each day, for example, because it has spent all day benevolently supporting our needs. "What a hard worker!" she writes, "It would be cruel not to give it a break at least at home. Being packed all the time, even when not in use, must feel something like going to bed on a full stomach."[41] Our socks especially warrant TLC: "Never, ever tie up your stockings. Never, ever ball up your socks," she admonishes. When inspecting one errant client's sock drawer, she reports, "I pointed to the balled-up socks. 'Look at them carefully. This should be a time for them to rest. Do you really think they can get any rest like that?' That's right," she adds. "The socks and stockings stored in your drawer are essentially on holiday. They take a brutal beating in their daily work, trapped between your foot and your shoe, enduring pressure and friction to protect your precious feet. The time they spend in your drawer is their only chance to rest."[42] When working with clients to curate their book collections on *Tidying Up*, Kondo suggests they first wake the books up, since they've been sleeping. She demonstrates this by putting her hand on a pile of books, then giving them a little shake to stir their energy.

As detailed as Kondo's advice is for caring for the physical needs of objects—socks should be folded, not balled; T-shirts should be rolled and laid side by side in a drawer, not stacked—she suggests that to be true stewards of our possessions, we must also tend to the needs of their spirit by expressing gratitude for their service. When we are folding, for example, "we should put our heart into it, thanking our clothes for protecting our bodies," as "folding is really a form of dialogue with our wardrobe," noting the ritualized folding methods for traditional Japanese clothing like *kimono* and *yukata*.[43] She describes the gratitude ritual she practices each day as she arrives home: "I'm home!" she announces to her empty house.[44] "Thank you very much for your hard work," she tells her shoes. "Good job!" she says as she hangs up her dress.[45] Finally, "You did well. Have a good rest," she says to her handbag.[46] The whole process only takes five minutes, she assures readers, encouraging them to try it. A staple segment of her Netflix show involves Kondo "greeting the home," paying her respects in a small ritual as she asks for its blessing. She kneels on the floor, closes her eyes, and sits silently for a few moments. As she finishes, she draws a small circle around her body with her fingertips, places her palms to the ground, and bows. After conducting this ritual with Margie, the grieving widow in episode 4, she assures Margie, "I will tell you, the feeling in this house is spectacular. So what I'd like you to remember as you go through this process is that you're not alone; the house itself and all your belongings are there to support you and are with you."

Discarded objects also deserve our respect, writes Kondo. "Can you truthfully say you treasure something buried so deeply in a closet or drawer that you have forgotten its existence?" she asks. "If things had feelings, they would certainly not be happy. Free them from the prison to which you have relegated them."[47] Although it may no longer set our heart sufficiently aflutter, each item has fulfilled the important function of showing us something about ourselves, and it should be thanked accordingly. Kondo encourages readers to take a moment and say, "Thank you for giving me joy when I bought you," or "Thank you for teaching me what doesn't suit me" before discarding an object or donating it so that it can perhaps spark joy in someone else.[48] Although many of us may see the benefits of practicing gratitude, I suspect that for many readers, Kondo's almost anthropomorphized view of objects may seem a bit too much. However, at a time when many people feel overwhelmed by the sheer volume of mass-produced goods in their lives, I believe it's also a large part of the appeal.

Kondo's perspective isn't new; in fact, it's ancient. Mortuary rituals for everyday items at the end of their life span have been performed for millennia and are still common in Japan. As Angelika Kretschmer writes in her study of *hari kuyō*, or requiem services held for inanimate objects: "*Kuyō* rites for objects are presently carried out for items as diverse as needles, chopsticks, combs, dolls, clocks, personal seals (*hanko*), knives, shoes, scissors, and semiconductors."[49] But the Japanese are hardly alone in attributing human characteristics to non-human objects. Anthropologist Stewart Guthrie argues, for example, that religions writ large are "systematic anthropomorphism" and serve the function of domesticating the unpredictable, ultimately unknowable world, translating it into something familiar and thereby reducing our anxiety by anchoring us to something relatable.[50] As Lyall Watson explains, in modern times, "such anthropomorphism is easy to understand, as it gives the engines which now run much of our lives a reassuringly human face."[51] Given that most of us living in globalized, industrial economies are forced to navigate a system in which the flow of products, information, and capital are far beyond our control or even comprehension, a discourse that personalizes the everyday products of that system may help to bring it all down to scale. If religious traditions historically served to make the world easier to understand through the anthropomorphization of objects, so too does the evangelical rhetoric of consumer culture, which increasingly suggests that every object has a personality and a story to tell. The gods may have changed, but the overriding logic has not.

For Kondo, the organizing function of objects—a kind of domestic jouissance—is key to one's sense of well-being, as they serve as conduits that connect us to ourselves and the world. The *Financial Times* describes Kondo as an "intuitive economist" because she offers antidotes to the issues that eat at behavioral scientists, such as status quo bias, opportunity cost, or the problem of diminishing returns.[52] Perhaps she is, but the psychology of choice Kondo offers sounds different from anything we might read in a consumer economics textbook.

If she is an intuitive economist, then she is also something of a therapist: "The whole point in both discarding and keeping things is to be happy."[53] Kondo's method and its legions of followers are situated squarely within what can only be called the happiness trend, a cultural juggernaut too massive to cover adequately here. What's relevant for our purposes is that KonMari, the personal organization industry—and object acquisition, curation, and storage in general—is one of the more populated lanes in the race to more happiness, wellness, and meaning that is currently underway in the more affluent and aspirational segments of U.S. culture. Proper management of one's possessions, as we've seen in the minimalist movements discussed earlier, is often cast as moral righteousness. Kilroy-Marac explains, "As the visible absence of clutter signals affluence, it may also signal virtue; the two are, in fact, closely intertwined. In the pages of home and lifestyle magazines like *Real Simple* and in larger public conversations about the merits of moderation, self-regulation, and self-discipline amidst endless possibilities for acquisition and accumulation."[54] She likens the discussion to the contemporary conversation about obesity: "As with talk about thinness versus fatness, talk about the proper and improper accumulation of stuff plays into a 'virtue discourse' (Halse 2009); those who consume too much or cannot manage their object worlds are seen as being out of control, lazy, and undisciplined."[55] Connections between discipline, well-being, and happiness pervade the culture right now, as evidenced by the booming popularity of books, wearable devices, and apps, all designed to help us track our exercise, calorie intake, sleep quality, mindfulness, and other good-for-us habits. Kondo even released *Life-Changing Magic—A Journal* in which to log one's tidying-up travails, peppered with such Kondoisms as "Letting go is even more important than adding" and "I can think of no greater happiness in life than to be surrounded only by the things I love."[56]

This latest instantiation of the quantified self resonates with a long tradition in Western culture. Classical scholars of rhetoric, such as Aristotle and Isocrates, for example, advocate the idea that everyday habits can lead to virtue, which in turn leads to happiness. Likewise, Benjamin Franklin, an ardent habit tracker, charts his progress via a system he created on several behaviors that he thinks contribute to virtues he wants to cultivate in himself: moderation, order, and cleanliness. In fact, Franklin's famous system is the model for writer Gretchen Rubin, who for her 2009 book *The Happiness Project* spent a year measuring her progress on twelve measurable goals in various areas (parenting, marriage, self-fulfillment, and so on). Perhaps you've heard the anecdote that one key to happiness is to make your bed every day? That comes from Rubin, who parlays that nugget, along with her enthusiastic testimonial about the happiness-generating power of an organized closet, into her second best seller, *Happier at Home*, which are followed by *Better Than Before* (2015) and *The Four Tendencies* (2017), not to mention a variety of happiness-related products such as a Happiness Project journal, coloring book, and a podcast called *Happier*. Her 2019 best seller, *Outer Order, Inner Calm: Declutter and Organize to Make More Room for Happiness*, provides her alternative to the KonMari Method.

As important as discipline is to success with Kondo's method, she adamantly parts ways with the microhabits strategy advocated by most happiness gurus like Rubin.[57] Although Kondo and Rubin agree that clutter (and an unmade bed) is a surefire happiness buster, Kondo rejects the popular notion that meticulously tracked, incremental change is the best path to the good life. Although infused with heavy doses of magical language, Kondo is unyielding in her insistence that tidying up be done in one fell swoop, what she calls a marathon, which may take days or even months. What's more, it must be done by category, not location. "If you have never succeeded in staying tidy to date, you will find it next to impossible to develop the habit of tidying a little at a time" she writes. "People cannot change their habits without first changing their way of thinking."[58] "The root of the problem lies in the mind," she writes elsewhere.[59] The big purging and organizing marathon Kondo advocates is meant to serve as a kind of reboot for one's mind, which has been erroneously clinging to objects that no longer serve. Unlike the more neuropsychology-based "habits beget mind-set" strategy, Kondo's philosophy has more in common with the magical thinking of the law of attraction approach, popularized by the film *The Secret* (2006), in which one has to first change his or her thinking, or get into the flow, before taking action. Her gentle tone notwithstanding, Kondo is something of an organizing drill sergeant, demanding that readers check sentimentality at the door and follow her model to the letter. One must trust and give oneself over fully to the process in order to realize the life-changing magic of tidying up.

The order in which Kondo's readers are to tackle the process— clothes, books, papers, miscellany, and mementos—is itself an escalation from those things least likely to inspire emotional attachment to those that will make choosing more difficult. Unused clothing and books, for example, are valued for their as yet unrealized potential. However, although it may be difficult to admit that we're unlikely to ever wear that trendy dress bought on a whim, or read the book on a topic that no longer interests us, the evidence is right there before our eyes, as these items lie dormant on the shelf or in the closet. Papers and miscellaneous items also hold the value of potential future usefulness, but their utility can be assessed relatively easily. "Starting with mementos," however, "spells certain failure," Kondo warns. "Things that bring back memories, such as photos, are not the place for beginners to start." If one adheres to the prescribed order, however, the psyche will be adequately prepared for the tough stuff later on: "As you gradually work toward the harder categories, you will be honing your decision-making skills," she assures her readers.[60]

Throughout Kondo's rhetoric, we hear the familiar slogan: Be present. An in-this-moment mindfulness is the most powerful weapon against clutter, she tells readers again and again. Although she doesn't address the extremes of hoarding directly, Kondo's targets are on the one hand a backward-looking sentimentality, and on the other hand a misguided belief in the utility of stockpiling objects for future use. These twin dragons of nostalgia and potential haunt those who suffer from an incapacitating reluctance to discard. Both have the tendency to take us out of the joyful now and mire us in the dead energy of past regrets or anxieties about the future.

Compared to the calcified stuckness of hoarding, Kondo certainly advocates a more fluid relationship to objects: If it doesn't spark joy, say thank you, and let it go. Unlike hoarders, who finds that discarding belongings is like losing a bit of themselves, Kondo promises that "truly precious memories will never vanish even if you discard the objects associated with them." Importantly, she continues, "We live in the present. No matter how wonderful things used to be, we cannot live in the past. The joy and excitement we feel here and now are more important."[61] Releasing those things that no longer serve you allows you to "process your past": "If you just stow these things away in a drawer or cardboard box, before you realize it, your past will become a weight that holds you back and keeps you from living in the here and now."[62]

Kondo is equally adamant that saving things for future use is taxing on the psyche. She tells a story of one of her clients, a young woman she calls M, who was making good progress, having filled thirty bags with items to discard or donate—that is, until her mother came into the room. M's mother began rummaging through the bags, rescuing items of potential use. Kondo relays the ensuing conversation:

> "Oh my, are you going to throw that away?" she said, pointing to a pink yoga mat on top of the pile.

"I haven't used it in two years."

"Really? Well, maybe I'll use it then," said the mother before collecting a few more things to keep.

Kondo continues, "When the room was quiet again, I sipped my iced tea and asked M, "So how often does your mother do yoga?"

"I've never seen her do any."[63]

For Kondo, latent potential is useless in this present moment: "I highly recommend that you get rid of excess stock all at once. Give it away to friends who need it, recycle it, or take it to a donation shop. You may think this is a waste of money, but reducing your stock and relieving yourself of the burden of excess is the quickest and most effective way to put your things in order."[64] She tells several stories of clients who have stockpiled massive amounts of things like toilet paper and toothbrushes—more than they could reasonably use. The stories are amusing, but only because her clients don't seem to exhibit the truly pathological symptoms of those who struggle with hoarding. But their reasons for stocking up are the same: the comfort of feeling that they are prepared, just in case. Kondo argues that such an orientation to the future diminishes one's happiness in the present: "For people who stockpile, I don't think there is any amount that would make them feel secure."[65] An *Atlantic* writer aptly describes her position as a rejoinder to the economic concept of opportunity cost: "The mental and physical toll of keeping an unused item around is greater than throwing it out."[66]

The Past and Future Value of Things

At first glance, the KonMari decluttering method may seem to occupy the opposite pole from hoarding if we were to think of the two practices on some sort of linear attachment spectrum, and in many ways it does. However, from a rhetorical perspective—that is, looking at the tropes, or linguistic commonplaces used in the popular conversation surrounding both—it seems that much unites these two responses to the current tsunami of stuff and the clutter it leaves in its wake.

First, as we have seen, the ways practitioners speak of both hoarding and the KonMari Method emphasize a kind of historicity of the object. Hoarders value the object's role as document, verifying what was. In this, their relation to objects is much like semiotician Roland Barthes's description of the testimonial power of the photograph: "In photography I can never deny that the thing has been there. . . . Every photograph is a certificate of presence. . . . An emanation of past reality . . . that-has-been."[67] For many of us, a departed loved one's watch may be as powerful a "certificate of presence" as a snapshot. Hoarders, however, assign meaning almost indiscriminately. All the objects in their lives are afforded this certificate status. Those objects provide the ontological record of a historicity that in turn hoarders come to see as constitutive of themselves. The excess of objects thus serves as an organizing principle that lets them make sense of themselves and to themselves. To remove, recycle, or otherwise dispose of the objects would be akin to purging a treasured memory or amputating a limb. Indeed, Frost and Steketee report "several cases in which hoarders have committed suicide following a forced cleanout" because the person has lost the sense of order their collection provides.[68]

"Konverts," in contrast, are encouraged to see objects as only transitory vehicles for history. That is, to prevent stagnation, one should keep the memory and discard the thing: "Just as the word implies, mementos are reminders of a time when these items gave us joy. . . . No matter how wonderful things used to be, we cannot live in the past. The joy and excitement we feel here and now are more important," writes Kondo.[69] Like shrine charms, all things eventually lose their vitality and must be released when they do. But if this seems like a strikingly different approach to the way objects constitute one's history, it nonetheless hinges on what is only a marginally different approach to historicity itself. Here, as with hoarding, objects are vehicles for history. But unlike hoarders, konverts believe that objects tire, that they have a finite life span, and that their capacity to serve as media for memories is eventually exhausted.

A second dominant set of tropes is future oriented, focusing on the potentiality of objects. As we have seen, many hoarders emphasize the possibility that they may one day have use for the things they save. As Irene describes it, "Life is a river of opportunities. If I don't grab everything interesting, I'll lose out. Things will pass me by. The stuff I have is like a river. It flows into my house, and I try to keep it from flowing out. I want to stop it long enough to take advantage of it."[70] Irene sees objects as ripe with possibility, even as they may be literally rotting in the unused piles that litter her home. Readers of Aristotle may be reminded of his theory of forms, suggesting that all things have two dichotomous characteristics. *Dunamis* (often translated as the Latin *potentia*) refers to his observation that an object's full "thinghood"—its potential—is embedded within it. Even if not yet realized, a thing has the power or capacity for change. *Energeia* (or *actualitas* in Latin) refers to the drive of all things to actualize themselves, to play out the role their form intends. In ways, some hoarders' attachment to objects seems overdetermined by their potential to such a degree their actuality may be thwarted as a result.

If life is a river of potential, then for Kondo it's one that must be allowed to flow freely, not bogged down by an obligation to the past or the future. That said, potentiality does play a large role in the KonMari Method. The value of objects is itself all about their potential to spark joy. Her book is filled with stories of clients who didn't think a clutter-free, ordered home was possible before devoting themselves to the life-changing magic of KonMari. Although her refrain when it comes to saving things like unread books or unworn clothes is "'sometime' means 'never,'" the real endgame (or telos) of the method is the promise of enjoying, once and for all, the clutter-free life of one's dreams. Kondo holds up her own life as an aspirational potentiality for readers:

> I never tidy my room. Why? Because it is already tidy. . . . I feel happy and content. I have time to experience bliss in my quiet space, where even the air feels fresh and clean; time to sit and sip herbal tea while I reflect on my day. As I look around, my glance falls on a painting that I particularly love, purchased overseas, and a vase of fresh flowers

in one corner. Although not large, the space I live in is graced only with those things that speak to my heart. My lifestyle brings me joy. Wouldn't you like to live this way, too?[71]

Unlike the rhetoric we hear from hoarders, Kondo discourages readers from getting mired in any one object's past or future value. Instead, she asks them to evaluate only whether it still has the potential to spark joy. However, she implores them time and again to imagine for themselves a future life in which they are finally in complete control of their material environment.

Like hoarders, however, Kondo invites her followers to connect to objects in a way that for many contemporary consumers must seem meaningful, even spiritual. She affords them a vitality and depth that offer novel patterns of engagement. In this, the KonMari Method also encourages a kind of empathy in overdrive, particularly for those objects still up to the task of sparking joy in an individual.

Tuning into the objects in our lives is, for Kondo, a psychological, even corporeal, experience: "When you touch a piece of clothing, your body reacts. Its response to each item is different. Trust me and try it."[72] As she told an interviewer, "When you touch something that brings you joy, your body, it feels like it rises up, it gives you a really positive vibe. But when you touch something that you no longer need, or you know doesn't give you a spark of joy, your body actually feels a little bit heavy, and low."[73] In her Netflix show, Kondo demonstrates for Frank and Matt, two young writers, the energy that surges in the body when an object sparks joy. She holds a shirt close to her chest, squeezes her eyes shut and then opens them wide, lifts onto her tiptoes, and makes a delighted "Szhoo!" sound as the two men chuckle and nod. Later Matt explains how he decided to keep a beloved book: "When I hold this I kind of feel this warm sensation, and it's slowly dawned on me, just like, 'Oh, this is what you're supposed to be feeling when you have that spark of joy.' The ones that I didn't feel connected to, it was immediately clear that I was ready to let those ones go."[74] Kondo writes that when you're done with the arduous process of ridding your home of extraneous items and you finally have things neatly organized, "you will feel your heart beat faster and the cells in your body buzz with energy."[75] Even the phrase "sparking joy," which Kondo uses often, is an English translation of the more visceral Japanese word *tokimeku*, which means to "flutter, throb, or palpitate." Only when we surround ourselves with things that literally make our heart sing, she suggests, will we experience the psychic, life-changing magic of tidying up.

The Accursed Share

So what's going on here? What unites these two seemingly different responses to the problem of overconsumption? To better understand the mainstream repudiation of hoarding on the one hand and the remarkable popularity of the KonMari Method on the other, I turn to Georges Bataille's influential concept of the accursed share. Bataille's three-volume treatise, *The Accursed Share*, written in the 1940s, heavily influenced many late twentieth-century observers of consumer culture, such as Jean Baudrillard and Guy Debord. Bataille proposes that to better understand what he calls the general economy, analysts must look not only at production and scarcity but also at consumption and expenditure. Bataille argues that a society's processes of consumption, or waste, tell us something important about that society. That is, analyzing what a culture considers luxurious will help us better diagnose the nature of the syndrome. Although we typically think of luxury as that which is exceedingly comfortable or extravagant, luxury is essentially what exceeds necessity. Indeed, the word *luxury* comes from the Latin *luxus*, "excess." For Bataille, the accursed share referred to the excess energy of any system, "the remainder, or irrecuperable difference," which cannot be easily contained.[76]

If modern capitalism can give us anything our hearts desire and our wallets can accommodate, it must by definition be producing more than we can possibly consume. As such, the accursed share is both the possibility of and a threat to our socioeconomic structure. For Bataille, the real question for any society is how to manage this excess, to dispel it, so that the rest of the system that benefits from that excess can remain intact.

Bataille suggests that economic systems are defined, at least in part, by their public, rhetorical rituals for managing the dispensation of their surplus. He cites a number of historical examples of these rituals of expenditure. The Aztecs, for example, constructed huge pyramids upon which they sacrificed humans, "so that the sun might eat."[77] Bataille describes, in great detail, the elaborate rituals in which slaves (but also warriors, prisoners of war, lepers, and other victims) were publically sacrificed in a rhetorical display meant to appease the gods. These violences, writes Bataille, "combined in an economy that put nothing in reserve."[78] Even as sacrifice eventually became less brutal—when humans were replaced by the ritualized destruction of animals or plants—it maintained its wasteful character. To simply communally ingest these things as food, say at a ceremonial feast, would not suffice. Bataille writes, "The victim of the sacrifice cannot be consumed in the same way as a motor uses fuel."[79] Consumption of this sort would be too utilitarian, too instrumental to do the rhetorical work of wasting the accursed share—that is, to put on display the distinction between ourselves and that which we discard.

Following Marcel Mauss's work on gift economies, Bataille, like Mauss, looks to the Pacific Northwest native tradition of the potlatch, a competitive gift-giving ceremony in which material possessions are given away or destroyed. The voluntary dispensing of property in the potlatch puts one's prestige on display for others. As Bataille writes, "It is the constitution of a positive property of loss—from which springs nobility, honour, and rank in a hierarchy—that gives the institution its significant value."[80]

How does the accursed share present itself in today's consumer-driven economy in what has been called aesthetic capitalism? What public rituals has contemporary capitalism devised to deal with its excess? Understood in this light, KonMari and hoarding represent different sides of the same ritualistic coin. Kondo's method essentially performs a highly aestheticized ritual of expenditure. She tells her readers that they should tune in to their possessions, take them into their hands, feel their pulsing or withering vitality, and decide whether or not they spark joy. On its face, this is admirable. If we are to stem the tsunami of ostensibly disposable but all too durable goods, we may indeed need to take things more seriously, not less. Perhaps Kondo's rhetoric may a bit too out there for some, anthropomorphizing inanimate objects as she does, but she does encourage us to pause and consider the role possessions play in our daily lives. The popularity of her approach indicates that many people are hungry for a more meaningful relationship with their stuff. And this is a potentially fruitful avenue to pursue if we are to cultivate a more intentional approach to consumerism.

Ultimately, however, for all her talk about things, Kondo locates all agency in the human subject. Things are important in the KonMari Method, of course, as they are the material means through which we can explore our inner selves and construct a living environment that is attuned to our needs. There is a karmic, mystical quality to Kondo's discourse that elevates tidying up to a deep, ritualistic dive into one's psyche. She writes, "While not exactly a meditative state, there are times when I am cleaning that I can quietly commune with myself. The work of carefully considering each object I own to see whether it sparks joy inside me is like conversing with myself through the medium of my possessions."[81] In the KonMari Method, the process of taking your possessions in your hands, one by one, is framed as an occasion for self-exploration. The argument for the therapeutic benefits of tidying one's home are on full display in her Netflix show, *Tidying Up*. In one episode, newlyweds Angela and Alishia describe going through the tidying-up process together. Angela: "It was really therapeutic in our relationship." Alishia: "Look, this'll change your life, seriously." Angela adds: "And it's not just about organization, it's really a lifestyle change. And it really is therapeutic and it'll change things in your life." "Oh, yeah," Alishia agrees, nodding. In another episode, Margie echoes the spiritual power of the process: "This process has been very therapeutic, I think. In many ways. It's sort of a rebirth for me." Margie's daughter, Lucy, observes after her mom has purged her home of a truckload of old clothes and books, "You can even feel the air and the energy in the rooms has changed."

Throughout her book, Kondo describes tidying as something of a ceremony, calling it "a special event,"[82] a "once-in-a-lifetime task,"[83] and "a rite of passage to a new life."[84] She even discourages followers from listening to music to pass the time while tidying, so they can more intimately connect with their things. The whole process should be treated as a sacred ritual. Tellingly, however, Kondo offers almost no specificity about the objects she discusses. We're given no sense of why, specifically, the beloved painting that she bought overseas gives her joy. We're told nothing of the material form of the dress she lovingly thanks at the end of the day. Is it the softness of its fabric? The flattering cut? The vibrant color? And when does the joy sparking moment occur? At point of purchase? Over time? Unlike hoarders, Kondo minimizes the role of objects as agents of story, either as mementos or as potentially useful and meaningful, but this resistance to signification does not seem to turn her attention to the material characteristics of the object form itself—at least not in the rhetoric of her massively popular book on the subject.

Perhaps Kondo neglects the material specificities of objects because, as she acknowledges, the discovery of what makes one's heart palpitate is a highly subjective, one might even say narcissistic, operation. As such, her method offers no mechanism for decision making beyond the vague "does it spark joy" principle. Given that corporations spend billions of dollars each year to make their products and brands do just that, the KonMari model isn't up to the task of slowing the ebb and flow of objects. Nor, really, is it meant to be. KonMari at its most ideal is a model for curation, not actually a method for addressing consumption per se. An object may thrill me today for reasons as diverse as it reminds me of my grandmother, I believe it is fashionably on trend, or its texture is pleasing to the touch. But given the fickleness of consumer culture, there's nothing here to stem the almost bulimic process of binging and purging in a never-ending cycle of joyful desire and the inevitable obligation to discard. As with many binaries, the positive term of KonMari (keeping things that give you joy) is ultimately usurped by its negative term (discarding those things that don't make the cut). The purifying ritual of elimination is KonMari's defining characteristic.

Indeed, one need only spend a few minutes scanning the tens of thousands of Twitter and Instagram posts (hashtagged #KonMari) to see what really sparks joy in konverts. It is not beloved dresses, heirloom teacups, or cherished teddy bears. Instead, a dominant motif of the various #KonMari feeds are piles of Hefty bags full of unwanted items awaiting disposal—the proud result of a successful purge. And, of course, there are images of thousands of impeccably organized closets, spice racks, and chests of drawers filled with skillfully folded T-shirts and socks. These are the before and after shots of the accursed share dealt with "properly," with empathy appropriately and ceremoniously reined in, the excesses of consumerism dressed in minimalist garb. Catharsis structures the process of expenditure for the konvert. It is the cleansing and ritualized release that provides excessive consumerism its alibi.

Bataille argues that humans are compelled to consume because it allows them to see themselves more as autonomous subjects than laboring objects at the mercy of an insecure future. "If I am no longer concerned about 'what will be' but about 'what is,'" he writes, "what reason do I have to keep anything in reserve? I can at once, in disorder, make an instantaneous consumption of all that I possess. This useless consumption is *what suits me,* once my concern for the morrow is removed. And if I thus consume immoderately, I reveal to my fellow beings that which I am *intimately*: Consumption is the way in which *separate* beings communicate."[85] Recall Kondo's admonishment of her clients who stockpile things like toilet paper or toothbrushes. These are people for whom anxieties about the future are precluding their bliss in the current moment. Like potlatch participants who get rid of possessions purely to show they have the ability to do so, Kondo and her followers celebrate less the actual objects they keep than the empowerment they enjoy when discarding the ones they no longer want. It is clear from Kondo's writings and her Netflix show that this is not the intention. Her rehearsal of gratitude for the discarded objects has genuine potential for inspiring empathy and a new way of engaging with our possessions. But not everyone has the luxury of destroying the accursed share in this way. As many critics have pointed out, it's easy to keep only those things that spark joy when you have the means to buy what you need when you need it. Other people might, by necessity, keep the tattered sweater missing half its buttons, or the toaster that smokes, or even the thirty rolls of toilet paper bought at a discount that will undoubtedly come in handy one day. One writer zeroes in on the classist nature of the trend, describing her reaction to KonMari as being "like that part in the Hunger Games when Katniss and Peeta are horrified to find that while people are starving in the districts, the people in the Capitol are binging and purging food for kicks."

Although it's clearly less violent than human sacrifice, these public customs of tidying up, so enthusiastically shared on social networks, are not so unlike other public rituals for managing the accursed share. The KonMari Method ritualizes, aestheticizes, and even fetishizes disposal. Again and again in her book she notes that "people may call this wasteful, but . . ."[86] In the most egregious example of this, she addresses the leftover artifacts of health fads to which readers may have fell victim: "Slimming belts, glass bottles for making kefir, a special blender for making tofu, a weight-loss machine that mimics the movement of horseback riding—it seems a waste to get rid of expensive items like these. . . . But you can let them go. The exhilaration you felt when you bought them is what counts."[87]

In the end, in KonMari, the joy seems to lie in getting rid of stuff, not in the items we keep. Marie Kondo, as genuine and lovely as she is, ultimately functions as global capitalism's Winston Wolfe, the fixer played by Harvey Keitel in *Pulp Fiction* (1994) who was brought in to expertly clean up the bloody messes left behind by hit men Jules and

Vincent. The trouble is, Kondo's enormously popular method does nothing to stop the Hefty bags from piling up like so many corpses in a Tarantino film. She simply tidies up the scene of the crime, leaving only beautifully organized closets in her wake.

Hoarders, by contrast, represent a different response to overconsumption, one that seemingly fails to manage the excesses of modern consumer capitalism. I suspect that most of us consume too readily, but hoarders have a more difficult time letting go, and the evidence of their attachment is all too obvious. One role that hoarders—especially popular culture's portrayals of hoarders—play is that of a cautionary tale; they offer examples of excess that allow the rest of us to feel normal. The "scariest reading of [the TV show] 'Hoarders,'" writes Rob Walker, "is that these freakish piles of stuff it documents simply reflect what plenty of us consume as a matter of course. . . . Our ability to dispose of the evidence properly is what makes us normal."[88] Or, as the show's producer puts it, "The line between the people on our show, who have very severe cases of the disorder, and, you know, most of the population, is kind of thin."[89]

Without minimizing or distracting from the very real psychological causes that might induce hoarding to the point where it harms the hoarder or others, hoarding is worth our attention as an emergent symptom of advanced consumer capitalism. Like the rise of self-storage, extreme couponing, and stockpiling, hoarding suggests one means of responding to the massive onslaught of consumer goods in our everyday lives, as well as the ever-present images and voices imploring us to consume still better, bigger, and cooler stuff. As Kilroy-Marac puts it, "One thing hoarding discourses and images of hoarders might do is show us examples of what's just too much," thus allowing us to say, "Oh, we're okay. I consume in a proper way, [whereas] that's excessive; that's pathological."[90] The popular fascination with hoarding may be explained by its role as the excessive alibi, the sign of a truly extreme relationship to objects that the rest of us can point to as counterevidence affirming our own, more moderate choices. Kilroy-Marac writes that hoarding disorder "hinges on *stuff*, it serves to distinguish supposedly normal late capitalist practices of accumulation, organization, and divestment from pathologized forms of being-with-things."[91] She notes that the disorder may be an example of what Ian Hacking has called "transient mental illness," in that it emerges within a population within an "ecological niche."[92] In this way, we might see hoarding as one of the many manifestations of this particular moment in aesthetic capitalism. As Steketee suggests, "People hoard for the same reasons that everyone saves their stuff, just more so."[93] The disorder afflicts individual people, but it is also a symptom of the systemic ecological niche that dominates much of the industrialized world.

Jane Bennett writes, "Perhaps hoarding is the madness appropriate to us, to a political economy devoted to consumption, planned obsolescence, planned extraction of natural resources, and mountains of discarded waste."[94] The kind of behavior portrayed on shows like *Hoarders* (2009–13) and *Hoarding: Buried Alive* (2010–14) is certainly extreme, and many people have rightly questioned the ethics of exploiting mental illness for entertainment. But when we look at the way hoarders talk about their relationship to their possessions, we see that several themes overlap with those expressed in everyday discourse. By foregrounding the complicated relationship between people and things, hoarding tells us something important about where we find ourselves at this stage of globalized, mass-produced consumer culture. With so much stuff on offer, it becomes difficult to moor oneself, to decide how much is enough, and to figure out what has meaning and what does not. As neuropsychology is increasingly demonstrating, hoarders' brains may be predisposed to an overattachment to things. But just because they may be the most vulnerable among us doesn't mean we aren't all subjected to the cultural conditions from which hoarding emerges. Put differently, hoarding tendencies may or may not be a modern phenomenon. Maybe they've always been there in a small handful of the population. But never before has there been such a plethora of things to acquire, and with such ease. Hoarders may be the canaries, but we are all just trying to find our way through the coal mine.

Ultimately, hoarders may be both an object of popular fascination and revulsion because they fail to adequately dispense with the accursed share. For the system to work, the excesses of consumer capitalism are supposed to go away, out of sight and out of mind. But hoarders essentially allow the landfill to take over the living room by refusing to destroy the evidence of acquisition gone awry. In fact, those cable TV shows devoted to hoarding nearly always end the same way: the hoarder is brought in line, and her home is normalized, often at great emotional cost. Indeed, the before and after shots, a staple of cable television, are essential to the narrative of a successful makeover, as they assure viewers that after a temporary deviance, all is again right in the world. If KonMari is defined by the cathartic purge, then hoarding is defined by disordered attachment, which is powered by empathy in overdrive for the objects that might otherwise make up the accursed share. Here it is cathexis, or the concentration of emotion, that threatens to disrupt the supposedly appropriate flow of objects: from factory to store to home to landfill.

While I acknowledge that hoarders exhibit a level of attachment that few of us likely aspire to, I want to suggest that much might be gained if more of us were to slow the purging impulse. Most depictions of hoarders in popular culture invite us to gawk at the pure oddity of the practice: "I just don't understand how someone could live like that!" But researchers who are starting to understand hoarders describe them with tremendous compassion and even a degree of awe. Studies consistently suggest that hoarders are intensely observant of the unique and detailed qualities of objects; they often see them as nodes of connection and meaning within a larger network of humans and the rest of the material world. Again, their affliction has been described as a kind of empathy in overdrive. Merriam Webster's dictionary offers two definitions of the word *empathy*, both of which are instructive here. First, empathy is "the action of understanding, being aware of, sensitive to, and vicariously experiencing the feelings, thoughts, and experience of another." Perhaps we don't have to fully understand hoarding in order to be sensitive to the plight of hoarders and perhaps listen more empathetically to what they have to tell us. But more to our point, empathy also means "the imaginative projection of a subjective state into an object so that the object appears to be infused with it."[95] This is the type of empathy that researchers tell us hoarders have in abundance, but that is a woefully scarce resource in our current mode of consumer culture. It may be that we care both too little and too much for the objects that surround us. We turn them into tokens, tools, or totems, always with the expectation that they are to do our bidding and are then expected to disappear when they are no longer useful or delightful. Empathy may be one step toward interrupting the dual fantasies that we are fully ever in control and that durable goods ever really disappear.

In the following chapter, we will visit what may be an unlikely, but familiar place: your local Target store. Target markets its objects as useful and delightful; it strives to create that joy-sparking attraction many consumers seek. As a so-called fast-design retailer, Target offers little in terms of slowing down the consumption–disposal cycle. However, Target's decisive emphasis on design contributes to a mainstreaming of interest in and awareness of the material and formal components of objects. Although not sufficient in itself, awareness is an important first step in opening up our perception of the manufactured world, thereby potentially providing insight into the ways objects and meaning are made.

TWO

On Target

Aura, Affect, and the Rhetoric of Design Democracy

If we once lived in a "system of objects,"[1] today we live in a world of things. The era of mass consumption, with consumers awash in cheaply made gadgets and gizmos, has given way to a world in which every object is more than merely an object. Each has become or has the potential to become a thing. These things are not oppositional but rather supplemental to the object. They are defined, Bill Brown suggests, "as what is excessive in objects, as what exceeds their mere materialization as objects or their mere utilization as objects—their force as a sensuous presence or as a metaphysical presence, the magic by which objects become values, fetishes, idols, and totems."[2] The thing contains within it magic and mystery—the stuff that dreams are made of.

Marketers and their corporate employers seem to understand, or at least intuit, this shift. Tasked with selling warehouses full of objects, they are increasingly transforming objects into things, or creating things outright in the hopes of sparking and fanning the flames of consumer passion and attraction. Today's capitalism is defined less by pastiche and a certain ahistoricity, as it was for Fredric Jameson,[3] than by an intensification of formal novelty—what Shaviro terms the age of aesthetics. Things help create a world, an aesthetic dimension that we

77

can assemble, inhabit, and presumably make our own, using the every-day items made available by the marketplace.

It is here that mass retailers like Walmart and Target work in concert as one of the many vanguards of modern consumer culture. Offering low-cost items with mass appeal, both retail giants promise customers happier, fuller lives through the acquisition of ever more stuff, increasingly novel things, ever-expanding surfaces on which to express their personal style. These promises are, of course, myths invented by advertising executives, the spinmeisters of commerce, but the point here is not to offer facile condemnation or to reveal the hidden truths behind the shill. What we see on the horizon of contemporary consumer culture has less to do with the branding and marketing of products than with the "thinging" of products, by way of an invitation issued by their physical composition: their design. The so-called big box stores have been enthusiastically embraced in some places and rejected in others, and they continue to amass high profits and saturate markets. My goal in this chapter, through an exploration of Target's celebration of design as a means to intensify attraction, is to begin to make sense of the role this big box retailer plays in the new age of aesthetics and what it means for the cultural dimension of the consumption of things. Enmeshed as we are in a growing world of things, in an increasingly aesthetic economy, we should take the opportunity to explore the mechanics by which big retailers are adapting to changes in consumption and pushing the boundaries and sensibilities of consumer sentiment.

In the last chapter, I suggested that empathy may be one affective avenue with the potential to slow down the process of disenchantment that causes us to cycle through objects with increasing rapidity. Mass retailers, aided and abetted by admonishments from lifestyle gurus like Marie Kondo to continually curate and edit our possessions, promote a mode of consumption in which the giddy experience of attraction reigns, and attachment is often cast as a sobering killjoy. Target, the focus of this chapter, offers an instructive case in point. "Our marketing creates a 360-degree *experience* that brings a touch of joy to everyday shopping, whether guests are walking into our stores, browsing Target.com, Pinterest or Instagram, catching our broadcast spots or print ads and more,"[4] says Rick Gomez, Target's current chief marketing officer. Target's modus operandi is to delight consumers with cute, clever, and sometimes useful objects. The stores themselves are designed to attract shoppers' attention to these objects, to give them a stylish, of-the-moment aura, at least until the moment of acquisition. In recent years, the company has sharply increased its focus on its online shopping experience to ward off the threat presented by Amazon. It has also intensified its long-standing practice of partnering with both well-known and up-and-coming designers, celebrities, and social media influencers on exclusive brands and product lines.

The art of attraction is about getting noticed and commanding attention—an increasingly scarce resource in a crowded marketplace. Marketers strive to lead consumers through a process dubbed AIDA by nineteenth-century advertising pioneer Elias St. Elmo Lewis: Attention, Interest, Desire, Action. This traditional marketing funnel, the manufacturing of desire that consumers feel compelled to satisfy, is still going strong and is on display in the showrooms of retailers like Target. The company's 2017 marketing campaign, "More in the Store," showcases its partnerships with a variety of cultural tastemakers with an eye toward celebrating what the company sees as its brand's unique point of view: "It speaks to the anticipation and the invitation, the excitement of discovery that every guest loves. . . . In our stores, we're not just crafting displays, but *destinations* that capture each brand's personality and encourage guests to explore and shop."[5] In retail, the Action that concludes the marketing funnel refers simply to that moment the customer swipes her card and completes the transaction as the clerk bags up today's chosen items. Grabbing attention, sustaining interest, and arousing desire are all in service of this moment. To the degree that consumers are invited to attach to Target's mass-produced objects, all bets are off after point of purchase. In fact, although typically depicted as a linear process, for mass retailers to stay afloat, AIDA must function more as a circular loop, in which the final "A" (the Action of purchasing) perpetually gives way to the initial "A" (the consumer's Attention must be grabbed by yet another thing to desire), and on it goes. Target may have perfected the art of attraction, but in the world of fast design, attachment—the sustained connection one feels to someone or something outside oneself—is a roadblock.

The Rise of Target

To better understand the rise of Target, we begin in that cosmopolitan city that never sleeps, New York, teeming with millions of would-be consumers. Yet this hub of commercial activity, where mom-and-pop retailers and upscale boutiques peacefully coexist, has at best an ambivalent relationship with the big boxes. Walmart, for example, has had a hard time making inroads in the Big Apple. In recent years, New Yorkers have nixed the company's plans for stores in Queens and on Staten Island, and Mayor Bill de Blasio has been a fierce critic of the company's tendency to drive down wages and put local retailers out of business. Given New Yorkers' apparent antipathy to Walmart, it would seem that the other big box retailer so popular in Middle America would be struck down by the same blow. After all, aesthetics aside, the so-called House of Tar-jay, like Walmart, imports much of its mass-produced merchandise from China, a country not known for its fair treatment of factory workers, and has fought the unionization efforts of its own employees. Despite the many institutional similarities of Target and Walmart, New Yorkers have a much more ambivalent relationship to Target.

Target currently has nearly thirty stores in New York City, with several new ones planned—part of the company's aggressive CityTarget strategy launched in 2017 to offer smaller-footprint stores in urban areas. Starting in the early 2000s, Target made inroads with Manhattanites through transitory pop-up stores, which open their doors for only a few weeks before morphing into something else. At the height of the 2001 holiday shopping season, for example, Target docked a 220-foot barge at the Chelsea Piers in New York Harbor to serve as a floating store. In 2003, it opened a temporary store in Rockefeller Center to promote its new line by the beloved New York designer Isaac Mizrahi, known for his car coats and schoolboy charisma. In the winter of 2006, a traveling Target in the form of a red double-decker bus emblazoned with Target's trademark bull's-eye made its way around Manhattan to promote a new line from British designer Luella Bartley—a line that would be available for only three months, after which another non-American designer would be spotlighted as part of Target's GO International campaign. In 2015, Target opened a holiday-themed "Target Wonderland" pop-up in Manhattan's Meatpacking neighborhood, featuring, among other things, a giant Etch A Sketch.

The GO International line, driven by the limited-edition collections of renowned designers from around the world, available for only ninety days, essentially turns the women's apparel department of every Target into a buzzworthy pop-up store of sorts, cleverly lending an air of exclusivity to mass-produced fare. Some have been more successful than others. Target's partnership with Marimekko, the Danish textiles company, known for its bold graphic prints, underwhelmed, while in 2015, Lilly Pulitzer's preppy florals, popular among the country club set, was so coveted that New Yorkers lined up around the block at the Bryant Park pop-up and Lilly fans overloaded Target's website, crashing it several times. The entire collection sold out in just hours. Target's 2017 line with style maven and former Spice Girl Victoria Beckham broke the company's sales records for such collaborations. Although the website did crash when the line launched, the "VBxTarget" collaboration avoided the frustrations of the Lilly Pulitzer launch by ordering significantly more merchandise. These urban pop-ups and in-store boutiques featuring limited-edition product lines function as what we might call "attraction attractions," ephemeral and alluring destination spots designed to attract consumers like moths to a flickering flame.

New Yorkers' response to Target's marketing schemes hasn't always been so enthusiastic. On blogs and in op-ed pages, some New Yorkers derided the sneakiness of these "moving Targets" (the double-decker with huge bull's-eyes on it was especially unfortunate in the wake of the very real London bus bombings the previous summer). However, these experiments in flash retailing are also highly profitable—both in terms of actual sales and surely in terms of creating a bit of buzz around Target, especially for those trendy Manhattanites who fear missing out on something exclusive and limited.

What seemed to spark more controversy for New Yorkers—and, really, members of the culturati throughout the United States—was Target's invasion not of their city but of their cultural bible: the *New Yorker*. In 2005, Target became the first single-issue sponsor in the magazine's eighty-year history, buying up the August 22 issue's entire ad space. The discount retailer from Minneapolis had made an ostentatious move indeed, commissioning well-known *New Yorker* artists to incorporate the company's logo into their pieces, adorning Manhattan landmarks and scenes with bright red bull's-eyes. The advertising industry, not surprisingly, saw it as a stroke of genius.[6] Others were not so enthused. Many writers pointed to the callousness of depicting targets on the buildings and subways of New York City a scant four years after 9/11. Others were appalled by the casualness with which the issue blurred lines of journalistic integrity.[7]

However, most of the complaints had to do with the highbrow *New Yorker* being besmirched by the middlebrow retailer from the Midwest. That is, they had to do more with aesthetics than with ethics.[8] Much to some readers' chagrin, the Target issue simply made it explicit that the *New Yorker* is, among other things, a brand—a brand that defines one as cultured and literate, but a brand nonetheless.[9] Target undoubtedly understood this when it orchestrated the *New Yorker* coup. By cobranding with the *New Yorker*, Target could better pursue what John Pellegrene, the former Target marketing guru, has described as the company's ideal market—"the person who drives a Rolls-Royce and those who drive Fords."[10] In doing so, Target took the next logical step in its evolution. After building an empire importing for the nation the cachet of sophisticated New York designers, Target was now coming to them—hitting the coveted "influential" class where they live—completing the marketing circuit between Fifth Avenue and Main Street,

U.S.A.[11] In the years since the controversy over its sponsored issue of the *New Yorker*, Target has worked to perfect its balancing act between highbrow and lowbrow, and has done so through a series of collaborations aimed at bringing design to the masses.

Design for All

Nearly two decades ago, Target launched a collection of housewares by the famous postmodern architect Michael Graves, in the first instance of what would become Target's marketing modus operandi: partnering with high-end designers to create everyday products at discount prices. Haute couture fashion designers such as Mizrahi, Cynthia Rowley, Proenza Schouler, and Jason Wu, as well as well-known interior designers like the Oprah-anointed Nate Berkus, Rachel Ashwell (known for her popular shabby chic flea market aesthetic), and Todd Oldham (the modernist DIY guru who has also designed furniture for the decidedly middlebrow La-Z-Boy and clothes for Old Navy) are now the most crucial components of the Target brand identity. In recent years, Target has expanded its partnerships to include lifestyle brands that bring with them preestablished followings, tapping social media influencers like Chrissy Teigen and fashion and shelter bloggers at YoungHouseLove, Who What Wear, Wit + Delight, Oh Joy, DesignLoveFest, and Poppytalk. It's also capitalizing on the success of HGTV and its stable of decorating and design stars, such as Emily Henderson, and Chip and Joanna Gaines of *Fixer Upper* (2013–18). Target may exceed $70 billion in annual revenues by selling toilet brushes, pajamas, and small appliances, but one could argue that these objects are just the media distributing what Target really sells: design itself. An ad from the early days of Target's design collaborations declares, for example:

Design inspires
Design shapes
Design shines
Design creates

Design transforms
Design moves
Design fits
Design protects
Design comforts
Design colors
Design unites

Target is at the forefront of a trend in Western capitalism in which aesthetics pervade every aspect of the marketplace, even, as Virginia Postrel suggests, "in areas where function used to stand alone." Aesthetics, she notes, is "not restricted to a social, economic, or artistic elite, limited to only a few settings or industries, or designed to communicate only power, influence, or wealth. Sensory appeals are everywhere, they are increasingly personalized, and they are intensifying."[12] Again, Target is an exemplar of the trend. Copy on its website describes the company's "focus on design" thus: "A trash can, a bottle of shampoo, a watch, a thumbtack. All perfect opportunities to add style, color, and smart function to your life."[13] As Target would have it, no item is too small, no moment of everyday life too banal, to serve as a venue for self-expression. In the new aesthetic world order, we are invited to ask ourselves, "What does my stapler say about me?" We have come a long way, for better or worse, from the early days of industrialization when Henry Ford could say that customers could have any color Model T they liked so long as it was black, and people would keep buying.

The success of the Target formula depends on consumers buying into a designer star system in which both established and cutting-edge product designers as well as lifestyle bloggers and TV personalities lend their talents to Target through highly publicized partnerships. As Target's ad copy puts it: "Bringing great design to every home is a big mission. . . . Our designers know how to create products you'll love to live with, at low prices you can't live without." Target understands well the nature of Shaviro's age of aesthetics—that for most of us, mass-produced commodities are the very stuff of our lifeworlds, and they constitute our everyday environments. Shaviro writes:

> The aim of brands like Nike, Disney, Apple, Microsoft, and Sony is to market an experience, an entire lifestyle; to commodify a total organization of feeling and behavior. To fashion a world. "The corporation does not create the object (the commodity)," Mauricio Lazzarato writes, "but rather the world in which the object exists. It also doesn't create the subject (worker or consumer), but rather the world in which the subject exists." It's Bill Gates' world, or Steve Jobs' world, or Disney's world; we just live in it.[14]

Target is careful to assure us again and again that if we entrust our world to it, we will be rewarded with an environment crafted by "world-class" design experts who know, presumably better than we do, how to "decorate and delight" and "offer the perfect blend of form and function."[15] Gone are the bad old days, Target tells us, when delightful surroundings were the privilege of the few. As Target CMO Rick Gomez puts it, "I'm especially proud that [Target's] work beautifully highlights inspiration for *everyone*."[16] Target's central message is that fine living, thanks to its pantheon of auteur designers, influencers, and the wonders of mass production, is now the right of the many.

Target's democratic rhetoric echoes that of the early twentieth-century Bauhaus architects and designers who, unlike many artists of their time, embraced industrialization as a way to bring beautiful living to the masses. The Bauhaus style was cheap, functional, and unabashedly mass produced. Bauhaus was an attempt to abolish the class-based distinction between the craftsperson and the artist, and to encourage the evolution from the craftsperson's workshop to the industrial laboratory. As Walter Gropius, architect and founder of Bauhaus, declares, "The Bauhaus believes the machine to be our modern medium of design and seeks to come to terms with it."[17] Mass production is incompatible with ornamentation, however, so for the Bauhaus designers, well-designed objects have to be reduced to their most essential forms, with smooth lines and only the most practical details. Gropius's ideals, put forth in the Bauhaus manifesto, are, as one writer describes it, "both aesthetic and practical: that all the tools of living, from a building to the objects within it, would be thoughtful but affordable, inspired but pragmatic, unique though mass-produced. Thus, everyday ugliness would be banished from the earth—by workers for workers."[18]

Given these rhetorical similarities, is Target's overwhelming success—its supposed democratization of design—evidence that we have finally reached what Gropius described as "the new structure of the future, which will embrace architecture and sculpture and painting in one unity and which will one day rise toward heaven from the hands of a million workers like the crystal symbol of a new faith"?[19] Has mass-produced design made good on its promise, putting beauty in the hands of the masses? After all, the packaging on Michael Graves's products, which launched Target's "Design for All" line, reads like a page out of the Bauhaus manifesto from a hundred years ago: "The Michael Graves product line is an inspired balance of form and function. At once it is sensible and sublime, practical and whimsical, utilitarian and aesthetically pleasing. Graves creates useful objects, which not only carry their weight, but simultaneously lift our spirits."[20] Today, Target's rhetoric continues in the same vein. In 2018, for example, Target launched a new line of home goods including over 750 items—all designed in a minimalist, pared-down style first popularized by the Bauhaus designers. The line is intended to attract millennials whose paychecks may not sustain their aspirations when it comes to home decor, a demographic it often loses to IKEA, another "democratic" design brand I'll discuss in chapter 3. Mark Tritton, Target's executive vice president and chief merchandising officer, echoes the Bauhaus insistence on making beautiful things available to everyone: "Made By Design is the ultimate expression of our DNA—a commitment to the democratization of impeccable design. . . . This line is filled with beautiful, purposeful pieces that our guests can count on for superior quality, style and value season after season."[21]

Despite its egalitarian, even utopian rhetoric and its subtle yet frequent references to the political posture of mid-twentieth-century populist design movements, the Target-led celebration of all things designed is worth interrogating. The Bauhaus philosophy, even if utopian, is predicated on the worker-citizen-craftsperson as the center of the project. It is an attempt to take back industrialization from the capitalist and reinvigorate a people's art—mass production as a means to beautiful craftsmanship, not the antithesis. Importantly, the masses are to participate at both the production and consumption end of the equation: beautiful things made by the people and for the people. So does Target democratize design? Despite what might seem like an obvious no, I will hold off answering that question for the moment. If our current political moment tells us anything, it is that democratization is a tricky business.

Sign Value

One interpretation of Target's success is that the company's version of the democratization of design is merely the branding of design. As Laura Rowley reports in her 2003 unabashed valentine to Target, *On Target: How the World's Hottest Retailer Hit a Bull's-Eye*, the designers with whom Target partners must never become larger than the Target brand itself. Isaac Mizrahi, Michael Graves, Alexander McQueen, Victoria Beckham, Philippe Starck, and Mossimo Giannuli must all be keenly on message—or, rather, "on Target"—in that their designs and personas are ultimately in service of Target's brand identity as the locus of low-end but fashion-forward products. As Target executive Robyn Waters tells *Businessweek*, the company makes a conscious choice to distinguish itself from Walmart by being explicitly design driven: "We soon developed a healthy respect for what design could do for the bottom line. We had started to see what the iMac computer did to Apple's stock or the [impact of] Volkswagen's redesign of the Beetle. Everyone at Target heartily and unanimously accepted that design can drive business growth."[22]

Because design is all about innovation, by allying itself with the design community, Target positions itself in the marketplace as the place to go for beautiful and interesting, even artistic, products. Indeed, Target began its partnership with New York's Cooper-Hewitt National Design Museum, part of the Smithsonian Institution, to launch the Target National Design Education Center, intended to introduce young people to the field of design. The partnership is a savvy move as Target works to be taken seriously by designers; the project offers a kind of design literacy program for the next generation of consumers. The specific designers featured in its stores may come and go (in fact, for the model to work, they must), but Target's message—that Target equals design—is what its brand managers work hard to perpetuate.

However, this interpretation—that design is essentially just a value added to the Target brand—is insufficient to explain the dynamic at work in Target's success. It's too simple. It suggests that Target's model of selling design simply overdetermines the sign value of design, that it merely extends its reach by way of a clever brand campaign—essentially labeling things "designed" as a way to add meaning to everyday objects. In this interpretation, design is simply another branding strategy, one that, like all brands, turns objects into signs. However, we are seeing something else at the forefront of consumer culture, something that cannot be adequately understood as branding. This new relationship between consumers and the objects they consume demands a theoretical approach that resists the tendency of much cultural theory to focus, often myopically, on systems of signification at the expense of attending to things.

Since as early as the 1950s, the political projects of critical and poststructural cultural theorists, in different ways, have been to destabilize the primacy of the subject, mainly by ushering in the apotheosis of the sign. Subjects lack integrity, we are taught, because, upon close examination, their apparent coherence gives way to a vast and fluctuating discursive field or plane of immanence on which no one subject is ever permanently localizable. Things are important in this tradition, but mainly in their capacity to signify (to mean in relation to other things) within a larger economy of signs. However, this model is insufficient if we are to understand the unique role that design plays in contemporary consumer culture—a culture in which things seem simultaneously to mean too much and not nearly enough. It also leaves those of us interested in the political and ethical opportunities in contemporary consumer culture (a culture of which Target is but one striking example) with a woefully limited arsenal of responses. It describes a model of cultural politics in which the only fight to be had is over the control of interpretations, when there is so much more at stake. To allow for a more robust relationship between consumers and products, between subjects and objects, we need to de-sign design. We need to look at things as things, not just signs.

To de-sign design is to take seriously the materiality of material culture. As philosopher Peter-Paul Verbeek suggests in his book *What Things Do* (its title a nice rejoinder to the assumption that things merely mean), "Not only has philosophy failed to recognize the significance of things and their materiality—so has contemporary postmodern industrial design, whose products are devised principally to serve as signs rather than material things, as symbols or icons for their owners' lifestyles."[23] Verbeek points to a collusion between structuralist and poststructuralist theories of signification, which tend to see things as merely "projection screens for our interpretations," and brand marketing, which treats things as mere vehicles for big ideas.[24] Both views erroneously reduce things to words. Verbeek argues, "Despite all the recent talk about the 'material world' and 'modern materialism,' we have managed to expunge artifacts of their materiality both in our thinking about and in our design of them. Now that we have survived the death of God and the death of the subject, we seem to be faced with the death of the thing."[25]

I take Verbeek's point—that critical theory is too caught up with signification—but before we start planning the wake of the object, we may want to visit the work of designers, that other group whose thinking Verbeek finds too limited. The work of Donald A. Norman, for example, may point us toward one way of thinking about objects that depends neither on a return to the subject as master of the material world nor on an overly romanticized notion of the object as that stable thing that unfailingly resists capture, hence serving as a kind of spoiler to the humanist subject.[26] Norman, an emeritus cognitive psychologist and computer scientist at Northwestern University, explores the role human affect plays in our interaction with things. In his books *The Design of Everyday Things* (2002), *Things That Make Us Smart* (1993), and *Emotional Design* (2004), Norman calls our attention to a variety of studies that allow him to make the strange supposition that attractive things work better. Why do attractive things work better? Is it because of something inherent in the objects themselves? Not quite. It is more accurate, following Norman, to say that we work better when we are in a state of positive affect. Our brain processing broadens, our muscles relax, and we engage with objects in a more sympathetic way.

In Norman's words, "Positive affect arouses curiosity, engages creativity, and makes the brain into an effective learning organism."[27] For example, if a device is fun to work with, like, say, the iPhone, then our brain is more primed to overlook and cope with minor problems, or to ignore otherwise irritating design flaws. Understanding human emotions, according to Norman, is crucial to understanding our relationship with the material world, because "emotion makes you smart."[28] Norman's work at least highlights an ambiguity in how we understand the materiality of objects. Are they in control, or are we? Who has the agency? Whereas cultural theorists have spent a lot of time critically investigating the subject, many are only recently critically investigating objects.[29] In an effort to better attend to the social life of objects, it might make sense to return to the thinker who most famously theorized objects in their commodity form: Karl Marx.

Marx argues that commodity fetishism reifies the social relations that bring products into the world and that capitalism lends an undue magical quality to commodities that lead to our confusion over the abstract system of exploitation that determines their value. Under market capitalism, things became important to us as a result not of their use value but of their exchange value—that is, the place they held in a larger economy. Commodities became valuable because of the money they could accrue, not vice versa.

In so-called postmodern capitalism, later theorists tell us, the fetishization of commodities takes on a new character. This second version of fetishization is no longer about the mystification of the commodity form; rather, it is about the mystification of the sign form. Here the commodity object is valued not for its use value or exchange value but for its sign value; objects are vehicles of representation. These varying conceptions of the commodity form correspond roughly to different historic instantiations of capitalism. The fetishization of the commodity has its roots in industrial capitalism, whereas the fetishization of the sign has its roots in what Jameson has famously called late capitalism. Despite the enduring popularity of Jameson's 1991 *Postmodernism, or The Cultural Logic of Late Capitalism*, Jeffrey Nealon convincingly illustrates new changes in the organization of capital— that is, postpostmodernism.[30] Here we begin to see the emergence of an arrangement that operates through intensification rather than the expansion of surfaces. Capital can no longer rely simply on an explosion of surface-level sign value. It must instead go deep, developing commodities that are imbued with value not through their production but through the various models of their use.

The iPhone, to pick an obvious example, gains its cultural cachet not simply from the sleekness of its interface but from the personalized content that gives each iPhone its unique identity. The iPhone works, in other words, because of the personality and depth created by the customized playlists and photo collections of each iPhone owner. As Shaviro writes: "The perpetual novelty of aestheticized commodities never actually leads to anything radically New. For capital itself cannot innovate. The New always comes from outside, from beyond, or from below; all a corporation can do is internalize this outside, by channeling the flows, appropriating the innovations for itself."[31] To understand the destiny of the object in an age of aesthetic capitalism, the previous relationships among use value, exchange value, and sign value need to be reconfigured. A new dimension of the object emerges, one best understood as combining aura and affect.

The concept of aura is most famously explored by Walter Benjamin in "The Work of Art in the Age of Its Technological Reproducibility." Aura, for Benjamin, is defined by the unique distance of any object in space and time. It is important to note that the concept describes a process by which objects gain their unique identity. This process is bound in ritual. High-society cathedrals have their wealthy congregations, paintings by the great masters have their special viewings, people bring out the good china for high tea. The point of these rituals is twofold. First, they highlight the distance between the unique object or artwork and the viewer by reserving them for special occasions and special audiences. This foregrounds their exclusivity. Second, rituals insert these objects into a system of class relations in which everyone presumably knows his or her place. These rituals give the object what Benjamin calls its "cult value," which raises the object to a status beyond mere thing and makes it something spiritual. Benjamin writes, "The artwork's auratic existence is never entirely severed from its ritualistic function. . . . the unique value of the 'authentic' work of art always has its basis in ritual."[32]

Benjamin predicts that mechanical reproduction will erase the distance between the masses and the auratic objects of class-based ritual. Instead of ritual value, the frequency with which objects could be reproduced would give them exhibit value, thereby replacing their mystic aura with indiscriminate accessibility. Benjamin's hope echoes that of the Bauhaus architects: access to the tools of industry would democratize design for the masses. For Benjamin, in the age of technological reproduction, art, "instead of being founded on ritual, is based on a different practice: politics."[33] Unfortunately, Benjamin's hope is in vain, for he could not have anticipated what Guy Debord, Pierre Bourdieu, Jean Baudrillard, and others would realize decades later: the role that sign value plays in creating new rituals for capitalism to commodify. That is, under what critic Mark Dery has called the "empire of the sign," brands and the privileges they confer have allowed consumers to mark themselves with status icons, initiating new rites of class differentiation.[34]

As a consequence, aura undergoes a transformation rather than a dissipation. With sign value, objects gain aura through their circulation and not their inaccessibility. This is how modern branding functions. It is perhaps this auratic value that some *New Yorker* readers feared was diminished by Target's commercial besmirching of the magazine. Although anyone can buy a copy of the *New Yorker*, not everyone presumably has the requisite taste that would prompt them to do so. By so audaciously partnering with a big box retailer, the magazine undermined, for some, its status as a luxury brand.

With aesthetic capitalism, however, we might say that aura is changing yet again. Now the ritual is the invitation to constantly make and remake one's lifeworld through the beautiful objects that design makes available. Gernot Böhme describes aesthetic capitalism as a system for which growth "is possible only through the enhancement of life, through the production of staging oneself, that is, through the production of aesthetic values."[35] This is more than simple brand identification. It is the users' manipulation of reality that is the new ritual value. Consider the current onslaught of design shows on cable TV, for example, or the curated collections of design images on Instagram and Pinterest, or the easy customization of everyday objects, from laptops to cell phones. All are venues for us to insert and remake ourselves, to make what geographer Nigel Thrift calls "connective mutations," in which we and the objects we live with constantly transform one another.[36] With this new ritual function, aura is no longer determined by distance or circulation but by a combination of user innovations and object integrations, a process that we might conceive as a sort of renaissance of use value. Böhme's description for this is "staging value," which he uses to account for this new aestheticized element of use value. Although his concept of staging is useful as a general descriptor of the larger cultural shift to aesthetic values, here I prefer "ritual," because it offers a degree of nuance that attends to the specific rhetorical ecosystems of meanings and practices in which we integrate aestheticized objects into our daily lives.

To understand how this material manipulation works, it is helpful to return to the concept of affect. Affect, as Brian Massumi defines it in his translation of Gilles Deleuze and Félix Guattari's *Thousand Plateaus* (1980), is not a personal feeling but "an ability to affect and be affected."[37] For Norman, affect, along with cognition, is an information processing system. It allows us to "make judgments and quickly helps you determine which things in the environment are dangerous or safe, good or bad. The cognitive system interprets and makes sense of the world. Affect is the general term for the judgmental system, whether conscious or subconscious. Emotion is the conscious experience of affect, complete with attribution of its cause and identification of its object."[38] Affect describes the response we have to things before we label that response with feelings or emotions. It is a visceral sensation that precedes cognition. Importantly, affect is about our physical interaction with material things. Indeed, it is what much design attempts to influence.

Aura explains why rituals allow us to invest objects with meaning. The combination of aura and affect may help us get at the processes of invention within the world of things. Affect comes about because of material manipulations, but the meaning of those manipulations is determined by the rituals in which we insert them. There is a difference, for example, between my moving the butter dish from the fridge to the counter and my taking hold of an OXO Good Grips vegetable peeler as I prepare dinner. The design of the hugely successful Good Grips line was inspired by the special needs of OXO International founder Sam Farber's wife, who has arthritis. As one writer notes, "The decision to include a wider range of user ability in terms of dexterity proved a masterstroke in creating more usable, enjoyable and stylish kitchen products," and the peeler has "become an icon."[39] The soft and supple Santoprene handle feels good in the hand, and "the patented flexible rubber fins, a device borrowed from bicycle handles, became a defining motif of the Good Grips range, communicating the functional benefits to customers in a tactile way."[40] OXO's success is due not to a cool brand that amps up its product's sign value but is due to a return to the simple concept of use value: the peeler is tactile and ergonomic, and it swivels to move easily over the contours of any surface. Its heft in the hand makes it a pleasure to use. Perhaps it is a small thing, but this little gadget makes an otherwise tedious kitchen chore a bit more special, more ritualistic. It has what psychophysicists and designers call "jnd," or a "just noticeable difference" in sensory perception that distinguishes one object from another. Apparently design experts agree: the Good Grips peeler has won more industrial design awards in the past ten years than any other household product has. As it happens, it is also available at your local Target.

This theoretical framework, combining affect and aura, may allow us to make better sense of Target's so-called democratization of design. Despite my argument that this interpretation is too simple, Target does, of course, engage heavily in branding—that is, turning things into signs. But even at this level, its model is a bit different from traditional branding, even personality-driven branding such as Martha Stewart's lending her name to linens and housewares for Kmart. As Graves puts it, his work for Target "is not blessing towels," suggesting that it is about something much more profound.[41] This hint that something mystical lies beneath the surface of—or, better, floats above—the objects we consume is part of what makes Target's commodification of design work. Nate Berkus bed linens might confer a certain status, but more than that, the linens allow us to tap into the genius of a high-end designer. The creative juices of haute couture become a crucial part of the formula. The value of design, at least as offered by Target, is garnered because it comes to us by way of an auratic, mystical process most of us do not have access to. However, through the miracles of mass production, we can presumably own a remnant of that process, thus permitting us to participate in it vicariously.

This third version of fetishization—the fetishization of the invention process itself—offers a parasitic model of consumption. For all its celebration of the inventors of everyday objects, Target's commodification of design glosses both the production of these objects (i.e., the factory is nowhere to be seen) and the design process itself. As consumers, we are invited to purchase these designed objects, to mix and match them to suit our individual style, to place them side by side in inventive ways, but that's about it. We are not encouraged to become designers ourselves, to interact with these objects beyond deciding how to display them in our homes or on our bodies. That is, they remain objects and are not part of a larger process in which we are agents. This further displacement of production may be one reason why Target has evaded the criticisms that continue to haunt Walmart. Consumers are encouraged to imagine the designer's workshop, not the factory, as the source of Target's wares.

Skinning and the Production of Meaning

To borrow a metaphor that Web designers frequently use to describe the aesthetic options for computer software, we could say that Target's democratization of design amounts to skinning. To skin something is to change its outward appearance without changing any of its underlying characteristics or functionality. Web browsers dressed up with the logos of the Seahawks or *Stranger Things* (2016–), Nintendo and Xbox-styled Air Jordan sneakers—these sorts of cosmetic skins may be important for an individual's aesthetic sensibility, but they typically are purely aesthetic. Similarly, Target's increasingly specific objects offer the opportunity to skin one's home, one's body, and one's lifestyle. Tellingly, the company is retiring its more mass-appeal apparel brands, like Mossimo and Merona, for more custom fare: "People are looking for something that is more curated and meaningful to their specific lifestyle," says Tritton.[42] For example, the success of Target's new children's clothing brands Cat & Jack and Art Class, tailored to specific age demographics, says Michelle Wlazlo, senior vice president of apparel and accessories, offers "validation of why we need multiple brands with unique aesthetics."[43] The Made By Design line of minimalist houseware basics is meant to serve as a foundation that consumers can skin with items from other of Target's more niche home lines, like the farmhouse chic accessories from Chip and Joanna Gaines's Hearth and Hand, or the "artisan-inspired" bohemian wares in the company's new Opal House brand. By playing bricoleur with an ever-growing cadre of specialized objects, one engages in a cosmetic mock-up, assembling one's individualism through the selection of handy and cheap fashion icons. This is a democratization of the epidermis of design, but nothing about Target's strategy scratches the functional tissue and bones beneath this skin. Target offers design as a pleasurable product to be consumed, not a process in which to participate. In this sense, our agency as consumers in this model is more analog than digital, more mixtape than remix.

That said, although making a playlist is surely more an act of assembling than making, it is nevertheless a creative act. To do it well, the assembler must consider the qualities and components of particular songs as well as the ways their individual tempos, moods, and themes might go together, build, and flow into a cohesive whole. Likewise, although shopping at Target can hardly be defined as production, the company's design ethos does create the conditions for bolstering design literacy for people who may have never thought about design much at all. By celebrating designers and foregrounding the relationship between form and function, Target begins to introduce the vocabulary and grammar of design into the mainstream consumer culture. As graphic design scholar Ellen Lupton puts it:

> More people can apply design in their own life and to me that's the most exciting development going on now. . . . Designers are not just creating things, they are creating ideas that are transferable. They are creating an information commons. . . . Usually when people talk about the democratization of design, they're talking about shopping. They're talking about how there are more stores where you can buy better stuff, which is true. Target, IKEA, Design Within Reach—they have done huge things in terms of raising peoples' awareness of and access to better stuff to buy. But there's another side to the democratization, which

isn't about buying. It's about making. It's about how you use what
you've got.[44]

By calling our collective attention to the form of everyday objects,
by encouraging us to find beauty in the mundane, Target, perhaps in
spite of itself, moves us a step toward a relationship with objects, even
mass-produced ones, in which they become a bit more malleable.

Let's now return to my earlier question. Does Target really democratize design? My answer is no—and yes. No, because to have any real
political potential, the process of design must be democratized. Target's ultimate success is in sparking that initial moment of attraction
rather than encouraging our long-term investment in the life span of
designed objects. Consumer responses such as ecodesign, crafting, repurposing, or the makers movement more generally—topics
addressed in chapters 4 and 5—are going much further than Target
ever could to invite users into the invention process, thus opening
up new opportunities for attachment. Yes, because skinning, as an
affective-auratic process of engagement with things, encourages consumers to become conversant in the language of design. Further still,
aesthetic capitalism succeeds via Thrift's connective mutations, via
the user-added value that makes every consumer an inventor of sorts.
Target, as an example of this new aesthetic order, cannot contain the
material effects, or affects, of its own products. It may intend a superficial democratization, but the eventual consequences may ultimately
be more robust than that.

By making consumers aware of design, by explicitly calling attention to its logics and languages, Target represents a first step in a
productive opening up of objects in mainstream consumer culture.
In the following chapter, I turn to another seemingly unlikely player
in this deconstruction of objects. Under the auspices of the international furniture behemoth IKEA, objects have the potential to open
up further still, both literally and figuratively, allowing consumers
to participate in the processes by which objects are made, and made
meaningful.

THREE

Some Assembly Required

IKEA, Project Value, and What Happens When Things Come Apart

The home-brew supply shop in the strip mall near my home in sub-urban Seattle recently added cheese and soda making to its course offerings. According to a 2013 report by the American Homebrewers Association, the industry is seeing significant gains in recent years, with new hobbyists getting started all the time. Beginner home-brew kits saw a nearly 25 percent increase in sales that year. "U-pick" farms are a rapidly growing phenomenon as family farms struggle to remain independent and nostalgic city dwellers long for ways to connect with agricultural traditions. According to a popular website catering to hobby farmers, u-pick operations are one of the fastest-growing segments of the small-farm industry. In Snohomish County, located north of Seattle, in the plains and foothills just west of the Cascade mountains, u-pick farms abound, inviting visitors to harvest their own pumpkins, apples, and just about every type of berry you can imagine. U-pick farms, not surprisingly, are especially popular with families, as parents look for ways to expose their children to the manual labors of farm life, if only for an afternoon.

But it's not just beer and berries. There seems to be something about participating in the production and harvesting—or at least the assembly—of the objects we consume that sparks an emotional investment in us. Although this emotional investment may or may not have always been the case, a certain nostalgia for handwork appears to be on the rise in this age of mass-produced efficiency and convenience. As Matthew Crawford laments, "Both as workers and as consumers, we feel we move in channels that have been projected from afar by vast impersonal forces."[1] As a result, many of us are seeking a more human-scale relationship with the things in our lives, to personalize and bring down to earth the web of relations that puts food on our tables and clothes on our bodies. Increasingly, for many people, that includes having a hand in the processes of production, however limited that participation may be.

Perhaps the best-known example of this is the lesson learned by General Mills in the early decades of mass production, when the company took its efforts to make baking quicker and easier for modern women a bridge too far by selling premixed cake mixes under its Betty Crocker brand in the early 1950s. Although Betty Crocker had been a popular brand for thirty years, consumers were slow to respond to its boxed cake mixes. When sales failed to improve, General Mills consulted two psychologists, who suggested the problem was that the mixes were just too convenient. The solution, it turned out, was eggs. As Susan Marks writes, the psychologists argued that "powdered eggs, often used in cake mixes, should be left out, so women could add a few fresh eggs into the batter, giving them a sense of creative contribution."[2] In its quest for convenience, General Mills was denying women the important ritual of baking for their family—a ritual in which cracking an egg on the edge of a mixing bowl is apparently crucial. This "just add an egg" anecdote is popular among contemporary marketers and designers who recognize they must not only design the products themselves but also design users' experience of products. This experience, more often than not, depends on how our interaction with a particular product invites us to see ourselves. Cracking the eggs for a cake presumably allowed a 1950s-era woman to see herself as a good wife and mother who, although busy, and maybe even working outside the home, still took the time to make a homemade treat for her family. As

Harry Brignull writes: "The egg, therefore, becomes more than an ingredient, and more than just an extra pleasurable step. It becomes a prop, enabling the customer to play a social role."[3] Importantly, this social role—nourishing one's family—is made possible because the cake mix arrived in one's kitchen incomplete. The consumer's participation is required, and in fact desired, if the product is to be made whole.

Harvard Business School professor Michael Norton and Duke University psychologist Dan Ariely have a name for our tendency to feel more attached to objects that are, in some way, the fruit of our own labor. They call it the IKEA effect, named after the Swedish home goods retailer that sells flat-packed furniture products that consumers assemble themselves. In a series of studies, Norton, Ariely, and their colleague Daniel Mochon found that, time and again, research subjects overvalued objects they had a hand in making. Their own labor, the degree to which they exerted effort in its making, imbued the object—an origami crane, for example—with a value subjects didn't see in structurally similar objects made by others. Ariely describes his surprising attachment to what he calls an "übermodern" IKEA toy chest he assembled for his kids. He admits that after a long struggle putting the piece together,

> I was very proud of my work, and for weeks afterward I smiled proudly at my creation each time I passed it. From an objective point of view, I am quite sure that it was not the highest-quality piece of furniture I could have purchased. Nor had I designed anything, measured anything, cut wood, or hammered any nails. But I suspect that the few hours I struggled with the toy chest brought us closer together. I felt more attached to it than any other piece of furniture in our house. And I imagined that it, too, was fonder of me than my other furniture was.[4]

Although one might assume that we overvalue things we make ourselves because we can customize them to suit our own tastes, studies of the IKEA effect demonstrate that the main reason we value self-made objects is because we value the effort we put into them. Norton and Ariely's findings essentially flip on its head the maxim that we labor for what we love, suggesting instead that we love what we labor over. In fact, when they tested for the customization factor, the researchers found that it was indeed primarily effort that accounted for the increase in value estimation. Instead of origami cranes, which could potentially be customized or simply look different according to the skills of the folder, this time, subjects were asked to assemble plain black IKEA boxes, with little possibility for structural variation. Their finding? When asked to bid on the boxes, subjects "were willing to pay a 63% premium compared to those who were given the chance to buy an identical pre-assembled box."[5] A follow-up experiment using Legos supported the results: subjects still overvalued the things they assembled themselves, even when they looked just like everyone else's.

The Gaps of Which Objects Are Made

Formal homogeneity notwithstanding, the IKEA effect studies foreground the role that the sheer expenditure of effort plays in the value we assign to an object we have assembled ourselves. If we spend an afternoon out of our life on our living room floor, Allen wrench in hand, lining up particleboard slabs until the familiar form of a glossy-white grid of shelves begins to take shape, we have made an investment. What was once a stack of disparate pieces bound in cardboard is now a useful and stylish piece of furniture, ready to house children's toys, sci-fi novels, or a beloved collection of vintage vinyl. Yes, those pieces were precut by the thousands in a factory in China, and the simplistic cartoon figure in the instruction book looks like a gender-fluid Ziggy, but assembling IKEA furniture is infamously difficult—so much so that mocking it has become something of a popular culture mainstay. The Marvel film *Deadpool* (2016) features a scene that pokes fun at the process, and the film's star, actor Ryan Reynolds, a new dad, filmed a comic video for *GQ* in which he struggles to assemble a Hensvik baby crib, muttering, "What's Swedish for 'f*#k you'?" before tossing the hardware and resorting to duct tape.[6] Comic Amy Poehler has joked that "IKEA" is Swedish for "argument." Psychological studies of couples seem to concur. When the power play that often accompanies a shared task like assembling IKEA furniture begins to escalate, "little things like putting a set of shelves together will bring up some ancient history with the partners," says psychologist Don Ferguson. Struggling with such a task may raise questions such as, "Do you trust me? Do you think I'm stupid? Do you think I have no skills? Do you wish your old boyfriend was here doing this?"[7] Even Allan Dickner, an executive at IKEA, acknowledges that the assembly is often harder than it looks: "A newspaper in Sweden described IKEA [furniture assembly] as something between civil engineering and captaining a submarine, and I think that's a good description," he admits.[8] Unsurprisingly, companies with names like Flat Pack Mates have emerged to relieve the furniture assembly burden from those who have more money than patience. And in late 2017, IKEA purchased TaskRabbit, the online marketplace for gig workers, where IKEA furniture assembly was already a common request.

Even though assembling an IKEA desk could not reasonably be described as making anything, and it requires relatively little skill to achieve, the process does, for some of us more than others, demand patience, perseverance, and, often, cooperation with another person. Although it may overstate things to call it skill, it does require a certain know-how to assemble IKEA products. As anyone who has assembled multiple such items knows, this know-how increases as one becomes more fluent in the material grammar and vocabulary of the process. However insignificant it may seem, an investment is made when one spends time, energy, and equanimity putting together even a by-the-book, mass-produced, prefabricated object. In turn, that expenditure shapes one's relationship with that object. The object becomes, in a real way, an artifact, or a document, testifying to the investment made.

Whether we call it the IKEA effect or the "just add an egg" phenomenon, the evidence demonstrating the relationship between participation and meaning is convincing. But why? Although psychologists, sociologists, and economists may have their own theories, perhaps no more productive lens exists than the ancient art of

A comic captures the prevailing sentiment about the ease of IKEA assembly. Courtesy of Andy Singer, http://www.andysinger.com/.

rhetoric, which is devoted to understanding how it is that humans make meaning. Over two millennia ago, Aristotle, in his famous three-volume treatise, *Rhetoric*, observes that people are most effectively persuaded when they participate in their own persuasion. A successful orator makes use of what Aristotle calls the enthymeme, a basic unit of rhetorical logic that he calls a "rhetorical syllogism." A standard syllogism is a form of deductive reasoning in which one draws a specific conclusion that is based on information provided in a general and a more specific premise. This classic example serves as well as any:

> Major premise: All men are mortal.
> Minor premise (more specific): Socrates is a man.
> Conclusion (makes a specific claim deduced from premises): Socrates is a mortal.

Written largely as a rejoinder to his teacher Plato's renunciation of the "charlatan" rhetoric and celebration of the philosophical dialectic, Aristotle uses the *Rhetoric* as the platform to make the case that rather than a false and shoddy version of philosophy, rhetoric is instead a true art of its own, though one with different aims. If the role of the logical syllogism is to map out the deductive path one's audience is to follow to the desired conclusion, then the rhetorical syllogism—the enthymeme—invites one's audience to collaborate in the journey. For Aristotle, this may be as simple as leaving unstated one of the argument's premises, forcing the audience members to fill in the gaps for themselves. A speaker might ask, "Of course Socrates is a mortal; he's a man, isn't he?" This leaves the audience to fill in the missing information (men are mortal), thus completing the deductive circuit. However slight this move, Aristotle argues that this act of contribution, of completing the circuit, makes audiences active participants in the persuasive process and hence coconspirators with the rhetor.

Two millennia later, when mass communication technologies have made it possible to broadcast messages across time and space like never before, the nature of the audience has changed fundamentally, stretching that circuit between message and meaning beyond what Aristotle could have imagined. Communication scholar John Durham Peters explains that for its critics, "'mass communication' became defined as a one-way, impersonal, distant, and an unprecedented product of new technologies, while communication per se—that is, interpersonal communication—was taken to be interactive, personal, face-to-face and direct."[9] Plato is concerned that writing—the new communication technology of his time—could potentially pervert one's message as it traveled across space and time as it is indiscriminately disseminated to whomever might read it. Indeed, although he begrudgingly avails himself of this new technology, he does so in the form of dialogues, simulating what he sees as the purer vehicle to discovering truth: unadulterated, face-to-face dialectical argument between intellectual equals. Similarly, one of the underlying critiques of contemporary mass communication continues to be that it is open in its address and indiscriminate in audience. In short, mass communication is not personal enough. This somewhat purist notion of communication is juxtaposed with those who celebrate its democratic potential, and Peters starts with none other than Jesus of Nazareth.

Peters explains that mass communication is like casting seeds in a field. Citing Jesus's parable of the sower, he explains that some seeds may be eaten by birds and others may lay infertile on the stony ground, but some will inevitably take root and flourish. Jesus's parable is about the storyteller's dissemination of a message to an audience. One never knows what the audience members may be receiving or what they may do with the message, whether it will lie fallow or take root. Peters notes, "When the loop between speaker and listener is distended, the audience bears the hermeneutic burden." That is, as Aristotle observes, communication happens in the space between, in the moment of collaboration between speaker and audience—when an argument arrives incomplete, not fully formed, and we, the auditors, must complete the circuit. Peters calls this "the gaps of which communication is made."[10] It is not through smooth transmission and completeness that we communicate; it is through filling in the gaps inherent in what is said. Communication is always a matter of interpretation.

Of course, Aristotle and Peters were talking about discourse, and in this discussion of IKEA, we are talking about the design and assembly of material things. But the IKEA effect illustrates that whether the subject is arguments or objects, we are more invested in each when we participate in their construction. This explains the pride some of us may feel at simply having assembled the object according to the instructions. However, for a host of people, assembly is just the start of a larger process of invention. Indeed, for the global community of IKEA hackers, the act of assembly is also an act of self-expression.

IKEA Hacking

IKEA probably isn't advocating DIY assembly to boost customers' self-regard or give them an empowering brand experience of some kind. The company offloads the assembly process to consumers because it's simply cheapest to do so. Nevertheless, IKEA's business model has the unintended consequence of opening up its products, both materially and figuratively, thereby offering potential new points of connection for those who interact with them. Consumers who sit down to assemble a piece of IKEA furniture, pieces spread out on the floor, are now tasked with closing the circuit. They must transform this hodgepodge of components into the modern Lack coffee table, displayed so stylishly earlier that day in the IKEA showroom.

As Aristotle taught so many centuries ago, we are more convinced of the value of something when we participate in the persuasive process, when we are forced to fill in the gaps. Further, as Jesus argues in the parable of the sower, when we open up the process, especially when we cast our seeds as far and wide as possible, we cannot always know how they will land—that is, how the circuit of meaning will be completed. The tension between on the one hand the uniformity of mass communication and mass production and on the other hand the desire for control over one's message has only intensified in today's age, when we can cast messages globally in seconds, and when one company can distribute, as IKEA does, half a million Billy bookcases a month.

But IKEA customers, like any audience, don't always consume its products according to the instructions, even if those instructions are offered in nearly thirty languages. IKEA hackers modify, enhance, and tinker with IKEA components, using them as source material for projects they design themselves. IKEA hacking may be a simple embellishment, such as adhering floral contact paper to a tabletop, but these types of decorative additions aren't quite hack-y enough to suit many in the global network of IKEA hackers. Indeed, these hackers have built a substantial online community where they share innovative projects that "may require power tools and lots of ingenuity."[11] IKEA hacks include things like hinging a large mirror to the wall that, with the help of an IKEA stool, can come down, Murphy bed style, to form a dining table. Hackers have discovered ways to make bookcases and other pieces appear built in with the addition of finishing touches like crown molding. Others have found ways of cutting and recombining pieces from several kits to create storage platform beds, or elaborate catwalks, or customized media centers. One couple converted their studio apartment into a one bedroom by building a frame and installing IKEA's PAX system sliding pantry doors. And in a controversial IKEA hack that went viral in late 2015, a mother shared how she modified IKEA components to create a multilevel bed designed to accommodate her entire family of seven.

IKEA hackers congregate online at IKEAhackers.net, a website started in 2006 by Jules Yap, a dedicated IKEA fan who lives in the Philippines. On the site, hackers post pictures, videos, and often step-by-step instructions for hacks they've completed. The comments sections are filled with kudos, questions, and ideas for additional modifications. Like many online venues in which a reputation economy thrives, sharing one's accomplishments online with others in the IKEA hacking community is a key part of the appeal. Most IKEA hacks are innovations designed to solve some functional problem in one's home. They're intended to be useful and are shared in the hopes of being useful to someone else. For these tinkerers, hacking is less an attempt to resist or thwart IKEA in some way than it is putting to use the tools IKEA provides to realize a vision of their own.

For others, however, IKEA hacking is more rhetorical than that. It serves as a vehicle for commenting on the mass retail behemoth itself and what it stands for. As design scholar Daniela Rosner tells Roman Mars on his *99% Invisible* podcast, these hackers are "not just hacking the materials, they're hacking IKEA. They're hacking the brand, they're hacking what that brand actually symbolizes beyond just the stores."[12] These kinds of products are often attempts to beat IKEA at its own game, designing solutions that are even more clever and efficient. Even more pointedly, some hacks are intended to highlight the homogeneous, standardized, mass-produced character of IKEA products. As Mars puts it, "They're mocking the modularity of IKEA, saying, 'This stuff is so Tinkertoy, I can mix and mash up the hell out of it.'"[13]

For these hackers, the practice is downright subversive. It becomes one small way to assert oneself as more than just another passive, brainwashed consumer accepting what is offered without question. In this sense (with apologies to Audre Lorde), IKEA hacking is akin to using the master's tools to tinker with the master's house.

In his podcast episode on the subject, Mars assists a friend in hacking an IKEA bed. He describes the experience of putting holes in "inappropriate" places in the process. He observes that doing so is "transgressive and crossing a boundary," but he acknowledges, "It's not destructive anymore, it's creation." He notes the pleasure that comes from evading the usual consumerist position of merely picking something from a menu. "We were *making* what we wanted," he says. Another hacker describes it this way: "It feels a little bit subversive, and a little bit bourgeois. It's like being a punk member of the mainstream."[14]

Whether or not we are willing to grant IKEA hacking "punk" status, this characterization is instructive. Customizing IKEA furniture, whether for function or politics, does subvert common patterns of consumption. But it's likely more accurate to call the practice IKEA modding, despite the rebellious sensibility the term "hacking" affords. Labels aside, the customizations that IKEA hackers produce are made possible because of, not in spite of, IKEA's ubiquity and homogeneity. Hackers are exploiting not a bug but a feature of IKEA materials. Nearly fifty countries around the world have an IKEA store, all filled with the exact same stuff. If a woman in Iceland shares a clever way to turn a shoe rack into wine storage and a man in Brazil wants to give it a go, he can do so precisely because his local store will likely have all the parts he needs. These objects, as many critics have jeered, are as standardized as Lego blocks. In this sense, as Mars puts it, "IKEA, in spite of itself, is the great leveler."[15]

For all its democratic leveling of the design playing field, IKEA has at best an ambivalent relationship with the IKEA hacking crowd. In 2014, the company became embroiled in a lawsuit with James and Susan Martin, a couple in Virginia who had for nine years been running the extremely popular online idea-sharing forum IKEAFans.com. Although IKEA had supported the site in the past by offering sample products and sweepstakes prizes, IKEA changed course and ordered the site be taken down. Although the Martins fought back with a countersuit and their followers rallied vociferously around their cause, the site ultimately folded. That same year, Jules Yap of IKEAhackers.net also received cease-and-desist orders from the company. Yap says she was devastated. She responded by posting a desperate plea for support from fellow IKEA hackers. The outcry online was substantial: Cory Doctorow called IKEA's move "steaming shit" on his hugely influential tech-culture website Boing Boing, and Gizmodo described it as "boneheaded" and "a huge mistake."[16] In this instance, IKEA backpedaled its legal bullying. An IKEA PR executive contacted Yap and apologized, saying that stymying innovation was "off brand" and that the company would like to make amends.

Yap was invited to IKEA's main bases in Sweden and the Netherlands, where she was treated to tours, workshops, and meetings with IKEA executives and designers. She reports that not one IKEA employee expressed an objection to the work she collects on IKEAhackers .net. "In fact, they were very supportive" she says. "Even the designers whose furniture we hacked, sawed, repainted, reshaped into things unrecognisable like what we do on IKEAhackers are pretty tickled to see their designs turned into frankenthings."[17] If IKEA hackers and their frankenthings are carrying on in the tradition of dada and even the now-defunct *ReadyMade* magazine it inspired, they are doing so in quite different cultural times. For example, today, fan fiction is seen by the film and video games industries as an inevitable and even welcome augmentation of commercial culture, as it allows enthusiasts to extend the conversation beyond the walls of the original text. George Lucas, although he was slow to embrace Star Wars fan fiction, ultimately came to understand its purpose. IKEA now seems to as well. It allows people to express themselves, to customize the mass-produced texts and objects to better suit themselves, therefore deepening their bond with the source material. What is IKEA hacking if not a kind of material fan fiction, augmenting, distorting, and often talking back to the original text?

Like most retailers, IKEA courts customers' identification with its brand, but its business model also provides its customers an opportunity to engage the object differently than is the norm in today's

consumer culture. People experience IKEA furniture as a deconstructed stack of parts—as objects. Only through the application of
effort will it materialize into the thing we want. In some cases, this
stack of deconstructed parts begins to take form in someone's imagination differently than it was intended. Its temporary formlessness
has the potential to inspire real innovation.

Project Value

This innovation differs from the artistic pastiche afforded by the
likes of Target. The mode of engagement that I, following Benjamin,
call ritual value perpetuates a fetishization of the object in the most
traditional Marxist sense. Ritual value, as exemplified by Target, invites us to delight in the object, to desire it, to use it in our rituals of
self-expression. But in this mode of engaging the object, we remain
blissfully ignorant to the conditions of its emergence. It is as if it arrived ex nihilo, the labors of both human and machine obscured from
view. Again, this is Marx's understanding of commodity fetishism. In
contrast, this exploration of participation in the creation of IKEA objects demonstrates yet another way we interact with the objects in our
lives. I call this "project value." Self-assembled objects speak to us
differently—or in a purely figural sense, speak *us* differently. Again,
rhetorical theory provides an instructive way of understanding these
distinctions. At stake between the two modes of engaging objects is
what rhetoricians like Kenneth Burke have called identification or what
critical philosophers like Louis Althusser have termed interpellation.

   With Target, as with much of mass retail, we are invited to identify
with a particular aesthetic style. The most banal of objects are offered
in an array of designs, allowing shoppers to choose the one that best
expresses the way they see themselves, or aspire to see themselves. Is
your home urban-industrial? Shabby chic? Organic modern? New
traditional? Glam? Rustic? Target has you covered with just the right
stapler, vegetable peeler, or toilet bowl brush. These objects, preas-
sembled and complete, await inclusion in our homes or our wardrobe.
But the art of bricolage, even when the source material is mass

produced, is not passive. Persuasion through identification is participatory. One layers a home, a wardrobe, even a life out of the bits and bobs they collect through a variety of means.

But participation in this model is largely about conjoining, or what Kenneth Burke calls consubstantiality: becoming one with a particular aesthetic or a group of people with shared tastes and opinions. Identification is arguably the dominant strategy of contemporary marketing rhetoric. We are invited to be an "Apple person" or part of the "Nike tribe." Or we may be asked to affiliate with some indie brand that wouldn't be caught dead associating with either Apple or Nike. As Burke explains identification: "You persuade a man only insofar as you can talk his language by speech, gesture, tonality, order, image, attitude, idea, identifying your ways with his."[18] Increasingly, as I explore in my book *OurSpace* (2007), retail brands seek our loyalty by attempting to speak to our values, to insinuate themselves into our lifestyles, and to compel us to associate with the fantasy world they create. Identification in this sense can be creative, but it is largely about reproducing, duplicating, and aligning oneself with an aesthetic or political sensibility already in existence. In the logic of identification, participation takes the form of association.

When it comes to marketing, identification through association is a double-edged sword, earning the scorn of those who resist the notion that we should identify with corporate brands at all. For many people, IKEA and its ilk epitomize the empty fantasy of consumer culture itself. Resistance to this fantasy is perhaps most famously characterized in the 1999 film *Fight Club*. David Fincher's film, based on the novel by Chuck Palahniuk, is an absurdist meditation on the malaise of the American consumer at the turn of the millennium. The narrator (played by Edward Norton), a jaded middle manager, sits in a beige and soulless office and explains: "Like many of you, I was stuck."[19] If the narrator's office looks like something out of a *Dilbert* comic, his home is an IKEA catalog. This is made explicitly so by an early scene in which the narrator describes the Swedish retailer as the source material from which he assembles his identity: "Like so many others, I had become a slave to the IKEA nesting instinct. If I saw something clever like a little coffee table in the shape of a yin–yang, I had to have it. I'd flip through catalogs and wonder, 'What kind of dining set defines me as a person?' [. . .] I had it all. Even the glass dishes with tiny bubbles and imperfections, proof that they were crafted by the honest, simple, hardworking indigenous peoples of . . . wherever." While the voice-over intones, we first see him on the toilet, catalog in his hands. He turns it lengthwise and opens it, as if admiring a *Playboy* centerfold. He then walks through his apartment, phone cradled in his neck, on hold with a FÜRNI (IKEA) operator, waiting to order Erika Pekkari dust ruffles. As the narrator makes his way to the refrigerator, viewers are treated to a tour of his apartment, outfitted with mass-produced designer bookcases, chairs, Venetian blinds. Graphic overlays of product descriptions and prices emerge under each object in IKEA's signature typeface.[20] The narrator concludes, "We used to read pornography. Now it was the Horchow Collection."

Fight Club is a satire, to be sure, but if it works as one, it is only because it struck a chord with turn of the twenty-first-century audiences. Corporations like IKEA want people to identify with their brands, to imbue their products with value. But often this identification falls short of what we might call meaningful. As *Fight Club* progresses, for example, the decorative veneer of identity through consumption begins to disintegrate as the emasculated narrator is increasingly subsumed by his alter ego, the virile and apocalyptic Tyler Durden (Brad Pitt), who delivers impassioned rants about the evils of consumer capitalism. Fueled by the adrenaline and testosterone generated at the underground Fight Club that the narrator/Tyler founds, the members embark on the next stage of Fight Club: the anticorporate Project Mayhem, intended to take down the credit card companies, those engines of consumer culture. If Wall Street is the big bad of *Fight Club*, IKEA is its lackey, the decorative surface luring the masses into a fantasy world in which one's identity can be cultivated through a particular choice of coffee table and membership in the global community can be found in the purchase of drinking glasses made by the "indigenous peoples of . . . wherever." *Fight Club* is a challenge to the marketing proposition that we can or should find meaning by associating with brands like IKEA. As Tyler Durden admonishes his disaffected young followers: "You are not your fucking khakis!"

As powerful and multifarious as identification can be as a motivating force in political and commercial culture, interpellation presumes no preexisting subject to discourse. A concept explored by many critical theorists in myriad ways, interpellation is most commonly understood by way of Althusser's well-known example of a police officer shouting, "Hey, you there!" The person who turns, who recognizes him- or herself as being addressed by the officer, is in that moment hailed into being as subject to the state, its laws, its ideologies, and so on. The address ("Hey, you there!") and the response (the person turning toward the officer) are what constitute both the officer and the respondent as subjects within a particular legal-juridical matrix. Unlike identification, in which subjects avail themselves of a preexisting identity, in the moment of interpellation, subjects are created, constituted as a subject, through participation in the act of discourse.

Recall the Betty Crocker "add an egg" anecdote. The original formula that included powdered eggs failed to persuade its target audience, as it relied merely on the power of the Betty Crocker brand. But it wasn't enough that a customer might identify as a Betty Crocker cook. The eradication of the small but important task of adding the egg meant the product failed to adequately interpellate women into the subject position of "baker," and by proxy "mother" or "wife." The act of cracking and stirring fresh eggs into the mix was the minimal act that allowed one to become so in the doing. Participation through mere association isn't always enough for people to value, in a meaningful way, their relationship to a particular brand or object. Indeed, although they may not use the vocabulary of interpellation, advertisers are beginning to recognize that it is not brands, or even products, that earn consumers' loyalty, but the experiences they have with certain objects and the discourses that surround them. As a *Forbes* headline puts it, "It's time to design human experiences, not just products."[21]

Interpellation and Commodity Fetishization

The claim that the IKEA brand experience is a pleasurable one is dubious, to say the least. Online memes, cartoons, and testimonials abound declaring people's frustrations with either the assembly process or the madness of the in-store shopping experience. Yet as one writer puts it, "Despite the infamy of these ordeals, the masses (myself included) continue to torture themselves with long, painful trips to IKEA, followed by long, painful days spent wrestling with hinges and balsa and instructions that at times seem to require a PhD in semiotics."[22] By the millions, year after year, people across the globe keep coming back to the blue-and-yellow behemoth for more. Perhaps they, as philosopher Slavoj Žižek might put it, *Enjoy Your Symptom!* IKEA, like Target, does invite a certain fetishization of the commodity. But it differs, in degree if not in kind, from the kind Marx described so presciently in the mid-nineteenth century.

Marx's concept of the commodity fetish depends on his notion that ideology is a form of false consciousness. In his words, "They do not know it, but they are doing it." When we engage in commodity exchange, we may think our boots are "worth" $90, but we neglect to see the multifarious human relations and exploitations associated with their production. Marx's understanding of ideology, as Žižek explains, "implies a kind of basic, constituitive *naivete*."[23] Instead of the familiar Marxian maxim, "They do not know it, but they are doing it," Žižek promotes Peter Sloterdijk's observation that we now live in an age of cynicism, and "the cynical subject is quite aware of the distance between the ideological mask and the social reality, but he none the less still insists upon the mask. The formula, as proposed by Sloterdijk, would then be: 'they know very well what they are doing, but still, they are doing it.'"[24]

For philosophers such as Žižek working in the Lacanian psychoanalytic tradition, the value of any commodity does not come from its truth being dissembled, hidden from view behind the false consciousness of exchange value. Its value comes from our collectively participating in the fantasy of its value. Take money as an example. It is the commodity form par excellence, as it has no value other than its role as a unit of exchange. If I'm in the middle of a jungle and I'm hungry, the $10 in my pocket is of little value. However, if I'm walking down the street near my university's campus and happen to pass my favorite burrito bar, that same $10 means lunch. The fact that the $10 bill can mean nothing in one context and sustenance in another is possible only because the teenager working at the burrito stand, his managers, the bank, and the entire U.S. and global economic system have collectively agreed to buy into the fantasy that money means something, that it has some sort of tangible value, which in nature it does not. Does that mean this value is fake? Not at all. This "fantastic" value makes very real things possible: health care systems, cities, wars, burrito lunches. But this value isn't exactly real either. Its reality is wholly dependent on our knowingly conspiring in a collective fantasy.

The experience of visiting an IKEA showroom is also to give oneself over to a kind of fantasy. Its massive stores are carefully designed to aid us in this surrender. Retail environments have long deployed strategies that encourage shoppers to check their prefrontal cortexes at the door and get lost in a consumerist haze of desire and impulse indulgence. Strategies such as maze-like layouts, an absence of windows, clocks, and way-finding cues, as well as easy access to food for weary shoppers all work to intensify the so-called Gruen effect, in which shoppers lose sight of their original intentions and begin aimlessly and compulsively filling their carts.[25] IKEA customers have proven exceptionally susceptible to the Gruen effect. Built environments scholar Alan Penn, in a study of IKEA, reports that 60 percent of the stuff people buy there wasn't on their original shopping list.[26]

As anyone who has shopped in an IKEA has undoubtedly observed, the stores are designed less like a maze than a giant labyrinth, with prominent arrows steering shoppers, herd-like, through a myriad of domestic vignettes. Over here is a child's room, modern and bright, with a clever storage system for corralling Legos, books, and stuffed animals. Over there is a stylish bedroom, with matching wardrobe, nightstand, and bed, made all the cozier by a colorful geo-print duvet and complementary throw pillows, curtains, and area rug. Along the way are kitchens, dining rooms, and breakfast nooks, each one contemporary and sleek, staged with elegant and affordable place settings, one for what looks to be a family dinner, another for an urban cocktail party. Further still are office scenes, each a study in the efficient use of space and form. Many of these vignettes are labeled by size, such as "375 square foot apartment," to demonstrate that no matter how tiny your abode, you too can live the fantasy of organized, cozy living. After all, as IKEA explains on its website, "'At home' isn't just a place. It's a feeling. Like being in the most comfortable space in the universe."[27] Thanks to IKEA, that feeling is incredibly affordable—until, of course, you factor in the hours of frustration you likely face re-creating that fantasy once you get back to your real home.

However fantastic the showroom may seem, if we are to follow the logic of psychoanalytic fetishization, IKEA customers are co-collaborators in the fantasy and active participants in the consumerist journey. Consider again the layout of IKEA stores. The unidirectional path leads shoppers out of the showroom, which ultimately morphs into a giant warehouse, a functional grid of shelving and flat packs, through which shoppers push huge carts and carry small slips of paper guiding them to just the right bin from which collect the components they'll later use to assemble their new Besta media console or what have you. As consumer psychologist Maria Pachaki explains, "IKEA offers two differentiated areas: the hedonic area and the utilitarian area. Each of those areas has a distinct layout that fulfills its aim and appeals to a different kinetic quality. In the hedonic area the consumer may lie on the beds to try them, sit on the couches and on the armchairs to see if they are comfortable extracting pleasure from them, while in the utilitarian ground floor he can easily navigate the spaces which have a simple and organized according to codes layout."[28] On display in this utilitarian warehouse, with its forklifts, industrial carts, and thousands upon thousands of flat-packed kits of particle board, is but another fantasy layered under the first, hailing us to collaborate in a fetishization of another sort.

In this phase of the IKEA fantasy, shoppers spill out of the hedonic labyrinth of sensory pleasures and are now turned loose, bin numbers and product codes in hand, into the sprawling grids of stock to search for the pieces they need. IKEA goes out of its way to make the search successful, of course, providing computer kiosks where one can look up stock availability and location, for example. But like all good treasure hunts, a degree of effort and navigational skill is required if one is to claim one's prize. Once shoppers have located their pieces and loaded them onto dollies, they make their way to the last stage of the journey, where they will wait their turn to place their spoils on conveyor belts to be scanned by waiting cashiers. Now, in these final moments, plants, candles, and other impulse items appear, ready to be added to the booty.

One could say (and many do) that the journey of shopping for, locating, transporting, and then assembling IKEA products is a harrowing one. But it is not without its pleasures. IKEA may have offloaded these tasks onto the consumer as a cost-saving measure, but the result is customers who are engaged at a level quite different than with other retail environments. Shoppers may or may not identify with the IKEA brand, but it is their interpellation as adventurer, navigating IKEA's labyrinth of pleasures and challenges, that cultivates the relationship between customer and product, subject and object. Understood in the vernacular of psychoanalysis, the IKEA experience—the process of admiring the images in its ubiquitous catalog, envisioning one's own home among the fleeting scenes of domesticity in the showroom, then steering one's way toward the acquisition of the flat packs themselves—is just the first stage in a larger journey. This interpellative process of fetishization, which begins as one browses the catalog or enters the store, doesn't really end until that final twist of the Allen wrench, when the circuit between matter and meaning is completed.

Herein lies a significant difference between a Marxist and a psychoanalytic conceptualization of the commodity fetish. For Marx, the commodity is presented in situ, as a complete and discrete object, silently guarding the secret of the human labor that birthed it. From this perspective, consumers' eyes are unknowingly veiled by the false consciousness of exchange value. They participate in a system they do not understand; "they do not know it, but they are doing it."[29] In contrast to the Marxist commodity, the psychoanalytic commodity is presented in fantasy. It is an object that doesn't quite exist yet, except in the imagery IKEA creates through its catalogs and stores, and the countless design blogs and shelter magazines it sponsors. Whereas the Marxist commodity arrives in situ, with IKEA, we encounter the object at a different stage in its life cycle. It holds the promise of becoming the thing we want, but it is presented as a thing to come. Although its completeness may be the stuff of imagination, the imagination is aroused nonetheless.

Ian Bogost, writing for the *Atlantic* about, of all things, the McRib sandwich, calls on Lacanian psychoanalysis to suggest that McDonald's yearly reintroduction of the "restructured pork patty" is more about inciting desire than sustaining it:

> McDonald's sells what it does not sell: the conditions of predictability, affordability, and chemico-machinic automated cookery that make its very business viable. When we eat at McDonald's we don't eat its food—Quarter Pounders or Big Macs or what have you—so much as we consume the mechanical predictability of its overall offering. Chicken McNuggets are the same everywhere. The same shape, the same taste, the same packaging, the same menu, the same uniforms, the same roofline, the same signage. Industrialism is also a kind of magic, the magic of the perfect facsimile.[30]

As with Marx's concept of the commodity fetish, the psychoanalytic tradition also understands commodities as being imbued with a kind of magical quality. But this magic doesn't do its work by way of mystification. As any sleight-of-hand master would acknowledge, the audience's collusion in the illusion is crucial to the enjoyment of the experience. As an impressive sleight-of-hand artist, IKEA, like McDonald's, is less duping its customers than inviting them to participate in the ruse. It diverts their attention from some aspects of the performance while focusing it on others. Herein lies the difference between the Marxist and psychoanalytic understanding of fetishization, although the difference is more one of degree than of kind. Even though fans of the McRib know they are consuming at best a facsimile of a slab of barbecued short ribs, they love it just the same.

If you indulge in the IKEA fantasy, then the labor that births the object will largely be yours, and you know that. IKEA customers are under no illusion that the slabs of compressed sawdust and glue they schlep home and put together themselves is bespoke Scandinavian furniture, or otherwise unique in any way. In the spirit of true fetishistic disavowal, they know perfectly well, yet this knowledge does nothing to quell their desire.

IKEA as Democratic Design

However, as we have learned from the Marxist-inspired design movements of the twentieth century, uniqueness isn't always what it's cracked up to be. For the likes of Bauhaus, the standardization wrought by factory production is precisely the thing that would make beautiful objects available to all of us rather than a handful of privileged elites. Yet the age-old tension between uniformity and individuality remains. How is it, in an age when we expect to tailor everything from sneakers to cell phones to suit our personal taste, that IKEA's simple, homogeneous designs have become so ubiquitous that they furnish homes across the globe, with little regard for the specificities of personality, place, or culture? Indeed, 85 percent of IKEA's products are common to all its stores around the world. The IKEA catalog—two hundred million items of which are shipped per year, rivaling only the Bible as the world's most distributed publication—displays scenes of domestic life designed to be as "placeless" as possible. Bill Mooridge, director of the Cooper-Hewitt National Design Museum, describes IKEA's design as "global functional minimalism," noting, "It's modernist, and it's very neutral in order to avoid local preferences."[31] That smiling, racially ambiguous family gathering for breakfast around their BJURSTA dining table could be nearly anywhere on earth—Budapest, Hungary; Tampines, Singapore; Amman, Jordan; Houston, Texas (all of which have IKEA stores). On the identification front, IKEA is casting a wide net indeed.

Like Target, IKEA appears to see itself as following in the footsteps of modernist movements like the Bauhaus, democratizing design by making thoughtful, stylish, and easily reproducible pieces available to the global masses. Like Target's "Design for All" manifesto, IKEA's familiar slogan, "Design for Everyone," echoes those Marx-influenced designers who sought to wrest factory production from the hands of the rich and produce objects that were beautiful, affordable, and designed for how everyday people actually live. Ingvar Kamprad, IKEA's famous founder, writes proudly in the preface to his company's constitutional document: "A well-known industrialist/politician once said that IKEA has had a greater impact on the democratization process than many political measures combined."[32] That may be, but the democratization of design is not without its critics. For all its aping of their rhetoric and formal aesthetics, IKEA seems to forget that modernist design movements—most notably Bauhaus, the International Style, and Le Corbusier and his followers—have themselves been heavily ridiculed precisely for the one-size-fits-all placelessness that defines the genre. Modern design's attempt to be all things to all people proved to be its Achilles' heel.

Perhaps the most famous and damning blow came from Tom Wolfe, who scathingly critiques the oppressiveness of modern architecture that so permeated Europe and the United States throughout the twentieth century. He opines, "Every child goes to school in a building that looks like a duplicating-machine replacement-parts wholesale distribution warehouse."[33] Even the mansions of those who presumably should know better live in buildings with "so many pipe railings, ramps, hob-tread metal spiral stairways, sheets of industrial plate glass, banks of tungsten-halogen lamps, and white cylindrical shapes, it looks like an insecticide refinery. I once saw the owners of such a place driven to the edge of sensory deprivation by the whiteness & lightness & leanness & cleanness & bareness & spareness of it all."[34]

Most of the various postmodern and organic design movements that emerged out of or railed against the sparseness of modernism were attempts to breathe some life back into the sterile world it had created. By attempting to offer design to the masses by paring down form to only its most functional features, its critics charge that the Bauhaus and its modernist comrades stripped design of its very humanity, asking us all to live just like our neighbor, in ugly, soulless boxes.

To Le Corbusier's famous description of houses as "machines for living," many essentially responded, "Who wants to live in a machine anyway?" As for the design movements that inspire it, democratization of design for IKEA is a double-edged sword. As Megan McArdle notes, "A visit to an IKEA warehouse brings home what progressives like, and libertarians hate, about Scandinavia: it's the Kingdom of *Lagom*, where everyone has exactly the same, perfectly adequate, stuff."[35]

IKEA as Lying Facade

Postmodern critiques of uniformity aside, for all its aesthetic similarities to modern design, its detractors charge that IKEA doesn't even offer *good* modern design, which, after all, was committed to producing innovative and high-quality objects. Although traces of the Bauhaus's populist rhetoric and ruthlessly modern aesthetic can be found throughout the IKEA landscape, the similarities break down around a key Bauhaus principle. Walter Gropius, founder of the Bauhaus, sought a true design by the people for the people, aided by the new technologies of industry. But, he insisted, never should mass production be an excuse for shoddy quality. He concludes his 1926 "Principles of Bauhaus Production" by arguing: "The dangers of a decline in the quality of the product by comparison to the prototype, in regard to quality of material and workmanship, as a result of mechanical reproduction will be countered by all available means. The Bauhaus fights against the cheap substitute, inferior workmanship, and the dilettantism of the handicrafts, for a new standard of quality work."[36] Gropius and the other Bauhaus designers were committed to producing authentic, high-quality objects, even if they were machine made. Gropius railed against what he called "lying façades" and claimed that the Bauhaus "aimed at realizing standards of excellence, not creating transient novelties."[37]

IKEA may produce stylish, often charming objects at affordable prices, but I suspect no one would argue that these are high-quality objects meant to stand the test of time. Artist Jeff Carter plays with the ephemeral nature of IKEA products with an installation piece directly addressing the differences and similarities between IKEA and the Bauhaus. For his project "The Common Citizenship of Forms," Carter built a scaled-down replica of the Michael Reese Hospital campus, designed in part by Walter Gropius, and which was demolished by the city of Chicago between 2009 and 2012. Carter's replica, which calls attention to the machinic nature of the modernist buildings of the complex, is constructed almost entirely of materials he acquired at IKEA. In a talk introducing his installation at the Illinois Institute of Technology, Carter explains that he was interested in "exposing information about IKEA that I feel is beyond the material substance that I use to make the work, looking for conceptual depth within the objects that are mass produced and marketed by IKEA."[38] Carter, like many contemporary artists and designers, seems ambivalent about the cultural influence of the Swedish mass retailer. He acknowledges the fundamental ways in which IKEA is a successful model of the modernist ideas of the Bauhaus: affordable, mass producible, with "an aesthetic of placelessness."[39]

However, Carter reminds us that the throwaway nature of the material runs counter to Bauhaus ideals. He hopes to foreground the simulacral quality of IKEA in his project: "The fact that even though this looks like wood it really isn't." In a nod to Gropius, he submits that "IKEA is nothing but lying façades."[40]

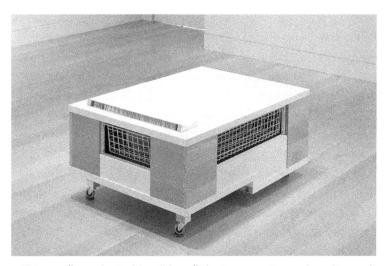

Jeff Carter, "Laundry Building," from "The Common Citizenship of Forms," 2010. Courtesy of Jeff Carter. Photograph by Nik Massey.

As one reviewer of Carter's project puts it, "While both the Bauhaus and IKEA promote simplified forms and the mass-production of goods intended for middle-class homes, IKEA sacrifices durability for cheap costs, relying on false surfaces to imply a quality that does not exist. Carter acknowledges this disjunct by exposing the unfinished sides of laminated MDF boards, as well as ragged gaps in his sculpture's edges that reveal flimsy cardboard."[41] Carter himself explains that "the reason I left a lot of the edges raw rather than unfinished, was exactly that, to show what is really inside. The idea of applying fine cabinet making skills to these materials, you know, could be done, but it seemed like a futile gesture . . . to try to cover up the edges and make sure you never knew that there's nothing but paper inside?"[42] As insightful as Carter's project is, revealing that IKEA materials are cheap is no revelation at all, because IKEA customers know this. In fact, to assemble a piece of IKEA furniture, one has to assess each board along the way to ensure it's put together with the veneer side facing out, lest the flimsy cardboard side show.

In her powerful 2009 indictment of discount culture, *Cheap*, Ellen Ruppel Shell devotes an entire chapter to IKEA, entitled "The Death of the Craftsman." Ruppel Shell echoes Carter's assertion that IKEA offers flimsy knock-offs of "good" design: "Flatpacks of medium-density fiberboard hauled out of sprawling warehouses and cobbled together with IKEA's notorious L-shaped six-sided Allen wrench are not tasteful, comfortable furniture. They are a facsimile of tasteful, comfortable furniture." Ruppel Shell argues, correctly, that IKEA sells design, not craftsmanship. Although she does not address the Bauhaus explicitly, her critique suggests that Gropius's lying facades have come home to roost, "convincing millions of people around the world that mass-manufactured furniture that looks, feels, and smells like extruded Lego blocks is not only affordable and stylish but *soulful*."[43] It seems that now, instead of mass-produced design being the liberator of the masses as Gropius had hoped, it is yet another cultural axis upon which the financial elites come out on top: "The combination of quality and value, once available to the many, is now affordable only to the few. For the rest of us, there is 'design.'"[44] In the IKEA version of design, design is more aesthetic than functional, more lying facade than quality artistry. Ruppel Shell notes, "Design may be clever, amusing, and eye-catching, but if executed without craftsmanship, it does not sustain us. Like a zirconium engagement ring, poorly executed design deceives: It has glitter but no gold."[45] Most of us are left with this ersatz design because true craftsmanship has become rare in an age when the trades are in decline and everything—electronics, shoes, furniture—is treated as temporary and disposable.

Disposability versus Attachment

IKEA is the epitome of fast design, a category of the home goods industry in which trendy yet cheaply made products are intended to be disposed with when they go out of style, whether they still function or not. The so-called fast category is booming across the contemporary marketplace, with fast fashion retailers like H&M, Uniqlo, and

Forever 21 enjoying record sales in recent years,[46] and fast casual food chains such as Chipotle Mexican Grill, MOD Pizza, and Panera Bread gaining significant ground against the likes of McDonald's by in part offering a more "designerly" dining experience. As with fast fashion, which allows people to participate in runway trends on the cheap, IKEA's products aren't designed to be family heirlooms. They're intended to serve a particular purpose, in an attractive manner, for as long as their components hold up. As Lauren Collins argues, "IKEA has made interiors ephemeral. Its furniture is placeholder furniture, the prelude to an always imminent upgrade. It works until it breaks, or until its owners break up. It carries no traces."[47]

This expectation of the "imminent upgrade" is actually an explicit mainstay of IKEA's public messaging. In the 1990s, when IKEA introduced itself to the United Kingdom, for example, it did so with a humorous two-minute advertisement called "Chuck out your chintz!" in which women (only women) scoured their homes, collecting their lacy curtains, flowery bedspreads, and dusty tchotchkes, tossing them into a huge blue-and-yellow IKEA bin for removal. We then see the women opting instead for less fussy IKEA decor: bright, casual, modern. IKEA's challenge to British women to ditch their doilies is even pitched as a feminist call to action. The campy song playing over the action frames chucking out chintz as something akin to tossing off the shackles of patriarchy: "We're battling hard and we've come a long way, in choices and status and jobs and in pay. But that flowery trimmage is harming our image, so chuck out that chintz today!" At this moment, the ad cuts to an animated woman laboring to lift huge block letters forming the word "frustrated" and replacing it with "liberated." Similar to the 1950s Betty Crocker cook being interpellated as a good wife and mother through the baking of a cake, IKEA was telling 1990s women that domestic freedom was as simple as modernizing the style of one's home, with liberation only possible because objects are, in the world of IKEA, utterly chuckable.

Ten years later, IKEA's message remained the same. IKEA's 2005 "Lamp" commercial, one that I often show in my undergraduate courses, linges on the fast, disposable nature of its products. Created by indiefilm director Spike Jonze (known for 1999's *Being John Malkovich*, 2013's *Her*, and music videos for the likes of Björk and Kanye West), the commercial opens with a young white woman in an urban brownstone apartment, unplugging her old lamp and replacing it with a stylish new one, presumably from IKEA. The woman then goes out into the windy, dusky night and discards her old (yet still functional) lamp onto the sidewalk with the trash. A melancholy, minimalist piano melody plays in the background; the lamp seemingly shivers and hunches in the wind and pounding rain as the sky grows dark. The camera pans up to the woman's apartment window, where the viewer, from the discarded lamp's point of view, sees her cozy up under the warm glow of her new lamp, then pat it lovingly before turning in for the night. Just as viewers' heartstrings are pulled taut, a soaking wet man wearing a raincoat breaks the fourth wall, addressing the viewer directly in what Ellen Ruppell Shell rightly describes as a bad Swedish accent: "Many of you feel bad for dis lamp. . . . Dat is because you are crazy. Duh lamp has no feelings. And the new one is much bedder!" At this point, my students, most of whom were reared on the narrative tropes of Hollywood, usually break into awkward laughter. Comparisons to other heartbreaking tales (*Toy Story* [1995], *The Brave Little Toaster* [1989]) in which a beloved familiar object is replaced by a newer model usually follow.

Spike Jonze's spot makes a clever rhetorical move, one that serves fast retailers like IKEA well. By goading viewers into deriding their own sentimentality, the spot encourages us to adopt a common posture of the hipster consumer: ironic, detached, decidedly unsentimental. An early adopter consumer attitude ("the new one is much bedder!") that's driven by the novelty of the "always imminent upgrade" is more or less harmless when ushering in the latest pop band or lifestyle blog. But the speed at which consumers are encouraged to discard consumer objects—shoes, lamps, cell phones—has very real environmental implications.

For Ruppel Shell, the problem with cheap, disposable furniture is that it perverts the natural order of things. It inverts the traditional relationship between us and the objects we live with. In failng to adequately do our bidding, we must accommodate them, rather than vice versa. She observes, "Millions of IKEA enthusiasts around the globe contort themselves to meet the needs of the brand." For example, "rather than burden poor Billy [bookcase] to the breaking point, they carefully confine their heavy books to the perimeters." As a result, "the idea of what constitutes a bookcase . . . is modified to accommodate the limitations of an object that is wonderful mainly for its sleek exterior and low price. In a very real sense, a Billy is not a bookcase but a subspecies of bookcase."[48] Essentially, Ruppel Shell seems to suggest, the demanding Billy promotes a way of living with objects in which the authority of the human subject is increasingly undermined. In this technology-driven, mass-produced era, our things seem to forget who's in charge.

Although not explicitly so, Ruppel Shell is arguing from the Marxist position that the use value of an object remains the core of its essential nature. Judged on those grounds, it can reasonably be argued that IKEA fails. Indeed, IKEA manufactures objects designed to delight rather than endure. But it also designs objects meant to address the challenges of urban living. Many people spend so much on housing—even tiny spaces—that little room or money is left for expensive, well-crafted furnishings. It's hard not to agree with Ruppel Shell's overall characterization of IKEA. Its products are indeed uniform and cheaply made. IKEA is among the most recognizable symptoms of what Julia Butterfly Hill calls the disposability consciousness of our current cultural moment.[49] Recycling programs and composting notwithstanding, we do live in an unsustainable throwaway culture, and what we might call true craftsmanship and stewardship of objects are on the decline. That said, like Carter exposing the unfinished edges of IKEA materials to show it's little more than flimsy cardboard, Ruppel Shell's argument rests on the revelation that IKEA's materials are cheap. I'm not convinced that this is much of a revelation to anyone buying its products.

More importantly for this discussion, however, I am reluctant to grant her concluding indictment: because of their inherent disposability, we don't attach to cheap and transitory objects. She writes, "Cheap objects resist involvement. We tend to invest less in their purchase, care, and maintenance, and that's part of what makes them so attractive. . . . Perhaps we don't even want the object to last forever. Such voluntary obsolescence makes craftsmanship beside the point. We have grown to expect and even relish the easy birth and early death of objects."[50] The implications of this indifference to the birth and death of objects are clear. It suggests that IKEA is, by design, a massive, global waste generator.

Concluding her chapter on IKEA, Ruppel Shell tells a poignant anecdote about a friend who, when moving from one state to another, was told by the movers that because of its poor quality, they couldn't promise her Billy bookcase would arrive at her new home in one piece. The friend decided to leave the Billy on the curb and replaced it with a solid oak bookcase she found at a flea market for a comparable price. Ruppel Shell relays that when visiting her friend, "Ten years later it is still there, marked with age and packed to groaning with big, heavy books and memories. My friend has lots more money now and could afford a brand-new bookcase, so I asked her if she plans to put this one on the curb. She looked stricken. 'Why,' she asked, 'would I do that?'"[51] If Ruppel Shell's friend looks stricken, it is because she feels emotionally bonded to this bookcase. It is imbued with history for her. It carries with it the stories of its former owners as well as her own. It seems likely she will pass this piece of furniture along to her children, or at least release it back into the secondhand retail pool from whence it came, allowing it to absorb the stories of its next owner. Regardless, it is doubtful she will discard it altogether, dooming it to live out the rest of its days on a landfill somewhere. I suspect nearly all of us have had this kind of relationship with an object in our lives. As I will argue in the next chapter, I believe it's worth exploring ways we might deepen this emotional attachment to objects.

I'm not willing to dismiss IKEA altogether as sheer fakery that resists emotional involvement. Recall that Dan Ariely believes that the toy box he assembled for his children "was fonder of me than my other furniture was." His research suggests he's not alone in this.[52] Ariely describes a sentimental attachment to that toy box that cannot so easily be called fake. And IKEA fans and hackers across the world are inserting themselves into the design process, modifying the company's products to suit their own aesthetic, utilitarian, and creative visions. They are transforming modular, supposedly disposable materials into something perhaps even more worthy of attachment.

Ruppel Shell and others' critique of IKEA tends to be based on issues of identity and tradition. If it is ephemeral and not with us for the long haul, this logic goes, then an object doesn't merit attachment. If it doesn't adequately do our bidding or fully realize its use value, then it doesn't merit attachment. This is a rigid understanding of authenticity, one that adheres to a romantic and ultimately unhelpful notion of the subject–object relationship. It's true that nobody is likely tending lovingly to their Billy bookcase so they can one day hand it down to their children, and admittedly this disposability does seem to run counter to the IKEA effect's thesis that we love what we labor over, or at least the notion that this love leads to anything like long-term commitment. But if the IKEA effect studies demonstrate anything, it's that our labor, even if it's just the act of assembling an object from a kit, produces real value. If we esteem an object we've assembled (however shoddy its material), it is because it serves as an artifact, a document testifying to our struggle, effort, and ultimate success. Whether assembling origami cranes or cardboard IKEA boxes, the subjects in the IKEA effect studies assigned greater monetary value to the objects they made themselves as a way to represent the emotional attachment they felt to that document and that experience. Tellingly, when rendered a commodity by the researcher's offer of cold, hard cash, the actual exchange value of these objects increased.

This is project value altering our traditional understanding of exchange value. It augments the commodity beyond its conventional form. Exchange value, as exemplified by the commodity form, does not only reify the object, obscuring the conditions of its emergence. Whereas Marx is concerned about the fetishization of objects wrought by our ignorance of the labor that went into them, what we see with project value is more a psychological fetishization. When we have a hand, however slight, in its creation, an object becomes meaningful because we believe it to be imbued with a little bit of ourselves. However frustrating it may be to visit the labyrinthine stores or assemble the item once the pieces have been taken home, IKEA shoppers both identify with and are interpellated by the experience. Although the fabrication of materials is still obscured, people who buy IKEA know that the stuff is coming prefabricated from Sweden, Eastern Europe, or, increasingly, China, and that they are not actually building anything. But in the process of assembly, a relationship between assembler and material is forged. Assembly may not result in long-term, sustainable commitment to the task of mitigating the inevitable disposability of IKEA products; this is a problem if we want to reduce the material waste on the planet. However, unlike Marx's commodity fetishism, which dissembles the human story behind the objects in our lives, project value gives us a glimpse into objects' material inner workings and asks us to participate in the story of its emergence. In a small way, these objects are no longer discrete, wholly formed talismans simply there for our pleasure and use. They begin to demand something of us as well. We transport them home, put them together, and, yes, even arrange our books carefully so as not to overburden their shelves.

Whereas Target's treatment of design encourages a new mystification of the commodity object by exaggerating the role and mystique of invention, the IKEA effect sees in design an introduction, however slight, into the material conditions of emergence for the objects hidden, inchoate, within the confines of those brown flat packs. By itself, the coffee table or the bookshelf or the bed frame doesn't arrive fully formed, bursting from the forehead of a creative design genius like Athena being born from Zeus. Instead, through the act of assembly, assemblers are invited to think of the invention of an object more broadly: more open, less mystified. Assemblers are not under the illusion that they created their new table, but they necessarily know more about how that table came to be because of their role in its construction. Invention, in other words, becomes less a mysterious, quasi-magical process done elsewhere by those with the competency and pedigree required to do so, and more a set of decisions that any consumer can make as he or she assembles, or even adapts, standard-ized objects as objects of their desire.

It is this raw desire that Ruppel Shell undervalues. The fact that IKEA furniture is disposable is absolutely true, but this is fundamen-tally beside the point that we need to understand if we are to progress to delineating how the era of design potentially changes how we relate to objects. The moment of attachment, of desire, for IKEA assemblers takes place at an earlier stage of the product life cycle. That it doesn't sustain itself through extended use doesn't imply an illegitimacy of that attachment any more than breaking up with one's first love implies a lack of true affection. The problem is that too often, the way we speak about attachment lacks the sort of nuance and granularity that would allow us to initiate a richer, more productive conversation about how we relate to and interact with objects. That will be the subject of the next chapter.

FOUR

The Value of Story

Extending the Value of Objects

I once built a mahogany coffee table on which I spared no expense of
effort. At the time I had no immediate prospect of becoming a father,
yet I imagined a child who would form indelible impressions of this
table and know that it was his father's work. I imagined the table fading
into the background of a future life, the defects in its execution as well
as inevitable stains and scars becoming a surface textured enough that
memory and sentiment might cling to it, in unnoticed accretions.

—*Matthew Crawford, "Shop Class a Soulcraft"*

Thus far, as we map the deconstruction of commodity objects, we have
looked at a variety of ways that consumers interact with things in the
age of design. In one model, exemplified by the fast fashions offered
by Target, design is largely an aestheticized add-on to objects, a stylistic skin that is often clever and even beautiful. As consumers, we
can combine these mass-produced objects in interesting ways, acting as bricoleurs of sorts, fashioning ourselves and our homes with
mass retail versions of the latest high-end designs. Target's rhetorical
emphasis on affordable design popularizes a material vocabulary, promoting a design literacy in consumers who may otherwise have little
interest in or access to such things. That said, Target's design rhetoric

ultimately does little to open the object up or to render it malleable. It remains discrete, congealed, easily fetishized. In the flat-pack boxes of IKEA, we begin to see the object as something more inchoate, an object yet to come that is made whole only by our own intervention into the evolution of its material form. The IKEA effect and what I call "project value" demonstrate that this more participatory experience of objects, although hardly revolutionary, invites a degree of affection for the assembled object, if only because it testifies to the effort we exerted bringing it to life.

But while Target has mastered the art of sparking delight at point of purchase, and while IKEA enjoys a degree of brand loyalty that its competitors envy, the attachment to objects that these two retail models encourage remains relatively superficial. The charming geometric pencil cup designed for Target by Nate Berkus is likely discarded once the novelty (or rose gold veneer) wears off. The IKEA bookshelf, too fragile to withstand a move, is left on the curb rather than preserved for future generations. Any attachment we feel to these objects is at its apex in the middle of their life cycle, when they sit beckoning to us from the in-store display, or, a bit later, as we admire our creation, temporarily gratified after spending an arduous afternoon with particleboard and Allen wrenches. Both companies have had great success bringing design trends to a mass market. But as a result, the actual durable goods they sell—various admixtures of wood, cotton, plastic, and glass—are vulnerable to what Vance Packard calls psychological obsolescence, a subset of the phenomenon he famously identifies as planned obsolescence, in which a rapid succession of stylistic changes and aesthetic upgrades are intended to ensure that consumer desire for any one object in particular is finite.[1] These companies' stock in trade is their capacity to inspire attraction, to sound the siren's call to humans trained by millennia of natural selection to pursue pleasure and covet the reddest berries on the vine. But as we know, the pleasure of discovering and consuming the objects of our attraction is inherently fleeting; our pleasure inevitably returns to the status quo, driving us to pursue the next red berry, or rose gold geometric pencil cup. Modern consumer culture, exemplified by the likes of Target and IKEA, is especially adept at exploiting the effects of this conundrum, what evolutionary psychologists call the hedonic treadmill.

Nothing in either Target's trendiness or IKEA's pseudo-DIY gratification is necessarily up to the difficult task of inspiring what we might think of as a genuine emotional bond between a person and an object such that the former feels obligated and committed to the latter—that is, the kind of attachment that inspires stewardship. Neither model forecloses this possibility, but surely we can do better. In this chapter, I explore the work of artists and activists who are experimenting with the power of story to imbue objects with meaning. Some apply stories to already existing objects in the hopes of extending their value and staving off their disposal. Others create objects that from their inception are designed to be malleable, evolving relational partners, with the capacity to tell their own story and to help shape our own.

Something Old . . .

The KonMari craze has been a boon to consignment boutiques and thrift shops as people empty their closets of uninspiring garments. "If you have a cocktail dress you'll never wear again," explains one consignment shop owner, "why not pass that energy on to someone else who needs it."[2] But even before Kondo's blockbuster book was published, a handful of secondhand retailers explored how to reboot the value of objects someone else no longer wanted. One strategy that seems to be gaining traction is to link objects to anecdotes from the past, thus inviting new owners to participate in their legacy. The Tales of Things and Electronic Memory (TOTeM) project, for example, was a collaboration among scholars at five major British universities. The project, which received a £1.39 million grant from the United Kingdom's Digital Economy Research Council, was an experiment in extending and augmenting the life of objects with diminishing value. Using QR and RFID codes together with a social networking site, the researchers created a platform through which people could tag items and attach video or audio of themselves telling stories about the role that object has played in their lives.

The highest profile of TOTeM's projects was "Remember Me," a collaboration with Oxfam charity shops in the United Kingdom in which people were encouraged to digitally tag the things they donated so potential buyers could learn a bit more about an item's history. By scanning the code with a handheld scanner, Oxfam customers were able to hear, from speakers scattered throughout the store, a tale about the thing in their hand. As proof of concept, Oxfam and TOTeM invited celebrities like Colin Firth, Kate Moss, and Scarlett Johansson to donate articles of clothing and record videos of themselves describing the significance the item had in their lives. Singer Annie Lennox, for example, tagged a dress she donated with a video in which she described wearing it to a birthday celebration for Nelson Mandela. Remember Me was launched during Manchester's Future of Things festival, and coordinator Jane MacDonald reported that every tagged object at that city's Oxfam store sold that day, propelling a 43 percent increase in sales for the shop.[3]

TOTeM principal investigator Chris Speed argues that story has the power to cultivate greater attachments and connections to objects: "You pick up these banal objects, and if it has a story, as soon as you hear it, it becomes something far richer."[4] The project's organizers surmised that this enriched view of objects could have positive social and environmental impacts: "The project will offer a new way for people to place more value on their own objects in an increasingly disposable economy. As more importance is placed on the objects that are already parts of people's lives it is hoped that family or friends may find new uses for old objects and encourage people to think twice before throwing something away."[5]

Such stories—of an object's travels, its use patterns, its history, its context—lend it an aura that can translate into value. Applying a modern technology (readable digital codes) to old items has the potential to reinvigorate their worth and hence extend their life. "A lot of scanning is about the price or about advertising right now," says Speed.

"This is a breakthrough in that you can retrieve memories of an object as opposed to what the organizations want you to know. You can scan an old shoe and hear its story."[6] It makes sense that items once owned by celebrities like Scarlett Johansson would fetch a big price, as there's a long-standing tradition of valuing things associated with famous people. Celebrity product endorsements have long made use of the power of association, but this is more than that. Frost and Steketee, the hoarding researchers, describe asking a class of undergraduates about their most meaningful possessions. When one young woman describes owning a shirt once owned by Jerry Seinfeld, the class unanimously agrees this was indeed valuable.[7]

Although it may seem unreasonable, humans have a long history of seeing objects as containing an essence of their previous owner—in this case, some sort of Seinfeldian mojo. (The fact that Seinfeld's shirt had been washed since in his possession did nothing to curb the students' enthusiasm about its worth.) Such items make us feel connected to something larger, perhaps a bit more special than we would be without them. As Frost and Steketee write, this sympathetic magic isn't just the sparkly stuff of celebrities: "It's the same whether we collect celebrities' clothing, a piece of the Berlin Wall, a deck chair off the Titanic, or five tons of newspapers. We can't help but imagine that some essence of the person or the event symbolized by the objects will magically rub off and become part of us."[8] In a study of children's attachment to transitional objects, child psychologists Bruce Hood and Paul Bloom find that kids believe their favorite blanket or stuffy to have a unique essence. When Hood and Bloom test their hypothesis using other objects, they find that children believe a goblet they were told had once belonged to the queen to be more special than that same goblet described as being made of precious metal.[9]

The TOTeM website (http://www.talesofthings.com/) offers a virtual space where everyday people can share anecdotes about the possessions they already own, precious or not, with the hope that they will come to value the item all the more by doing so. Although the website has fallen out of use, hundreds of people have posted stories since

its 2010 launch, sharing stories of the significant and mundane objects in their lives. A few examples:

> This manual coffee grinder has been an important part of my morning
> routine since 2006, and has followed me from Dresden, via Zurich to
> London.

> The tale of The Red Boy [describing a china plate painted with the
> image of a boy in red]: As a child, this plate hung in the lounge of my
> parent's house, which was directly under my bedroom. I never liked
> the picture which made me feel very uneasy. I used to have nightmares
> where my bed fell through my bedroom floor, and I landed in front of
> The Red Boy. A few years before she died, my mother gave me the pic-
> ture which now hangs in my bedroom (without attendant nightmares!)

Here is a diary of a homemade stuffed monster:

> He was born in a strange eastern country, and came to Levallois,
> France, by a windy day of December along with his family of 4. Some
> disappeared, some left and went to Paris. Here comes the story of just
> another Monster.

The people posting on the TOTeM website aren't selling the objects
they describe. They're telling the story of an object that has meaning
for them. Even if no one reads these biographies, the act of recording
them, testifying to a thing's sentimental value, itself may deepen the
human–object bond.

Although exploring the meaning of things is hardly a new phenomenon, digital media have offered people new ways to share and
reflect on their relationship to objects. Podcasts like *RadioLab* and
99% Invisible regularly offer meditations on material culture. WNYC
public radio, in its 2012 series "The Story of New York in 10 Objects,"
offered deep dives into the histories of such Big Apple icons as the
subway token and the Greek coffee cup. The podcast was a mini version of "The History of the World in 100 Objects" by the venerable

BBC that same year, in collaboration with the British Museum. Museums, long serving as showcases for objects as art or historical artifacts, have broadened their reach through interactive websites and YouTube channels to expand the conversation about people and their stuff. The Portland Art Museum (PAM), for example, has had a rotating exhibit running since 2010 in which everyday people share stories about an object significant in their lives. The museum records these stories and shares them on its YouTube channel. Portlanders offer stories of meaningful objects, such as one young man's tattered old wallet, given to him by his mother, or another's stone owl, which he's had since childhood. The people and stories vary, but they each do the work PAM intended: they disrupt the traditional structure that both endows the authorial voice of the museum and questions the types of objects worthy of our reflection. The project invites people to consider the meaning and value of everyday objects, and in so doing encourages new ways of seeing and relating to things.

While less high-tech, a for-profit enterprise in Japan is, like TOTeM, banking on the idea that knowing the biography of an object will make it more valuable to consumers. The Pass the Baton chain of thrift shops in Tokyo is successfully overcoming the Japanese distaste for second-hand clothing by attaching stories and pictures from previous owners about the object's meaning in their lives. As its name suggests, Pass the Baton's mission is to use objects as vehicles to connect one person to another; one person hands off a belonging to the next, who may find new value in it. Part of that value comes from knowing something about the object's history. As one writer puts it, "Even just one sentence can place an everyday object in a new light, adding almost a sense of duty upon the next owner to treat it with care."[10] For example, seller Kou Machida, a poet, writes of his Pelikan fountain pen, "I received this 13 or 14 years ago, and used it to write thank you letters and such."[11] A local newscaster adds a note to a Diane von Furstenberg dress: "The print was too flashy for me, but I bought it as an adventure when shopping with my friend."[12] Pass the Baton even allows buyers the opportunity to write a note to the previous owner, thereby completing the link and extending the potential network of stories and meaning.

Pass the Baton founder Masamichi Toyama sees his shops as using story to reinvigorate traditional Japanese values like thrift and community. He explains:

> In the Edo period, which was over 100 years ago, recycling was very common among people. Then, after the economic growth that followed the war, the era of mass consumption began. However, now we realize we wasted so much and we should cherish old things. Every person has their own history, culture, and aesthetic, so it would make for an interesting world if people express and exchange those with each other. It would not just be items mingled, but also stories . . . and that creates a new culture.[13]

Toyama says he was motivated to start Pass the Baton as an ethical intervention, an effort to quell *mottainai*, which seems to pervade modern consumerism: "*Mottainai* is the sense of regret that occurs when the value of a product or resource is not properly utilized and wasted," he explains.[14] *Mottainai* is a core value of the Japanese environmental movement. It is an ancient Buddhist term meaning "essence," and it encourages a sense of respect and gratitude for resources. Pass the Baton and TOTeM create venues that seek to make explicit a role already played by many objects: that of memory host. By foregrounding this role, the hope is that the objects will be less easily discarded.

By connecting secondhand objects to stories from their past, TOTeM and Pass the Baton establish a sense of legacy. Those who purchase an object from one of Toyama's stores, for example, also inherit its history, or at least a snippet of it. However small the gesture, the veil of anonymity is lifted, and shoppers are encouraged by the context to see a given object as specific, individual, and unique, even if the object's story began on an assembly line where it was but one in vast number of identical copies. Through the application of narrative, our perception of the individual object is opened up. As current owner, I am but one link in a potential chain of owners, one instantiation of ownership in the longer life span of the object. This shift in sensibility from the norms of contemporary consumer culture is slight but significant because ownership now carries with it the potentiality of duty and stewardship. We do not want to be the ones to break the chain.

Mass retailers are now starting to see the rhetorical power of story. Advertisers are routinely changing their titles to "storyteller," and Amazon offers hundreds of business books hailing the importance of narrative when establishing brand identity. The J. Peterman Company, for example, has long made storytelling a central piece of distinguishing its brand of high-end travel apparel. In the company's catalog, each product is accompanied by a story, usually told in the voice of founder John Peterman himself, situating the item in the historical moment that inspired its design or the exotic locale in which it was discovered. Here, for example, is just the beginning of a description for a women's caftan (called the Goddess) from J. Peterman's spring 2016 collection:

> I was received in the double drawing room which had been expertly painted in a weathered shade of blue known as Stolen Moments. There was a man sitting at a desk laughing into a rotary phone. She'd just had her dog's ashes put into a family heirloom and asked if I found it appropriate. I told her it was a tasteful receptacle that went well with the decor.
>
> Evidently I passed the test.
>
> These are the things one endures to find the good stuff.

The pretentious tone of the J. Peterman brand is famously spoofed in a long-running gag on *Seinfeld* (1989–89), in which Elaine works as an assistant to the company's eccentric, globe-trotting founder. Jokes aside, the company's brand identity is inextricably tied to its use of story to imbue otherwise ordinary retail goods with a distinctive personality and sense of history.

The outdoor clothing retailer Patagonia vigorously promotes good stewardship as a way to extend the longevity of its products and the authenticity of its brand, and it uses the power of storytelling to do so.

The company's website offers a series of user-generated testimonials called "the stories we wear" featuring personal stories from customers detailing their adventures while wearing Patagonia products. Stories of backpacks, sleeping bags, and parkas being battered and worn, but no less beloved, support the company's mission to encourage mending rather than tossing their gear. Customer Jason Antin of Golden, Colorado, posts that his jacket, "Ol' Blue," has served him well through "great adventures and milestones": "The folks at Denver Patagonia have come to know Ol' Blue quite well—they've given her a new zipper and mended some unsightly battle scars thanks to an unwieldy ice axe. . . . This jacket has been with me during many life changing moments and adventures far and wide. Unfortunately, the bumps and bruises it's seen have forced me to stop wearing it to business meetings. But that's ok! There's lot's of places I'd like to go where she'll fit in just fine!"[15] The company's slogan, "Worn Wear," insists that its products are intended for the long haul. The main page of its website features manifestos from its CEO, entitled "repair is a radical act!" and "if it's broke, fix it!," which include instructions for how to maintain Patagonia products. The company offers not one but five entry lines for the familiar "This jacket belongs to" patch inside its children's coats, and it explicitly promotes the resale or handing down of their products, thus enabling multiple people to participate in the story of each object.

In a similar vein, high-end Swiss watchmaker Patek Philippe advertises, "You never actually own a Patek Philippe. You merely look after it for future generations."[16] Brands that emphasize the longevity of their products, either as a result of quality materials or classic styling, often position themselves against the ephemera offered by the fast fashion brands in their category—Old Navy, Target, IKEA. In an era when even designs with the toniest of origins can be brought to mass market within months, it comes as no surprise that legacy, tradition, and even minimalism arise as the markers of class distinction. If anyone with even a bit of disposable income can get the latest runway looks from the likes of H&M, it makes sense that we see a simultaneous rise in brands that promise meaning and objects infused with story.

Although these commercial storytellers seldom open up for the consumer the conditions (environmental, human labor) of the object's manufacture, as some critics might understandably prefer, stories do potentially serve as points of connection that invite consumers to consider more carefully not only the past use patterns of the object but its future as well. As the narrative connectivity demonstrated by projects like TOTeM and Pass the Baton become more commonplace, consumers may be encouraged to see themselves not merely as owners (and eventually disposers) of the things in their lives but as temporary stewards of these objects, participants in a larger life span that will exceed this particular encounter. A host of companies like Patagonia, especially so-called American heritage brands like Danner, Filson, Carhartt, and even Levi's, are hoping to capitalize on exactly that sense that the relationship between a person and a product is part of a grander narrative of attachment, authenticity, and legacy.

Signifying Objects

If stories have the power to afford objects a sense of authenticity and meaning, thereby bolstering our attachment and devotion to them, does this logic hold when the stories themselves are inauthentic? Two cultural critics set out to answer just that question with their Significant Objects project. Significant Objects was "a literary and anthropological experiment" conducted by Rob Walker (*The Art of Noticing: 131 Ways to Spark Creativity, Find Inspiration, and Discover Joy in the Everyday* [2019]) and Joshua Glenn (*Taking Things Seriously: 75 Objects with Unexpected Significance* [2007]), two writers who explore consumerism and material culture. Their hypothesis: "Stories are such a powerful driver of emotional value that their effect on any given object's subjective value can actually be measured objectively."[17] To test their theory, Walker and Glenn purchased a number of inexpensive objects, such as a souvenir snow globe, an owl figurine, a *Charlie's Angels* (1976–81) thermos, and other trinkets from thrift shops. Their purchases averaged about $1.25 each.

They then recruited a variety of writers, some well known, like Jonathan Lethem and William Gibson, and others less so, like comic book writers and staff writers for *The Daily Show* (1996–). They assigned each writer an object and asked him or her to write a story around it, with the hope that adding narrative might produce meaning in the otherwise insignificant tchotchke. Once they received the stories, Walker and Glenn auctioned the objects on eBay, posting the fictional narrative in lieu of the typical item description. The starting price was listed at whatever they had originally paid for the item. Importantly, Walker and Glenn explicitly acknowledged that the story was a work of fiction and provided a link to their website, which offered an explanation of their experiment. Thanks to the stories, as well as the buzz the project generated in the press and blogosphere, Walker and Glenn's experiment was a resounding success. Through the mere application of story, they turned $128.74 worth of insignificant merchandise into $3,612.51 cash (which they distributed among the storytellers). As they summarize the experiment in their book documenting the project: "Via our experiment, the exchange value of these unwanted and sometimes unlovely objects was increased by more than 2,700 percent!"[18]

At its base, Significant Objects functions just like traditional corporate branding. It's not so different from the tall tales one might read in the J. Peterman catalog (although the stories Glenn and Walker collected were arguably better). Branding, of course, takes an ordinary object and attempts to imbue it with significance by embedding it in a story—one that makes us laugh, that pulls at our heartstrings, or tells us that by consuming this or that product, we'll finally get the girl, the job, or the life we covet. In the logic of branding, objects are the vehicles, the distribution mechanism, for what is often really being sold: the brand itself.

Independent of story, the thrift shop items that Glenn and Walker rescued remain relatively insignificant. That is, they fail to adequately signify something outside themselves: a memory, an emotion, an ambition. The Significant Objects project examines and makes explicit the logic of branding and its power to imbue objects with meaning through the attribution of story. But unlike corporate branding, Significant Objects deploys story in an effort to revitalize discarded objects that may otherwise, in KonMari parlance, no longer spark joy. A significant object is something that is infused with secret or special meaning. The word comes from the Latin *signum* (sign) and *ficare* (to make or do). Signification is the making of a thing into a sign, and signs are the basic unit of meaning. The Significant Objects project was an attempt to prolong value through layering, or adding to Baudrillard's sign value, discussed in chapter 2. Glenn and Walker's experiment with manufactured significance value updates and deepens Baudrillard's concept—a move that would likely delight the late philosopher, who had a keen appreciation for simulacra.

Significant Objects also introduces yet another nuanced version of Böhme's staging value. By embedding these otherwise meaningless objects in fictional, sometimes fantastic narratives, staging them on eBay, and generating social media buzz around the whole endeavor, Glenn and Walker, as well as the people who buy the objects, grant these objects a kind of story value. They are staged as part of a story larger than themselves—something quirky, sweet, adventurous, or relatable. One can imagine the possibilities if retailers of secondhand objects were to consider the staging and branding of their merchandise as carefully and methodically as behemoths like Target or IKEA. The opportunities to reboot and extend value of otherwise disposable objects are, well, significant.

Although Significant Objects may have started out as a "life-affirming cheeky stud[y]" on the quantifiable value of story, its admittedly less than scientific findings offer us the real insight that some kinds of story may be more valuable than others.[19] For their edited collection featuring the first hundred of the Significant Objects stories,[20] and on the Significant Objects website, Glenn and Walker devise a taxonomy of object significance types based on how specifically each is featured in its story. The categories are:

Fossil: bears mute witness to a vanished era way of life
Evidence: Implicated in a crime or public event
Totem: Offers wisdom from the natural world, and acts as a tutelary spirit

Talisman: Magical, lucky, and/or alive

Idol: Has no special power, but intense contemplation lends it an aura

The top three earners by far were Fossils ($1,126.14), Evidence ($906.89), and Talismans, ($864.90), whereas Idols ($377.86) and Totems ($336.72) garnered the least.

Glenn and Walker also consider the objects by way of Marshall McLuhan's "cool/hot" dichotomy, taken from his 1964 book *Understanding Media*. Hot media, in McLuhan's estimation, are those that require little interpretation on the part of an audience, whereas cool media invite more participation in the meaning-making process. Again, while hardly a scientific study, Glenn and Walker's findings are compelling:

> Cool narratives about talismans . . . generally speaking, are highly effective at increasing an object's significance value; hot narratives about talismans are less effective in that regard—best to keep the object's significance mysterious. However if one is writing about a fossil (an object that bears witness to a vanished era or way of life, including childhood), one's best bet is to employ a hot narrative mode—i.e., come right out and state the object's significance.[21]

Although Talismans were the third earner overall, the two most prized objects in the study were hot Talismans—open-to-interpretation tales of objects that took on a life of their own. At the top of the list was novelist Doug Dorst's story in which a Russian figurine commemorates the fictional folk legend of St. Vralkomir, who saved his village from certain death one cruel winter by lighting a fire with the sparks that emanated from dancing feet. Vralkomir danced and danced all winter long before dying of exhaustion in the spring. "My grandmother said that on frigid and moonless winter nights, effigies of St. Vralkomir may come to life and begin dancing, throwing sparks from their wooden pedestals," writes Dorst.[22]

If Glenn and Walker's small experiment in significance value is any indication, stories in which objects act as testimonials of the past (Fossils, Evidence), or stories in which objects come alive in the present or are otherwise infused with magic (Talismans) seem most likely to capture our imagination. This may also be the lesson to be taken from hoarding and the KonMari Method. The promissory power of future usefulness has its lure, as evidenced by the tendency of hoarders (and the rest of us, really) to hang onto presently useless things, just in case. But meaning is not something that exists *in potentia*. How many of us hang onto an object because we think, "One day, I will feel emotionally attached to this"? Emotional attachment is an effect of shared history—or, often, it is the inexplicable, magical attraction we feel for something in this moment.

As clever as Significant Objects was, its adherence to brand logic ultimately leaves objects at the mercy of the stories that give them meaning. The object remains the vehicle of meaning that is grafted on from an external source, real or imagined. The object itself is still objectified. Of their project, Glenn and Walker conclude, "It turns out that once you start increasing the emotional energy of inanimate objects, an unpredictable chain reaction is set off."[23] They're right. But one lesson we can take away from their experiment is that perhaps there are ways of manipulating the trajectory of the reactions people have to objects. This will take more than just refining the stories we tell about objects. It will require an approach to design in which an object's material form—its shape, texture, appearance, footprint—is enlisted in the storytelling process. Objects, like humans, age. They bear the scars, soft edges, and worn finishes that testify to their history, their relationships, and their patterns of use. In the remainder of this chapter, I will look at a set of design principles and practices that capitalizes on the mutability of objects and which, in doing so, invite us to collaborate in the production of meaning.

Emotionally Durable Design

In "Couch Arm," David Scher writes about his attachment to a piece of furniture from his childhood:

> Our sunroom couch was the scene of battles and parties, the stuff of
> forts, the extra bed, the TV couch. But one corner belonged to Mary

Grace: Mom, not only to her nine children but also to scores of others, including her children's friends and their friends.

When she wasn't feeding us, doing ten loads of laundry a day, starting a new school, running her own business, catching a blues band at a local bar, or marching for civil rights, Mom was on the couch resting her bunions drinking thin black coffee, smoking a long-ash Pall Mall, or enjoying an icy Coke with an egg salad sandwich. The television was always on but she could read the papers, do the Twins scorecard, tape a Columbo re-run, and pay attention to us at the same time. Late at night while everyone slept she would find some time alone there playing solitaire with a Manhattan. The woman slept very little.

After many hard years of service, the couch's time ran out. It was beat up pretty bad. My brother Paul called: "Dad's buying Mom a big easy chair, the couch is being tossed. What do you think?" I asked him to saw the arm off, the one with Mom's patina. The one with the cigarette burns. The dog-chewed, ketchup-stained, Miracle-Whipped, pawed-by-a-thousand-little-hands arm. He brought it to New York where it is screwed to a wall once in a while. Her grandchildren hang around it, leaning on it as though Mary Grace were there.[24]

I start this section with David Scher's poignant reflection because it illustrates the marriage between story and matter that makes some objects in our lives more meaningful than others. Scher's prose certainly provides context for those of us who will never know Mary Grace. His loving and detailed description of his mother going to jazz clubs and civil rights marches between loads of laundry and Pall Malls paints a vivid portrait of a woman worth knowing. But the couch arm, with its finish worn off by years of Mary Grace resting her weary arm, itself has a story to tell, a story that made its disposal unthinkable to her son.

While projects such as Significant Objects and TOTeM attempt to extend the life span of otherwise disposable objects through the application of stories told by ourselves or others, a growing number of product designers are experimenting with the ways the material, formal elements of a thing can invite us to attach emotionally to it, perhaps interrupting the typical life cycle of objects in which they are ultimately (with escalating rapidity) relegated to the trash bin. They are designing objects that they hope will eventually, like Mary Grace's couch, tell their own story.

In their studies of how people attach to consumer products, design scholar Ruth Mugge and her colleagues at Delft University of Technology find that "attachable" objects tend to engage us at an emotional level and attain a special meaning over and above mere functionality. But objects take on this special meaning for different reasons. In one study, for example, they observe a distinction between attachment to a product variant versus attachment to a product specimen. An example of the former might be if a person really loves the design of a particular product, say the Mini Cooper driven by the dashing hero of a blockbuster spy film, or the Kanye West–designed "yeezy boost" sneakers for Adidas. Attachment to these product variants induces special meaning in that they are aesthetically pleasing and are believed to afford the owner a desired identity, some kind of tribal membership by way of association. In this form of attachment, one feels bonded less to the specific car or sneakers and more to the design itself.

Attachment to a product specimen, in contrast, is when one feels bonded to a specific object, such that "another physically identical product cannot completely replace such a product, because the context in which the object was obtained or used is inimitable."[25] For example, I might feel particularly attached to a necklace because it was given to me by my father for my high school graduation, or to a specific pair of Levi's 501 jeans that I've broken in just so after years of wear. I may like the cut of 501s in general, but that doesn't mean that a replacement pair would hold the same meaning as the pair I wore on various adventures that bear the battle scars to prove it. In this case, the "personal signs of use," like nicks, scratches, and patina, "may be important for the product's special meaning, because they may serve as proof for certain events."[26] A couch of the exact same model and design as the one belonging to their mother would never suffice as an object of attachment for Scher and his siblings, as this specimen in particular is imprinted with their specific stories and memories. As a testament to these special events, these objects are woven into our identity and inspire our devotion. As the tag line in an ad for Swiss watch manufacturer Swatch puts it, "In twenty years, it has become a part of you."

Designers particularly interested in promoting sustainable consumption see stimulating attachment to product specimens as a promising path to reducing environmental waste. Because so many durable goods are replaced even when they're still fully functional, "a possible eco-design strategy to address the psychological lifetime of products is to strengthen the person–product relationship."[27] Most product design, as we have seen, focuses mainly on cosmetic upgrades to durable goods that, while lucrative for the companies that sell them, perpetuate an untenably wasteful cycle of stylistic obsolescence that excites in consumers short-term desire followed by their inevitable dissatisfaction when a new model is launched. This cycle is perhaps especially problematic when applied to consumer electronics like cell phones, which, when not disposed of properly, leak heavy metals and noxious chemicals into the soil and groundwater. But durable goods in general (shoes, tables, clothing, coffee cups, cars), at unfathomable rates and in huge quantities, are being tossed into already heaving landfills, where they will live out the rest of their often very long lives — this despite the fact that many of these items are still fully functional: "Freezers that still freeze and toasters that still toast—their only crime being a failure to sustain empathy in their users."[28] In essence, our current model of production and consumption in the industrialized world has resulted in a tasty but toxic cocktail that mixes physical durability with ephemeral sentiment. Thanks to modern material science, we can make objects that last nearly forever. Yet at the same time we have cultivated a culture in which our relationship to those objects is fickle and fleeting. "It's actually very easy to design and manufacture a toaster that will last 20 years; that can be done," explains design scholar Jonathan Chapman. "What's not so easy is to design and manufacture a toaster that someone will want to keep for 20 years, because as people . . . we haven't been trained to do that."[29]

Some professional designers committed to making more sustainable products are attempting to address the first ingredient of the cocktail, working with recycled or compostable materials, for example. Although it offers an important piece of the complicated puzzle of how to address the role of consumption in environmental degradation, this version of sustainable design is often more concerned with the suppression of symptoms rather than with the practices that support good health overall. As a result, Chapman argues, this emphasis on symptoms rather than causes means "sustainable design resigns itself to a peripheral activity, rather than the central pioneer of positive change it potentially could be."[30]

Chapman and his students in the Sustainable Design program at the University of Brighton in the United Kingdom experimented with what Chapman has dubbed "emotionally durable design" in his influential book of the same name. Emotionally durable design is an attempt to extend our emotional attachment to durable goods, to make objects that will be cherished over time rather than discarded as trends wane. For example, PUMA, the German sportswear company, partnered with students in Chapman's program to explore possible uses for emotional durability in the company's designs. For a PUMA-sponsored design contest, student Emma Whiting submitted a design for "stain sneakers," to which she applied an antistain treatment in the pattern of a series of PUMA's logo. As the white canvas high tops take on the dirt and grime of daily wear, the pattern emerges. Whiting's stain sneakers are an effort to flip the traditional fate of worn sneakers, which are devalued as they age. Bethan Laura Wood used a similar process to create teacups that takes on a pattern over time as tea stains develop on the inside surface.

Japanese designer Hiroki Nakamura, founder of the Visvim menswear brand, sells upscale jeans under his Social Sculpture line. He borrows the phrase from the twentieth-century artist Joseph Beuys, who theorizes that everyday art objects have participatory and revolutionary potential. Nakamura's affinity for what he describes as the "power" of vintage denim inspired the line, for which he reimagined the textile mainstay "from the yarn up" in order to make jeans that mold to one's body with repeated wear. "I loved the way my vintage jeans faded after months of wear, and I designed our Social Sculpture denim with this in mind," he says. "We developed a yarn from scratch by intentionally mixing yarns with different slub lengths, so that the resulting fabric displays both visual and tactile unevenness that becomes more pronounced over time."[31] Although he doesn't describe his jeans as "emotionally durable" per se, Nakamura's designs utilize his knowledge of textiles to create garments that will evolve with their users, endearing themselves along the way. He writes, "Denim follows your life, it shows your life, it shows your character, and as you wear it more, the more you come to like it. The denim that you come in and pick up from one of our stores . . . that is just the starting point."[32]

Picking up a pair of Nakamura's jeans doesn't come cheap. They retail in the United States at places like Bergdof Goodman for over $400. Although for most of us such a price tag is prohibitive, Nakamura's philosophy—to make garments that will stand the test of time, evolving as they do—offers a compelling rejoinder to the disposability we're seeing in the fast fashion marketplace. When an interviewer for *GQ* asked him to justify the price point, Nakamura cited his painstaking experiments in Old World fabrication and handmade craftsmanship that go into his designs: "I'm also introducing the option that, maybe instead of buying five jackets, you can buy one that will last longer. I want to create things that can be vintage in the future. That's my goal: Future vintage."[33] Like a growing number of designers, Nakamura is considering the ways that the materials and construction of objects might prolong people's attachment to them. This requires taking a longer view of objects, designing with the aging process in mind.

The origins of his products are as important to the story as their destination. Nakamura travels the world seeking ideas and time-tested techniques for crafting textiles. He cites Japanese kimono, Amish quilting, Native American blankets, and the Harris tweeds of Scotland

Aging gracefully: a teacup that takes on a pattern as it stains. From "Stain" series by artist Bethan Laura Wood, 2006. Courtesy of Bethan Laura Wood.

as inspirations. As one magazine puts it, Nakamura's company "is the antithesis of fast fashion. Rather than throwing away these insights every season, [Nakamura] seeks to evolve the brand's archetypes so they become even more durable as the years go by."[34] By considering both their past and the future life, Nakamura's "future vintage" is an attempt to offer imprintable objects that, through use, will eventually tell their own story.

For emotionally durable design, the object is not merely a vehicle for story, as we see in the brand logic highlighted by a project like Significant Objects. In branding, story is grafted onto the object from outside. The object is made sign, (sign-ificant), by way of association. Even those things we consider mementos of our own experience are meaningful because they remind us of a story or person that has special meaning. What emotionally durable design is attempting to produce is an object that may or may not have a meaningful origin story (e.g., the scarf was a gift from my beloved Aunt Lupita, or this was the dress I wore to my prom), but that, as a result of the physical properties of their form and content, have the potential to bear memories both symbolically and materially. The hope is that they become externalized manifestations of memory.

There is a long tradition of conceptualizing memory in this material way. In the classical era in the West, thinkers—for example, Plato, Aristotle, Cicero, and, later, Thomas Aquinas—describe it as something akin to a wax tablet, the writing surface used in early inscription. Aristotle writes in *De memoria et reminiscentia* (On memory and reminiscence) that experiences leave an image in our memory "just as persons do who make an impression with a seal."[35] The metaphors change as inscription technologies change, but the basic mechanism through which people in the West understood memory continued. As Douwe Draaisma notes, "Long after the wax tablet had given way to the codex and the codex had in turn been replaced by parchment and later by paper, 'imprinting' and 'impression' remained intact as images for the retention of information."[36] Even today, when we better understand the neurological realities of how memories are formed, retained, and recalled, it is common to use metaphors of inscription. We say a person has a photographic memory, or that our brains are like hard drives, imprinted with memories, storing the data of our experiences.

Emotionally durable designs, with their intentionally malleable, inscribable surfaces, serve as the wax tablets of memory, bearing witness to their own evolution over time. Take, for example, the wedding ring designed by the Japanese firm Torafu Architects. The band has a thin silver finish intended to wear off over time, revealing the eighteen-karat gold beneath. As the finish erodes in a nonuniform pattern, at the points where fingers rub together, or where repeated tasks, like typing, are performed, one can track the passage of time (and presumably one's marriage) by observing the evolving patina of the ring. The company describes the ring as having a "facial expression," noting that "the time shared between two people can thus be felt with the wearing of this ring."[37] The material form of the ring evolves as one's marriage evolves and as what one might call "wear" discloses a deepening and enriched object that becomes so only through enduring commitment to the ring and the relationship it represents.

Readers may be familiar with the Japanese aesthetic concept of *wabi-sabi*. An outgrowth of the Buddhist emphasis on the imperfection, impermanence, and incompleteness of all things, *wabi-sabi* is the art of finding beauty in the inevitable flaws in objects. As one writer explains, *wabi-sabi* "celebrates cracks and crevices and all the other marks that time, weather, and loving use leave behind. It reminds us that we are all but transient beings on this planet—that our bodies as well as the material world around us are in the process of returning to the dust from which we came. Through wabi-sabi, we learn to embrace liver spots, rust, and frayed edges, and the march of time they represent."[38] Product designers are increasingly exploring how they might create objects that will develop this *wabi-sabi* character as the objects age. San Francisco designer Remy Labesque argues that even electronic objects, like an iPhone, have this potential to age with dignity. Labesque compares favorably the way his aluminum-shelled iPhone ages compared to his plastic Canon camera with a metallic finish. Whereas the iPhone "acquired a polished patina over its aluminum shell" after three years jostling among his keys in his pocket, the effects of use on his Canon merely rubbed off the faux metallic finish, revealing the molded plastic underneath. "At this point the Canon's shell looks like garbage while the iPhone's is starting to resemble something more like an heirloom pocket watch," he writes.[39]

Etsy blogger Chappel Ellison agrees: "The nicks and scratches on our pricey objects shouldn't be lamented; wear and tear could be celebrated as evidence of a gadget's resilience, reflecting the journey it takes with you throughout your own updates and developments."[40] This is a central theme in emotionally durable design discourse: signs of wear testify to the durability of a well-made object and the longevity of the relationship to its owner.

Limitations to Emotionally Durable Design

As a tool in the arsenal of sustainable design and consumption practices, emotionally durable design is useful and well worth developing. It would reduce waste if we could slow the rate at which we replace perfectly functioning objects by cultivating an aesthetic appreciation for the traces of wear and the stories they tell. Extending our relationship to some objects in our lives is an important piece of the sustainability puzzle. Yet some qualifications are in order. First, emotionally durable design is not applicable to all durable goods, especially the most toxic ones. Although it's easy to see how a well-worn leather jacket may become a treasured object, the idea that consumers will come to see things like their cell phones and laptops as heirlooms is a much harder sell. Although resilience may be one reason people love their electronic gadgets, it's certainly not the only, or most compelling, one.

Marks of time are most rhetorically powerful for material objects whose worth is already linked to values like longevity and tradition. Take, for example the ivy that often engulfs the arches and edifices of long-standing university or governmental buildings. The tangled vines are considered charming, even authoritative; they represent the storied and hallowed halls of tradition and power. For the elite U.S. universities that are members of the Ivy League, the perennial vine materially conveys the historical gravitas of those institutions. But imagine an airport covered in ivy. Such an aesthetic, considered lovely on a university campus, would be utterly counterproductive in this context. The last thing people about to board a machine that will hurl them through the sky at six hundred miles an hour want to see are "charming" signs of age and decay.

Airports, like most high-tech objects and spaces, are designed and showcased as state of the art—as artifacts of the most advanced technological capacities of this moment. The high-tech style—what R. L. Rutsky has dubbed "high techne"[41] to emphasize the relationship between aesthetics and technology—is not about celebrating tradition, memories, or even longevity. It is decidedly future facing. Likewise our electronic devices. While Labesque's scuffed iPhone admittedly looks kind of cool, its condition conveys something that more often sounds the death knell for our personal devices: it's out of date. I'd wager, for example, that few people are so enamored by the worn spots on the remote control of their old SD television that they're immune to the allure of the latest Ultra 4K HD model. Although a laptop may have been the vehicle for many a fulfilling project, Skype session with a loved one, or episode of a favorite Netflix show, any loyalty you feel to it as a piece of hardware will be short lived when one of its components break, or it ages out and can't run software designed for later models. Labesque's encomium to the *wabi-sabi* beauty of his iPhone's case comes as he is replacing it after three years because the touch screen has stopped working. Devices like cell phones are often connected to memories, but this is so because they provide access to our photos and music (which now live in the cloud), not because we cherish the dings and scratches they acquire while doing so.

A second qualification to the celebratory rhetoric surrounding the emotionally durable design of objects is that human emotion is not what one could convincingly call durable. Humans are fickle creatures. Although we undoubtedly imbue objects with emotion and meaning, what of those objects that no longer spark joy because we have moved on? As much as objects can be an outward declaration of our identity, identity itself is a shape-shifty thing. Ani DiFranco gives voice to this in her song "Pale Purple," in which she remembers "regretting things I've worn when I was still playing roles."[42] When are we not playing roles of some form or another? I have, for example, over the course of the last thirty years, worn Birkenstocks, Doc Martens, and vintage kitten heels—three styles of shoe that communicate vastly different cultural identities and contexts. Objects may hold memories, but in some cases, that's just the problem. Take those perfectly broken-in Levi's 501s I mentioned earlier. It's true that they remind me of traveling and grad school and other happy adventures. But I can also recall feeling no small degree of resentment toward those very jeans, seemingly taunting me from the back of the closet during those years when, thanks to childbirth and the advent of middle age, they no longer fit so well, rendering them more relic than companion.

If identity is a fluctuating phenomenon, what of romantic relationships? Consider again that inventive Japanese wedding band that reveals its core of precious gold, but only after years of wear. While it may be true that the value of a marriage is cultivated and actualized over time, try telling that to a young bride who, reared on Hollywood rom-coms and *Bachelorette* (2003–) finales, has come to expect a sparkling token of abiding, unadulterated, pure love right now. In this instance, a wedding ring that promises to dazzle in years to come is woefully inadequate to the important task of publicly declaring "forever" on one's wedding day.

This leads me to a final caveat to the rhetoric surrounding emotionally durable design, which is that it's simply so easy (and lucrative) to fake. Chapman declares that "design must challenge our social desire for a scratch-free, box-fresh world. The onset of ageing can concentrate, rather than weaken, the experience of an object."[43] Chapman understandably calls on designers to ramp up cathexis, to deploy the tools of design to make malleable, imprintable objects that will serve as nexus points around which our emotions and memories might distill as we and the object age. This is a noble and worthwhile goal, one that might well foster longer-lasting relationships between humans and the objects they might otherwise too quickly discard.

The trouble is, other designers and manufacturers are capitalizing on our love of all things storied and vintage by offering up mass-produced, simulated versions of classic, well-loved objects by the cargo ship full. As the market for a well-worn aesthetic grows, so too does the lure of the knock-off. Take, for example, the flourishing "new vintage" trade on eBay. After more than twenty years of matching buyers and sellers in its online auction house, eBay has collected a vast amount of data illuminating what kinds of things potential buyers are searching for. eBay then sells that information to manufacturers, who quickly create new versions of the most popular items. "We send [manufacturers] data about what people are looking for on eBay and they respond and turn it around incredibly quickly," says president of eBay Marketplaces Devin Wenig. "We have a really big China export business to Europe and the United States. And they respond very, very quickly to consumer taste, whatever it might be. It's really remarkable to see how quickly the manufacturing base adapts to the demand signals they get."[44] Not surprisingly, nostalgia is big business on eBay. Remember those vintage messenger bags that were so popular a few years ago, the ones with the logo of the defunct airline Pan Am? Such an outdated brand becoming trendy decades after its demise may have been sparked by consumers' affinity for relics of the *Mad Men* (2007–15) era, but it was made possible by eBay and its manufacturing partners offering up affordable simulated copies. eBay doesn't try to pass off the new-fab bags as authentic. Like other popular retailers— IKEA, West Elm, ModCloth—it's just capitalizing on people's ongoing obsession with the midcentury modern aesthetic.

Based on the sheer volume of the goods on offer, and on my own admittedly unscientific observations while working on a large university campus in a major West Coast American city, consumers seemingly cannot get enough of this fabricated nostalgia. Take for example the popularity of vintage-style graphic T-shirts. A perusal of the men's graphic T-shirt section on Target's website yields no fewer than forty-five T-shirts featuring logos from 1970s and 1980s pop culture, as well as imagery from Star Wars, Mr. Rogers, Atari, Volkswagen buses, AC/DC, and Pink Floyd. These T-shirts didn't just sport old-school content. The shirts themselves have been made to look faded and soft, their silk-screened images cracked to simulate years of wear. The description for a Star Wars (1970s version) T-shirt reads, "Add some vintage flair to your wardrobe with the Star Wars Tie Fighter Men's T-shirt. This trendy heather gray tee shirt features a chest-front graphic with a tie fighter and the iconic Star Wars logo set over faded blue, yellow, and red for a touch of color. A distressed wash gives this tee a genuine retro look."[45] Interestingly, while many of the Target T-shirts featured throwback cultural icons like Cheech and Chong, boom boxes, and *Saved by the Bell* (1989–93), which convey a kind of "dude, remember this?" campiness, the vast majority were faux vintage renditions of pop culture properties enjoying huge mainstream success today in newly reincarnated versions. Star Wars, of course, but also Marvel characters like the Hulk, Captain America, and the rest of the Avengers crew were featured not in their current, Disney-owned Marvel Cinematic Universe instantiations, but in the original, presumably allowing the wearer to signal to others they've been true blue fans since back in the day.

Target is certainly not alone in meeting the demand for vintage style with mass-produced knock-offs. Mass retailers like Old Navy have been churning out their versions for years, often featuring vaguely and not so vaguely racist advertisements for fake products and restaurants like "Poncho's Seafood Fiesta!" (Old Navy), "Ghettopoly" (Urban Outfitters), and "Pizza Dojo: Come in and Wok Out," featuring an egregious stereotype of a Chinese chef (Abercrombie and Fitch). One blogger has dubbed the trend "kitsch vintage," explaining, "These T-shirts are not camp but *kitsch*—a cheap copy of the real thing. Old Navy provides buyers with a quick, easy way to get the campy feeling you have when you wear a vintage campy T-shirt from a campy place, but without *actually* wearing a *real* vintage campy T-shirt from a *real* campy place. You can have a cheap imitation of an ironic experience."[46] Whether camp or merely kitsch, the popularity of these T-shirts demonstrates that nostalgia—in both its ironic and sentimental forms—sells. But even if you hate the "vintage" T-shirt trend, Target's got you covered. Of the graphic T-shirts for men on the Target website, all were faux vintage, save one that, in a sneering rejoinder to the others, declared in bright, nonfaded letters, "Screw Vintage, this shirt is from the future."

It's not just T-shirts simulating a well-loved aesthetic. Although fashion writers have heralded the impending demise of the distressed denim trend for years now, flip through the pages of any fashion magazine or take a quick trip to your local mall and you'll see it's still going strong. Celebrities like Beyoncé and Kim Kardashian are frequently seen in faded, worn designer jeans, with the knees ripped out and tears often ascending both thighs. At the time of this writing, a pair of men's skinny jeans "updated with edgy distressing" (the knees are ripped out) in "vintage blue" by Saint Laurent are available on the Saks Fifth Avenue website for $750. For those of us unable or unwilling to shell out that kind of money for preripped jeans, the usual suspects in mass-produced apparel—Old Navy, Gap, Loft, Urban Outfitters, American Apparel, H&M—all offer more affordable versions. "Rugged style, with no breaking-in required!" says an Old Navy ad from a few years ago. "Unique wash layers subtle color over durable denim. Distressed hems and handcrafted abrasions create a thoroughly lived-in look."[47]

Perhaps the most egregious example of the lived-in denim trend came in the spring of 2017, when Nordstrom offered Barracuda straight-leg jeans from PRPS, an American–Japanese denim brand that specializes in paint-spattered, dirty-looking jeans that retail for as much as $900. The Barracudas were made to look as if they'd been splattered in mud after a long day digging ditches. Nordstrom's website description reads: "Heavily distressed medium-blue denim jeans in a comfortable straight-leg fit embody rugged, Americana workwear that's seen some hard-working action with a crackled, caked-on muddy coating that shows you're not afraid to get down and dirty."[48] The Internet was quick to mock the jeans and their $425 price tag on Twitter and in the comments section on the Nordstrom website. Now since deleted were comments such as, "The perfect match for my stick on calluses!" Mike Rowe, host of the Discovery Channel's *Dirty Jobs* (2003–12) and a longtime advocate of manual laborers, may have best captured the problem in a Facebook post that's been shared over 16,000 times:

> Forget the jeans themselves for a moment, and their price, and look again at the actual description. "Rugged Americana" is now synonymous with a "caked-on, muddy coating." Not real mud. Fake mud.

Something to foster the illusion of work. The illusion of effort. Or per-haps, for those who actually buy them, the illusion of sanity.

The Barracuda Straight Leg Jeans aren't pants. They're not even fashion. They're a costume for wealthy people who see work as ironic—not iconic.[49]

Kirsty Major, a writer for a British women's magazine, rightly points out the irony of haute couture fashion houses and their mass-retail imitators reanimating a look that was originally meant as a symbol of rebellion against the trendiness of consumer capitalism. Of the British retailer Topshop (recently arrived in the United States as a department within Nordstrom's), Major writes:

According to Topshop's website, each £42 pair of jeans "are toughened up with rips and tears to add some 'edge.'" A well educated guess is that the "edge" Topshop is referring to is a nod toward the youth sub-cultures of punk, heavy metal and grunge, who all adopted distressed denim as a visual symbol of social dissent. For punks, wearing jeans until they ripped in was a symbol of the fact that they refused to par-ticipate in capitalism; wearing jeans until they literally fell off your legs reduced the number of jeans purchased and was a big economic mid-dle finger to shops and advertisers.[50]

However, she reminds those buying them, "You didn't rip those jeans climbing into empty buildings and sitting on curbs drinking Newcastle Brown. No, you bought them from the high street and those rips were put there by a migrant worker in Mauritius who got paid 22p per hour. There is seriously nothing less edgy in the whole wide world."[51]

Aping punk and working-class style is well-trod ground in the mass-apparel landscape. Historically, as we know, denim was the textile of choice for work clothes, as its flexible yet durable weave made it com-fortable enough for those doing hard physical labor and tough enough to endure long-term wear. Whether consumers are conscious of it or not, this history is embedded in our collective cultural memory and the symbolism of jeans. When denim, in the form of jeans and jean jackets, transitioned to a fashion textile in the 1950s, thanks to icons like Jack Kerouac, James Dean, and Marlon Brando, it did so because it afforded the wearer a kind of working-class legitimacy, regardless of one's actual occupation or socioeconomic class. Perhaps this is why jeans, especially those that look like they've been worn nearly to death, are so popular at this particular moment in Western culture, when manual labor may feel increasingly remote and even romantic to consumers who spend their days working retail or sitting at keyboards in office cubicles.

More problematic than the inauthenticity of what Thomas Frank describes as commodified dissent[52] is the material conditions in which distressed denim is actually made. "Here's the problem," writes Jacob Brogan. "Artificially weathered jeans perpetuate myths about work that obscures the real toils of those who make our clothes. When we casually pretend to be a cowboy or a car mechanic, manual labor starts to seem a little less real, and a little less substantial."[53] Workers who make distressed jeans do so under incredibly perilous conditions. Although this style of jeans has been popular in various forms since at least the 1990s, major denim retailers like Levi Strauss and H&M only started to ban sandblasting in 2010, after public pressure to do so from a workers' rights group called the Clean Clothes Campaign. Until then, factory workers in Bangladesh, Turkey, and other countries would literally blast the denim with abrasive sand shot through a hose with an air compressor—a practice that causes silicosis, an incurable, sometimes fatal illness that occurs when dust particles from the sand embed themselves in the lung tissue.

The connection was discovered by a Turkish doctor who was alarmed by the high number of cases of silicosis in young garment workers who were enlisting in the military. Despite many large retailers' public ban on sandblasting, companies often don't have (or enforce) complete control over their supply chain. In 2013, the Clean Clothes Campaign investigated six factories in the south China province of Guangdong, a region that the group says is responsible for half of the world's entire population of blue jeans. It found that "sandblasting seems to be morphing into a more covert operation, potentially creating an even deadlier workplace environment."[54] Alternative methods for distressing jeans—chemical treatments, hand sanding, and polishing, for example—have also been found to cause health problems, largely because these factories lack proper training and equipment to ensure the process is done safely.[55]

By asking us to reflect on potential limitations to emotionally durable design, I do not mean to dismiss its potential as a strategy for intensifying our commitment to objects. Experimenting with how to create objects that invite attachment strikes me as a fruitful avenue for slowing down the disposal of at least some of the objects we acquire. But banking on the *wabi-sabi* charm of distressed denim or flea market furniture is insufficient, given how easily it is simulated. Further, given the fact that brand rhetoric's central focus is to imbue objects with story, the lines between product specimen ("Grandma's weathered coffee table bears the marks of my childhood on the coast of Maine") and product variant ("This factory-distressed coffee table from Restoration Hardware captures a beachy aesthetic that appeals to me") are increasingly blurred.

A piece of this puzzle over product attachment has to do with the effort consumers are willing to put into objects. Writer Dan Medeiros suggests that most are not willing to put in much, if any, effort. He offers a damning critique, for example, of the faux agrarian heirlooms on offer at shopping mall staples like Crate and Barrel and Pottery Barn. "Never mind that people who live in actual New England farmhouses generally can't afford such items," he writes.

> The point is to give people who live elsewhere (urban areas, primarily) a kitschy shortcut to the feeling of being rustic without putting out the effort of:
>
> Moving to New England
> Finding a farmhouse
> Building your own furniture [...]

Distressing it through the age and the wear of fingers and bodies
against wood in ordinary use

Letting the natural veneer crack in an appealing way (but not too much)

And finally passing the furniture down for a future generation

"Actual antiques take time and effort. These just take money." He quotes Umberto Eco's analysis of the wax interpretations of famous works of art at the Palace of Living Art: "The Palace's philosophy is not, 'We are giving you the reproduction so that you will want the original,' but rather, 'We are giving you the reproduction so *you will no longer feel any need for the original.'*"[56] Like Mike Rowe's suggestion that those fake mud-splattered jeans epitomize the reality that most Americans prefer the aesthetic illusion of manual labor to actually doing the work, Medeiros argues that consumers are simply too lazy to put in the time and effort it takes to bond with objects, especially when the marketplace makes it so simple to purchase products with an authentic veneer.

Perhaps we consumers are too lazy to put in any effort or connect with the objects we acquire. But let's look at the work of one last designer who is banking on the notion that the opposite is the case. Hyerim Shin, a Korean designer based in San Francisco, has developed a series of cute, pastel-colored robot appliances—a toaster, a vacuum cleaner, and a trash can—intended to mimic the qualities and behaviors of human babies, which are undeniably powerful objects of attachment. The toaster sneezes when its crumb tray is emptied. The trash can turns its face from the user and plays hide-and-seek when it needs to be taken out. And, yes, when it's full, the vacuum cleaner wiggles its behind and "poops" its dust bag out onto the floor, alerting its owner that it's time for a fresh one. Shin's working premise is that part of why we attach to babies and other young creatures is that they demand our care. Our investment of time and energy into their well-being helps cement our bond and our role as caretaker. By assuming responsibility for its maintenance, the value we place on the object of care intensifies, producing what we might even call affection. Recall

Lovable appliances. Hyerim Shin's "Be My Mother" series, 2016. Courtesy of Hyerim Shin.

the IKEA effect scholars' observation that "we love what we labor over." Shin describes her "Be My Mother" project this way:

> Based on empirical research on specific cuteness features I created design rules to create a cute appearance and behaviours to systematically trigger positive responses in consumers. These home appliances are examples of how my rules of cuteness can be applied in order to encourage affection for products to encourage care and maintenance without feeling like a chore. Emotionally durable design through the soft power of cuteness.[57]

Although Shin's appliances don't invite the material imprinting of memories in quite the same way as other objects designed to age gracefully, they do gain their value from a narrative logic that is imbued with value and meaning and which interrupts the traditional consumer–object relationship. "It needs me" can be a powerful foundation for attachment.

Emotionally durable objects may indeed require more care and investment than those created and purchased with easy disposability in mind. But as we have seen, many consumers will not only tolerate but may indeed crave a bit more investment in the things they own. Although hyperreal knock-offs of cherished heirlooms and faux vintage apparel won't likely be out of vogue anytime soon, another powerful trend demonstrates that the market for all things handcrafted, bespoke, and small batch is undeniably on an upward trajectory. If Target's model is one in which objects are wholly closed and discrete, then in IKEA's self-assembly we see them opening up ever so slightly. Further, emotionally durable design offers a way of seeing objects as instantiations of one moment in a larger historical trajectory of which we are but a part. In the next chapter, we will observe objects opening up further still, as more and more people engage in a more participatory mode of consumption—trying their own hand at crafting, making, and inventing objects.

FIVE

The Handmade Tale

Crafting, Making, and the Lure of the Artisanal

> The nearest kind of association is not mere perceptual cognition, but,
> rather, a handling, using, and taking care of things which has its own
> kind of "knowledge."
>
> —*Martin Heidegger, Being and Time*

In an era when Marvel superheroes dominate the cineplex, one might
not think a quiet documentary about the painstaking methods of an
eighty-seven-year-old sushi chef would particularly rivet audiences'
attention. But David Gelb's 2012 film *Jiro Dreams of Sushi* was celebrated at international film festivals, enjoys a 99 percent review on the
review aggregator site Rotten Tomatoes, did a respectable $2 million–
plus at the box office, and is now a Netflix staple. Gelb's beautifully
shot film chronicles the work of Jiro Ono who, although considered
one of the world's best sushi chefs, continues to work in a modest ten-
seat counter near the entrance to a subway station in the basement of a
Tokyo office building. A twenty-minute meal at the famed Sukiyabashi
Jiro Michelin three-star restaurant costs nearly $300, and customers
must reserve their seat three months in advance.

The film demonstrates why the sushi counter warrants such
adoration. Jiro's exacting standards for himself and his apprentices—

including his fifty-year-old son, who is expected to one day inherit the restaurant—are nearly impossible to sustain, and he is constantly striving to further perfect his craft. Jiro couples a deep knowledge of his source materials—perfectly vinegared rice, the freshest fish—with a meticulous process honed over years of practice to create what is, by all accounts, the meal of a lifetime. For Jiro, cutting corners is utterly unacceptable. Whereas, for example, he used to massage a piece of octopus only thirty minutes to tenderize its meat and bring out its flavor, he now massages it for forty-five minutes. One apprentice notes that Jiro taught him to "press the sushi as if it were a baby chick." Gelb joins Jiro as he visits the morning fish market, carefully inspecting each piece and discussing its quality with the various vendors he has clearly done business with for years. The fishmongers are themselves fastidious specialists; one specializes in tuna, another eel, each offering only the best-quality product. One sympathizes with Jiro's dutiful apprentices, to whom he doles out trust in small and hard-won doses. They spend weeks practicing wringing out the warm towels just so for customers to clean their hands, or learning to slice an egg to Jiro's specifications. The crucial task of actually slicing the fish is a reward that comes only after years of observing the master.

Roger Ebert describes *Jiro Dreams of Sushi* as a "portrait of tunnel vision." He marvels at Jiro's powers of observation: "Standing behind his counter, Jiro notices things. Some customers are left-handed, some right-handed. That helps determine where they are seated at his counter. As he serves a perfect piece of sushi, he observes it being eaten. He knows the history of that piece of seafood."[1] It is this capacity to notice things, to know the history of one's materials, to inherit a set of skills through apprenticeship and hands-on repetition, and to command control over each step in a larger process that characterizes craftsmanship of the kind we see in Jiro. "Jiro is described as a shokunin—a person who embodies the artisan spirit of the relentless pursuit of perfection through his craft," writes Silvia Killingsworth in the *New Yorker*.[2] Jiro's customers are willing to pay the equivalent of $300 for a seat at his counter because doing so allows them to become

the beneficiaries of his nearly eighty years experience.[3] They are temporary heirs of his skill, inheriting the fruits of a process decades in the
making. In an age when everything seems designed for convenience,
Jiro's degree of devotion to his craft is rightly celebrated as a thing of
rare beauty.

The success of *Jiro Dreams of Sushi* is one example of a much larger
trend across popular culture, a seemingly insatiable appetite for
what we might call process narratives. Marx's insistence that one's
very humanity is at stake in the process of creation is alive and well in
television shows, documentaries, YouTube videos, blogs, and books
detailing the methods and techniques of handworkers of all stripes,
from master crafters to embalmers. On the heels of the success of his
first film, Gelb created the widely acclaimed Netflix docuseries, *Chef's
Table* (2015–), in which world-class chefs from around the world get
the Jiro treatment. Nearly all the available reviews of the show aptly
dub it "food porn" for its lush lighting and loving close-ups of skilled
hands preparing intricate dishes. The show also focuses on the biography and philosophy of its subjects, affording cooking the status of a
true art or techne—which, of course, it is.

It's not just prestige Netflix shows like *Chef's Table* that give viewers a glimpse into the lives and work of skilled craftsmen and -women.
Basic cable channels like HGTV, DIY Network, and even PBS regularly offer process-oriented fare like *Craft Wars* (2012), *Craft Lab*
(2015), *Handcrafted America* (2016–17), and *Craft Corner Deathmatch*
(2005–). Some of these shows, like *Chef's Table*, focus on true master crafters, such as Animal Planet's unlikely hit, *Treehouse Masters*
(2013–), which, for nine seasons and counting, has followed treehouse builder Pete Nelson as he designs and builds from scratch
elaborate custom treehouses tailored to the specific space and vision
of his well-heeled clients. Nelson's goofy charm and joking banter
with his small team of carpenters is entertaining, but the real appeal
of the show is the jaw-dropping creations, each completely unique,
that Nelson conceives and executes. Each episode ends with a basic
cable reality show staple: the big reveal to clients, who are often moved

to tears. But unlike, say, the now defunct *Extreme Makeover: Home Edition* (2003–13), the big reveal is not merely a venue for product placement—the aggregation and arrangement of generous donations of tile, carpet, and cabinetry by corporate sponsors—but a testament to the thirty years Nelson has spent honing his craft.

American Public Television's *A Craftsman's Legacy* (2014–) each week features the methods of a master crafter—a cowboy hat maker, a yarn spinner, a decoy duck maker. The show's website perfectly articulates the value that so many people find in handcrafts: "In today's disposable, 'get-it-the-next-day' consumer world, one might even struggle with the question 'Why is a Craftsman important?'" The answer, in refrain, is,

> It's personal.
>
> And it goes back to our very core as people. When you first made a hand-turkey in grade school, and gave it to your Mother, was it ever about the piece of construction paper and how accurate the feathers were? No. It was meaningful because it came from you. Your hands, your talent, your imagination and creativity. And that's why your Mom never threw it away. It was a part of you and that's not something she ever wanted to lose.
>
> . . .
>
> It's personal.
>
> Maybe we don't need a hand carved set of salad bowls on our dinner table, but it doesn't mean they don't still represent something important. It only means we've lost our ability to appreciate the quality and the fact that someone put part of themselves into that creation.[4]

This notion that handcrafted objects contain, in their material form, some piece of the person who made it has long been a part of how we understand craftsmanship. That these narratives are enjoying a renaissance now, as many of our connections exist digitally and in the cloud, makes sense. Handcrafts seem to provide a more authentic sense of human connection, made tangible through the vehicle of a material object.

The celebration of the personal touch afforded by skilled crafters is playing out with maker videos that feature watchmakers, sword makers, and even a woman who makes gold lamé boxer shorts in the French countryside. Etsy, not surprisingly, offers perhaps the most prolific showcase for makers, with its "Handmade Portraits" series of maker bios and process videos. Although each is different, the portrait of wool harvester Susan Gibbs captures Etsy's overall ethic well: building community through making. Gibbs, a former CBS News producer working in Manhattan, gave it all up for a small patch of land on Martha's Vineyard, where she raises sheep and spins yarn from their wool. Following the community-supported agriculture model made popular by small-produce farms, subscribers to Gibbs's business—themselves crafters looking for quality yarn—invest in her farm and share a portion of each season's yield. The Etsy video features Gibbs in rubber wellies and a tattered hoodie feeding sheep as the sun comes up, joking about how her mother and sister, who still live in the city, fear she's letting herself go, and tell her, "Oh lord, we have gotta get those roots done." What Gibbs misses out on in the city, she says, "doesn't matter so much here," as she has found the deeper meaning that manual labor provides. She says that her customers find more meaning in this mode of exchange as well. She invites her subscribers to the seasonal shearing, making a communal event out of the harvesting process. "They get a big box of yarn at the end of the season, so they're really excited," she says. "They also get weekly updates. So they know the animals really well, like they know their personalities. So when they get their yarn, it's sort of much more special to them, because they know where it came from."[5]

Comedy Central's sketch comedy show, *Portlandia* (2011–18), mocks this desire to know the history of the things we consume in a sketch in which a couple in a restaurant ask increasingly detailed questions about the biography of the chicken they'll be eating tonight. The server, unfazed, retrieves the chicken's file, complete with photograph, to assure the couple that "Colin" was raised humanely on an all-organic diet of soy milk and hazelnuts, with four acres of pasture in which to roam freely. Fred Armisen's character pushes further, wanting to know if Colin had friends to "pal around with."[6] This episode of *Portlandia*, along with the many other spoofs of artisan culture, are funny precisely because they point to the preciousness, not to mention elitism, that permeates much of the discourse around all things pasture raised, handcrafted, heirloom, and bespoke.[7] That said, we needn't throw the baby out with the small-batch bathwater. Although much of the rhetoric emerging from artisanal economies in places like Portland and Brooklyn can indeed come off as the self-important yearnings of economically privileged, usually white, millennials, this doesn't mean the renewed interest in process and human-scale production permeating the culture at large isn't a sign that positive changes are afoot.

However, before we can understand what might be productive or progressive about the themes emerging from crafting culture and the values it espouses, it is useful to ask why its popularity is on the rise at the same time the overall trend is toward elegant, seamless, ubiquitous design. Crafted objects appeal to many of those who find the current slough of factory-made objects devoid of humanity. Today's objects feel too standardized, too homogenous, even when everything is supposedly customizable. While these same people may eagerly buy the highest tech devices they can afford, the sleek black-box aesthetics and systems of production characteristic of early twenty-first-century capitalism leaves them wanting something else—something more tangible.

Writer David Sax explores the rising popularity of seemingly outdated media like paper, board games, and film. Such things—Moleskine notebooks, tabletop games like *Settlers of Catan* (1995)—have a sensual, tactile appeal that simply cannot be captured by digital means, he argues. Sax describes the intimacy of listening to vinyl records with a friend:

> The experience of listening to a record was less efficient, more cumbersome, and not necessarily sonically superior to a digital file played

on the same stereo. But the act of playing a record seemed more in-volved, and ultimately more rewarding, than listening to the same music off a hard drive. . . . It all involved more of our physical senses, requiring the use of our hands, feet, eyes, ears, and even mouth, as we blew dust from the record's surface. There was a richness to the vinyl record experience that transcended any quantifiable measurement. It was more fun precisely because it was less efficient.[8]

Listening to vinyl records does not amount to making anything, and vinyl records themselves are machine made. But as with crafting, they require one to involve oneself physically in the experience, to en-gage rather than just consume, which is precisely what makes them enjoyable.

Another reason we may be seeing a rise in the practice and con-sumption of crafting is that people increasingly seem to recognize that when we consume, no matter the reasons for our choices, we are committing to a legacy of sorts. When we buy a ceiling fan from Am-azon instead of the hardware store down the road, we buy into more than that fan. Objects, all objects, are documents. They are records of a larger system of natural or manufactured processes that brought them into being. The fact that the Amazon fan can be so cheaply and conveniently acquired is an effect of Amazon's cutting-edge use of al-gorithms, data analytics, robotic warehouse management systems, and worldwide distribution networks. The fan is a document of that system—and in no small way our assent to that system. Although we might not always think of it in such explicit terms, participating in sys-tems that are so far beyond our (or really any) control is unnerving. No matter how well we may try to educate ourselves, wrapping one's head around all the human and environmental costs exacted by global sys-tems of this scale is no easy task.

Hacking the System of Objects

Not all those invested in making things themselves produce objects that we could call handmade. Those in the broader maker movement

respond to the same slick black-box world as those pursuing more traditional crafts such as woodworking or weaving. But whereas these
crafters respond by reaching for the traditional tools and techniques
of yesteryear, today's high-tech makers hijack the system of objects
and bring it back to human scale. They do so less by shunning it than by
hacking it. They take advantage of the technologies and machines capital has created. In their own related ways, crafting and making—and
such a distinction is not easily made—intensify the project value we
saw in the IKEA hackers in chapter 3. They also echo an insistence on
the agency of objects we heard from the emotionally durable designers
in chapter 4. They provide objects as documents with a different legacy
than much of what is on offer in the current consumer marketplace.
Their practices identify and make available new surfaces and openings
through which we might connect and attach to objects differently.

Regardless of our ability to fully conceive the impacts of our own
consumption, or perhaps because it is so difficult, a growing number
of people are considering what documents they might prefer to inherit
when they do consume. Whether they make things or not, for consumers, human-scale techniques and processes, of the kind we see in those
popular process shows, seem to offer a comforting antidote, bringing
the circuit of making and consuming back down to earth, giving us
something we can relate to in a more tangible way.

In 1917, Marcel Duchamp, under the pseudonym R. Mutt, famously
submitted his *Fountain* to an art exhibit of the Society of Independent
Artists in New York. Although the group refused to display what was
obviously just a porcelain urinal, Duchamp took the opportunity to
make a public and controversial case for what would become known
as the dada artistic posture. He defended the fictional Mutt this way:
"Whether Mr Mutt with his own hands made the fountain or not has
no importance. He chose it. He took an ordinary article of life, placed
it so that its useful significance disappeared under the new title and
point of view—created a new thought for that object."[9] Duchamp
championed the notion that all art was nothing but what he called
readymades—things already produced, often mass produced—and

that it was evidence of the art community's hubris to think it could be otherwise. He argued that although artists could not produce something new, they could engage everyday objects in conversation, thereby changing their context and subjecting them to a new process of meaning.

Duchamp's celebration of the readymade was the inspiration for a now defunct magazine of the same name, which was a leader in the early years of the current DIY and repurposing craze. The influential *ReadyMade* featured inspiration and tutorials for Gen X and millennial hipsters on how to recycle and repurpose everyday objects—to make art, fashion, and housewares out of the trash of mass culture. *Ready-Made*, claiming to be for "people who see the flicker of invention in everyday objects," was at the forefront of the trend toward a larger DIY sensibility, encouraging twenty- and thirty-somethings to make "chairs out of satellite dishes, lamps from old blenders, and skirts from broken umbrellas."[10] *ReadyMade* as a magazine may be out of publication, but the movement it helped launch is thriving.

ReadyMade was just one early instantiation of a now booming crafting and making ecosystem in which amateurs and professional makers share their ideas and inspirations online and in person at workshops, fairs, and expos across the globe. Many makers frame their return to the handmade arts in terms of a socially conscious insistence on buying sweat-free goods that allow producers and consumers to enjoy more individualized products. As Janelle Brown puts it, "Since cookie-cutter consumerism makes it difficult to be unique when everyone is buying the same Pottery Barn place mats, the new crafties have found a way to express individuality, showcase personal design sensibilities and make a small statement against conspicuous consumption by taking production into their own hands."[11] As *ReadyMade* founder Shoshana Berger explains, referring to Benjamin's observations about our relationship to art under industrial capitalism, "There's a real yearning for slowing down the pace of our culture, which is run amok. I think in this age of mechanical reproduction people are intrigued by the aura of the original."[12] In another context, Berger says, "We're sort of indy-rock hackers. . . . We're hacking our homes, hacking our furniture, hacking the stuff on our persons."[13]

Berger's use of hacking as a metaphor for the crafting movement is an apt one. Unlike skinning, which, as I described in chapter 2 is more or less a dressing up of objects based on a prescribed aesthetic, hacking material culture, like hacking computer programs, is an attempt to recontextualize mass culture and make it do something new. Rael Dornfest, editor of O'Reilly's Hacking Culture book series, describes hackers as "citizen engineers" who are making technology and mass culture better fit their own lives. "The difference between a hacker and a consumer," Dornfest explains, "is a consumer [who] says 'I wish it would work this way.' A hacker says, 'I've got a screwdriver and a few minutes.'"[14] A hacking ethic—or more to the point a hacker aesthetic—seems to appeal to a generation raised on hip-hop and techno (both of which rely on sampling found music) and who spend a great deal of time cutting and pasting text, images, videos, and music on their devices. Many are now adapting that same strategy to the everyday things left over from mass culture, thereby turning trash into environment. The movement is certainly one response to the wastefulness and unfair labor conditions of contemporary consumer culture, but it is also inspired, as Duchamp was, by an artistic desire to create art out of mundane objects and to decide for oneself the meaning of things.

Design and Craft

The tricky business of distinguishing between design and craft (to say nothing of art) is fraught and complicated, and it is not an endeavor I will attempt here. However, it is worth making some observations about the ways the two practices are taken up in mainstream American consumer culture—that is, outside the purview of seminars on design theory or anthropological studies on the role of craft. Although as we've seen many brilliant and thoughtful designers are applying their knowledge and skills to solve problems big and small, addressing questions that range from "What's the most seamless way to dispense dental floss?" to "How can we design a carbon-positive building?," others still are experimenting with the relationship between form and function, producing beautiful innovations to everyday objects. But the version of design that tends to enjoy the lion's share of the public's awareness about design is that offered by the likes of Target and its many competitors. This version, as we explored in chapter 2, perpetuates the aesthetic cult of the celebrity designer, the designerly brand, or, more recently, bloggers and HGTV personalities, capitalizing on and expanding their already formidable followings.

This version is essentially a designer-label, branded version of design. The form of the objects matter. Are the jeans skinny or flared? Is the flatware modern industrial or global eclectic? The materials tend to matter less—leather, vinyl, who cares if it's cute? What perhaps matters most is that the object was designed. But again, the aura of the designer does little to open up the object through, say, an exploration of its processes of production, or even the design process itself. Such objects are abstractions of their material components or the conditions of their creation, and they remain as vulnerable to the capriciousness of trends as designer labels have always been. This mode of design mystifies. It obscures the material life of the object. It *designates* in that it relegates objects to the role of sign. As consumers of this type of design, what we inherit is a system that seems to birth the object ex nihilo, with no identifiable history, as well as a future that is utterly dependent on the trends of the moment.

In IKEA, we are offered a glimpse behind the veneer of the mass-produced object. By participating in at least one step in its creation, we are rewarded with a memento not just of an afternoon shopping at a box store but of the efforts of our own labor. This, as Dan Ariely and his colleagues have demonstrated, accounts for the so-called IKEA effect, in which people see more value in objects they have a hand in assembling. But what IKEA objects really document is the massive global system of timber harvesting, factory production, and distribution that IKEA affords. My successful attempt at assembling a Billy bookcase is possible only because of the precision and efficiency of the monolithic IKEA machine—the compression of the wood composite, the flat-packing techniques and the cheap labor force that allow items to be shipped all over the world on the cheap. The cool design of the objects is surely a draw, but what makes IKEA successful is its design of the larger system, which makes IKEA's offerings so ubiquitous and affordable.

Design at its best is invention, and here I mean invention in all its guises—innovative, imaginative, original. It is a process of discovery (the Latin *inventus* means "to discover"). Crafting, while often including invention, is better understood as creation. It is the hands-on, skillful know-how that comes from working with materials—leather, metal, wood, glass. *Craeft* in Old English means "power, physical strength, might," but later it comes to mean "strength" or "skill." In Old Norse, *kraptr* means "strength" but also "virtue." This sense of practical virtue continues to permeate how we think of crafting.

Craft as Critique

Both Thomas Jefferson and Benjamin Franklin were avid inventors and tinkerers. Jefferson invented or upgraded a wide array of useful tools and gadgets, including moldboard plow, a polygraph for duplicating handwritten documents (not interrogating suspected criminals), a revolving bookstand, and even a machine for making macaroni, for which he acquired a taste while in the Old Country as secretary of state. Franklin invented the lightening rod and bifocal eyeglasses, but also a urinary catheter, the Franklin stove, and an armonica, a musical instrument inspired by the sounds of running one's fingertip over a wet glass, which Franklin declared as the invention that gave him "the greatest personal satisfaction."[15] Despite the widespread adoption of several of their creations, neither Jefferson nor Franklin took out patents, and they actively encouraged others to utilize their work however they saw fit. "As we enjoy great advantages from the inventions of others," Franklin writes, "we should be glad of an opportunity to serve others by any invention of ours; and this we should do freely and generously."[16] Democratic access to ideas and tools was an essential component of the early American ethos.

But Jefferson and Franklin were hardly unique in their abilities as makers. The waves of immigrants coming to North America included skilled craftsmen and -women working in a variety of fields, and their industriousness was embraced as the catalyst that would propel the new democracy. Sociologist Richard Sennett points out that an Enlightenment-era conception of citizenship was intimately tied to the virtue of craft:

> The pages of Diderot's Encyclopedia affirmed the common ground of talents in craftwork, in large principle and in practical detail, because a view of government rested on it. Learning to work well enables people to govern themselves and so become good citizens. The industrious maid is more likely to prove a good citizen than her bored mistress. Thomas Jefferson's democratic celebration of the American farmer-yeoman or skilled artisan stands on the same ground, the practical man being able to judge how well government is built because he understands building—an adage Jefferson unfortunately did not apply to his slaves.[17]

In addition to honing one's capacity for sound judgment, achieving skill in craft also made one self-sufficient—another crucial virtue for early American settlers seeking to separate themselves from British rule. Maker movement ambassador Dale Doughety writes, "Franklin might be the first famous maker in America. He is practical but endlessly curious. He is the self-made man, starting out as an apprentice, lacking much formal schooling and learning from real-world experiences."[18] As Dougherty points out, a maker sensibility may be part of the American ethos, but it is certainly not America's alone: "The maker mindset can be found as an element of any nation or culture, although it may be expressed differently in each one. It is not a uniquely American trait, although our national pride makes us think so."[19] Nonetheless, the rhetoric and values that animate many crafting and making communities today echo the same political sensibilities on which the United States was founded in principle if not always in

practice: equality of access, self-determination, sharing, the ennobling effects of practical know-how.

The technical innovations of the late nineteenth century made it
possible for a slew of new objects to be manufactured quickly and efficiently, although not usually of particularly high quality. Factory
production required the objects to be pared down to their most essential components so they might be more easily reproduced ad infinitum.
Whereas the Bauhaus embraced machinic production that, once in the
hands of the working class, they believed would abolish the old class-
based distinctions between craft and art as well as democratize access
to beautifully designed objects, their contemporaries in the Arts and
Crafts movement were more suspicious. The central figures of the Arts
and Crafts movement were influenced by the writings of John Ruskin,
an art critic in Victorian England who became so disgusted with the
disheartening ugliness wrought by industrialization that he turned his
critical eye on capitalism itself. Ruskin invested his family inheritance
into the Guild of St. George, intended as a more humane alternative
to what he saw as the spirit crushing grind of factory work. The guild
was modeled after the medieval crafts guilds Ruskin admired, which
empowered craftsmen with training in an apprentice system as well as
job security in an honorable trade. Like those earlier guilds, the Guild
of St. George set up a network of small farms and workshops and inspired his followers to start thriving businesses making things like
apple juice, sweaters, and jam. The Guild of St. George is still active
today, nearly 150 years later, as a charity supporting the "arts, crafts,
and the rural economy."[20]

Ruskin's most prominent follower, William Morris, went on to become a textiles designer famous for reviving ancient techniques and
his medieval-inspired botanical designs, many of which are still in
production today, printed on fine stationery, wallpaper, and fabric.
Morris was also a poet, an artist, a novelist, and a prolific advocate for
the cause of socialism. Morris's many speeches and pamphlets critique the woeful conditions of laborers under industrial capitalism,
which he argues robs them of their natural right to take pride in their

work: "A man at work, making something he feels will exist because he is working at it and wills it, is exercising the energies of his mind and his soul as well as of his body. Memory and imagination help him as he works. Not only his own thoughts, but the thoughts of the men of past ages guide his hands; and, as a part of the human race, he creates." Anything less than that, Morris notes, is "slave's work" and amounts to "mere toiling."[21]

Like Ruskin, Morris champions the crafts guilds of medieval Europe as the model for a modern socialist brotherhood, in which craftsmen could "work together with a common purpose: to glorify God through the practice of their skills."[22] Although the Arts and Crafts movement is known for its celebration of the beauty found in the organic imperfections of handmade objects, its adherents were not necessarily antimachine. Although the machine's role was a matter of some debate within late nineteenth- and early twentieth-century design circles, many Arts and Crafts advocates acknowledge that the more tedious, repetitive tasks of crafting could be relegated to the machine, leaving the crafter to focus on those elements that demanded a keen mind and skilled hand. More than the machine itself, Morris and his comrades are opposed to the division of labor popularized by factory production—essentially a machine made of workers, distributed across a larger system of manufacture in which they had little control. This mode of production, unlike that of the crafts guilds, separates workers from the intellectual aspects of creation, and "without dignified, creative human occupation, people became disconnected from life."[23]

Morris and others in the Arts and Crafts movement share many of the sensibilities of Jefferson and Franklin a generation before them. Although Morris may have been more aesthetically inclined, like his American predecessors, he saw practical knowledge—handwork—as a path to self-determination. He was committed to democratic access to those processes that he believed makes us human: "I do not want art for a few any more than education for a few or freedom for a few," he writes.[24] He also sees crafting as a moral endeavor, as a kind of material virtue, ennobling both the crafter who makes the handcrafted object and those who take pleasure in its use.

Craft Makes Us Human

Morris echoes a crucial component of Marx's famous critique that industrial capitalism reduced each worker's responsibility to one small part in a larger sequence of functions that brings a product to life. Unlike the craftsmen and -women before them, factory workers endlessly repeat the same action—say, installing a hubcap, over and over, relegating their role to essentially that of a cog in a machine. For Marx, what is lost in this mode of production is nothing less than what it is to be human. He argues that such mechanized and distributed labor estranges humans from their *Gattungswesen*, or "species essence." The worker, he writes, "does not feel content but unhappy, does not develop freely his physical and mental energy but mortifies his body and ruins his mind. The worker therefore only feels himself outside his work, and in his work feels outside himself."[25] As many scholars of contemporary capitalism have argued, this central experience of being separated or alienated from one's work and its products is not necessarily alleviated if one escapes into so-called knowledge work or joins the creative class.

If one watches a number of the maker videos I described earlier, a central theme emerges. Again and again, people who spend time working with their hands describe the process itself as well as the community that takes shape around it as allowing them to be more human. Makers describe feeling more connected to their ancestors, for example. A YouTube channel called How to Make Everything, which deconstructs the processes that create everyday objects, features a "Meet the Maker" series (online retailer Need Supply has a series with the same name, as does Condé Nast Traveler). One video features Kyle, a leatherworker, who suggests that working with leather puts him in touch with a central element of human history. "I like working on leather as opposed to any other medium," he says, "because it's been around through pretty much all of human development from the first things we threw over our shoulders. It's been bags, shoes, hunting equipment, it's been armor. This has kept people alive in every way from shelter, to clothing, to weaponry."[26]

Brooklyn knife maker Joel Bukiewicz, with his thick beard, MFA, and story of a failed creative writing career, seems straight out of central casting for the hipster artisan role in a *Portlandia* skit. Founder of the successful Cut Brooklyn, Bukiewicz's knives are in high demand, thanks in part to the booming indie food movement in the borough. In the edgy black-and-white promotional video produced by "Made by Hand," viewers are invited into Bukiewicz's workshop as he describes the very human process of trial and error as he taught himself to make top-quality cutlery: "The difference between my knife, that spends fifteen hours, say, in my hands all the way through the process, and a knife that gets made in Germany by, like, ten different robots over like a fifteen-minute period is all really in the details. There needs to be a human element in the making of these things."[27] Like many millennial makers, Bukiewicz did not apprentice under a senior craftsman; he is self-taught. But he has found community through his craft nonetheless. He suggests that the real value of what he does is in the comradeship forming among people like himself who are seeking greater control over their labor and the satisfaction that comes from making a quality product:

> I think probably some folks getting into it just sort of think there's like this great opportunity. That the streets are just paved with gold in the handmade world, and that couldn't be farther from the truth. Where the currency is really rich is in community, in the friendships you develop, the fact that you get to do what you want to do and not get bossed around. That's where it's rich, in quality of life, it's rich. This tag 'handmade' on its very basic face value, means quality. If it's made by hand it's made with great quality. Like when you think of a handmade suit, you think of something that's like, perfect. That's why you pay more for it.[28]

What one is inheriting with the consumption or appreciation of a crafted object, in other words, is the application of human know-how to work with and through a medium. Sign value is at work here, to be sure. "Handmade" may not represent a corporation, but it is a brand of sorts, a signifying memento of a project or process that one may experience directly or indirectly. Like all brands, it can serve to gloss over the specificities of the individual material object, little more than an add-on, generating exchange value by making it seem more special. But it also has real potential to invite both makers and consumers of handmade goods to experience form and matter in useful ways. Handmade goods offer different tactile, narrative, and emotional values than those coming off an assembly line. Textile artist Celia Pym explains why for her "craft still matters in a digital world":

> I value craft for informing my relationship with materials. I value knowing the touch, the weight, the hand, the smell, and the color of the materials. Craft develops your ability to work with your hands and hold the knowledge in your body of how you play with the materials. This is an intimate knowledge and can be fun. For me, working this way makes me very aware of scale because if I'm using my hands and my muscles to construct something the scale is always in relation to my body.
>
> This is one way that craft feels different from industrial production. The scale, quantities, and volume in industrial production can be so large, and this feels quite abstract. Craft, by comparison, feels pretty concrete and close to the body.[29]

This attention to the thingness, or the unique aspects of a material object that can only be known through direct experience, is echoed again and again by those who craft. Craftspeople must know both their materials and tools intimately. Crafters must enlist their bodies and memories in the process. Good technique is developed over time, through patience and perseverance. Unsurprisingly, makers report that they themselves feel transformed though this transformation of matter into form. Peter Korn, in a lovely meditation on life as a furniture maker, writes that whereas earlier crafts were simply to make things of use, "contemporary craft, being economically marginal, is created primarily to address the spiritual needs of its *maker*."[30] This spiritual experience comes from cultivating the technique and material know how that developed only though attention to the specific, not the abstract. He describes the detailed process of making a cabinet:

> In furniture making, beginnings are critical. For a simple frame-and-panel cabinet door to stay flat over the long haul, and not become too tight in summer or overly gapped in winter, success starts with the choice of timber. Not just what species or which plank, but also from which part of the board one saws the stiles and rails, how dry the wood is, the method by which it was dried, and how it was stored and handled. All this before the actual work of milling the timber flat and square, laying out and cutting the joinery, making and fitting the panel, assembling, trimming, fitting, hinging, latching, and finishing. Throughout the entire process, the quality achievable at each stage is utterly dependent on the care with which the craftsman has accomplished every previous step.[31]

Korn's depiction captures much of the value makers and crafters say they gain from the practice. To do it well demands attentiveness to a wide range of details, an ability to see the ways each piece fits in the larger puzzle, and a recognition that good quality is often the sum of mundane parts. The lessons that one learns from handwork are useful in all aspects of life as a human. They are character building.

For Matthew Crawford, old motorcycles provide the best education. Crawford laments that today we are offered few opportunities to exercise judgment—a crucial component of human intelligence. In order to effectively judge, say, a mechanical problem on an old bike, one cannot simply contemplate the issue in some detached, abstract way; one must attend to the specifics of the situation at hand. Doing so, writes Crawford, encourages "the development of what we might call a subethical virtue: the user holds himself responsible to external reality, and opens himself to being schooled by it. His will is educated—both chastened and focused—so it no longer resembles that of a raging baby who knows only what he wants. Both as workers and as consumers, technical education seems to contribute to moral education."[32]

Actor Nick Offerman (*Parks and Recreation*'s [2009–15] Ron Swanson) is an avid woodworker and something of a celebrity ambassador for the skills making develops. He's written two popular books on the subject, *Paddle Your Own Canoe* (2013) and *Good Clean Fun* (2016). He describes the intellectual challenge and satisfaction that come from handwork:

> One of the things that's so addictive about woodworking is that it is just a sequence of problem solving: How can I use these tools and these hands and this pencil to turn this stack of tree limbs into a beautiful chest of drawers? It requires a tinkerer's brain. . . .
>
> What's beautiful about the human being is that there are those of us who have a propensity for problem solving. We say, "Okay, this screen door keeps blowing open. How can I most conveniently solve that problem?" The majority of people wouldn't have the inclination to go into their box of miscellaneous hardware and say, "Here's a spring, here's a hinge, here's a shim—how can I MacGyver these into a solution?"[33]

Like their forbearers in the Arts and Crafts movement and others who recognized the power of craft, these testimonies accentuate the intellectual, ethical, and even spiritual aspects of working with one's hands. Those who may not have the time, resources, or inclination to make things themselves are increasingly exposed to the work and process narratives of those who do. The consumer market for handmade objects is booming, and the venues for consuming both those goods and stories of their making abound.

Although purveyors of cheap, mass-produced products, such as Walmart, Amazon, Target, and IKEA, clearly dominate the retail market, it's hard to ignore the massive growth in the handmade sector.

Indeed, the fact that I can even plausibly write the words "handmade sector" is noteworthy. Harvard economist Lawrence Katz has dubbed this growing segment of the U.S. marketplace the artisan economy, noting the increased attractiveness both for workers and consumers of participating in a more human scale process of manufacture and exchange. "Historically," Katz tells PBS, "an artisan is somebody who did the entire work largely by themselves—conceive a project, put it together, make it." Today, he adds, "there's the potentially hopeful scenario of, in some sense, being able to bring back the old mass production artisanal work with new technologies of today that allow a lot of customization and creativity in the same way that hand work did in the past."[34] These new possibilities, enabled by online retail platforms and increasingly affordable fabrication technologies, are contributing to a thriving, if not all together 'scalable,' handmade economy.

Much of the enthusiasm over the marriage between technology and crafting is being driven by Etsy, the popular e-commerce site in which artisans open online shops to sell their handmade wares. Now over a decade and a half old, and facing stiff competition from Amazon's recent "Handmade @ Amazon" venture, Etsy continues to be a major force in the online retail market for handcrafted goods. Etsy stock has gone up and down over the years as it has grown, but at the time of this writing, it's on a clear upswing. In an effort to get in on the craft supply action it helped generate, in 2017 Etsy launched Etsy Studio, a sister site with the same peer-to-peer format, allowing vendors of craft supplies to sell directly to crafters. Etsy is also moving into more mainstream retails spaces, as I will discuss in the following section, partnering with a variety of brick-and-mortar stores with Etsy pop-ups. The success of Etsy serves as proof of concept, demonstrating to the mainstream economy the appeal of craft.

Corporate Crafters

William Morris's romantic celebration of the handmade as an antidote to the bureaucratization and uncertainty of modern life is as popular today as it was in the early twentieth century. For activists such as those in the Arts and Crafts movement, "cultivating an appreciation for objets d'art was thus a form of protest against modernity, with a view to providing a livelihood to dissident craftsman," writes Crawford. However, he points out,

> it dovetailed with, and gave a higher urgency to, the nascent culture of luxury consumption. As [historian T. J. Jackson] Lears tells the story, the great irony is that anti-modernist sentiments of aesthetic revolt against the machine paved the way for certain unattractive features of late-modern culture: therapeutic self-absorption and the hankering after "authenticity," precisely those psychic hooks now relied upon by advertisers. Such spiritualized, symbolic modes of craft practice and craft consumption represented a kind of compensation for, and therefore an accommodation to, new modes of routinized, bureaucratic work.[35]

Today's retail giants recognize this "hankering" for authenticity in today's consumers and are increasingly positioning themselves as the venue for meaningful objects made by human hands. Much as Target uses design to get customers through the door, where they'll likely also pick up less designerly items like toilet paper and toothpaste, other mass retailers are increasingly showcasing artisanal goods as a way to increase traffic and distinguish themselves from their competitors at the shopping mall. Williams Sonoma, for example, purveyor of gourmet kitchen wares, hosts a monthly Artisans' Market, where they partner with local vendors specializing in handmade food products like small-batch pickles and exotic spice rubs. "We're proud to support local artisans, who are truly experts in their craft, by giving them a marketplace in our stores," enthuses a corporate press release about the project.[36] Nordstrom, West Elm (a trendy furniture chain owned by Williams Sonoma), and Crate & Barrel's kid-centric brand, The Land of Nod, have all partnered with Etsy's wholesale division to add a mix of handmade products to their mass-produced offerings. In 2016, department store monolith Macy's got on the Etsy bandwagon, with a boutique-style Etsy Shop in its flagship Herald Square store in New York City that rotates items from Etsy artists every month or two.

Even Target is attempting to feel more like a neighborhood store through the promotion of local, small-batch goods. Target has partnered with menswear designer Todd Snyder in a project they're calling "Local Pride." The description on the company's website is vaguely noncommittal yet characteristically on trend: "Target is tipping its hat to the same movement that has urban consumers gobbling up farm-to-table cuisine and patronizing neighborhood boutiques. Rather than buy mass-produced products, these consumers want to know details such as who the chef is, or where an item of clothing was produced—preferably locally."[37] Like its many competitors dipping their toes into the handmade marketplace, Target is a big box that clearly wants in on the artisan action.

Whereas these retailers are diversifying their usual offerings with unique handcrafted items for mall-weary customers, other corporations are positioning themselves as the craftsman, wrapping factory-made goods in the rhetoric of artistry. Perhaps because there's a clear appeal but also limitation to how much handcrafts can scale, we see advertisers grafting the language of crafting onto things that are decidedly not what we would think of as crafted. Despite the growing appeal of handcrafted objects and narratives of the creative, industrious souls who make them, not everything can or should be made by hand. Take cars. Nowhere is the corporate rhetoric of crafting more pronounced than in the marketing of perhaps the least likely of factory-produced consumer goods: the automobile. The small and exclusive community of handmade car hobbyists notwithstanding, truly handcrafted cars make no sense on any kind of scale.

Of the corporations flocking to align themselves with American workmanship, the postgovernment bailout marketing rhetoric of Chrysler beginning in 2010 is undoubtedly the most explicit in its celebration of the nation's craftsman heritage. Employing the talents of Wieden + Kennedy's Portland, Oregon, office, the brains behind such successful campaigns as "Just Do It" for Nike, Chrysler offered the plight of Detroit as the symbolic American überstory and the Jeep Cherokee as its comeback kid. In recent years, Chrysler products had suffered a reputation for poor quality (exacerbated by its purchase by Fiat a year earlier[38]), and this campaign was an attempt to remedy that by using the rhetorical and visual tropes of craft. Let's look at a few of the ads.

The Things We Make, Make Us (2010)

The opening image of the "The Things We Make, Make Us" (2010) campaign for the Jeep Cherokee is a steel spike being driven through a railroad tie, its telltale clang synchronized to the opening downbeat of Johnny Cash's haunting "God's Gonna Cut You Down"[39] (1957), a plodding, percussive stomp—clap rhythm that is both tenacious and industrial. Over a march of gritty images celebrating American crafts-manship big and small—a steam locomotive, a biplane, calloused female hands carefully chiseling metal machine parts—the narrator says:

> The things that make us Americans are the things we make. This has always been a nation of builders. Of craftsman. Men and women for whom straight stitches and clean welds were matters of personal pride. They made the skyscrapers and the cotton gins. The colt revolvers and the jeep 4X4s. These things make us who we are. *As a people we do well when we make good things and not so well when we don't.* The good news is this can be put right. We just have to do it. And so we did.

The images of American industry then give way to more specific scenes of Jeep Cherokees lovingly crafted by way of a mix of human hands and state-of-the-art technology: meticulously stitched leather uphol-stery, high-tech robots assembling a chassis, a worker's hand welding parts, all interspersed with a shiny new Cherokee off-roading through a pristine forest. The narrator continues: "This, our newest son, was imagined, drawn, carved, stamped, hewn and forged here in Amer-ica. It is well made and it is designed to work. This was once a country where people made things. Beautiful things. And so it is again."

This ad is the first in a long while to offer consumers a look behind the scenes of automobile manufacture. For years, car commercials have cast their products as sleek or rugged technological marvels that can take us anywhere, yet seemingly come from nowhere. SUVs negotiate jagged mountain roads, sports cars filled with laughing multicultural twenty-somethings navigate spotless city streets with ease, and massive pickup trucks bear the weight of muddy bulldozers. Car advertisements tend to invite us to covet the car—or the freedom, luxury, or brawn it affords—but nary a factory is seen. The production process is rarely part of the brand identity.

One exception to the trend was General Motors' now-defunct Saturn brand, an attempt in the 1990s and early 2000s to compete with the Japanese for the Gen X market, in ads featuring factories and autoworkers demonstrating that Saturn was a different kind of car company. Saturn ads foreground happy workers in clean factories who actually host family reunions in which loyal Saturn drivers are invited to visit the plant to share a meal and a shake hands with the workers who made their cars. Despite the feel-good spirit of the campaign, Naomi Klein derides Saturn as offering little more than a "new age nostalgia factory" designed to associate Saturn with "a simpler time, a time when goods were made in the countries where they were consumed, when people still knew their neighbors and nobody had ever heard of an export processing zone."[40] However, Klein concludes, "the ads—though purporting to take us behind the glitz of advertising—were there not to illuminate the manufacturing process, but to obscure it."[41]

What might we make of this latest return to the factory, or at least manufacturing processes, on offer from Chrysler? Its vehicles are supposedly "imagined, drawn, carved, stamped, hewn and forged" by the hands and instruments of real people, representing the best of American industry. Chrysler's recent ads are no more authentic than Saturn's, of course. They offer highly stylized, overly romantic images and sentiments intended to give mass-produced objects a more human touch. But the fact that craftsmanship, or at least its rhetorical trappings, are such fertile soil for advertisers to till suggests that consumers are craving and potentially responding to appeals that invoke the human hand.

Imported from Detroit (2011)

Wieden + Kennedy was behind another emotionally powerful ad celebrating the renaissance of American auto manufacturing. In the third quarter of the 2011 Super Bowl, Chrysler ran a two-minute spot, the longest in Super Bowl history, featuring Detroit's favorite son, rapper Eminem, driving through the city's streets in a new Chrysler 200. The spot, which reportedly cost Chrysler nearly $9 million to make, contains a montage of Detroit landmarks and homages to the city's industrial history. Over images of, for example, Diego Rivera's colorful 1930s Detroit Industrial murals of autoworkers and the Joe Lewis fist monument, a gravel-voiced narrator begins:

> What does this city know about luxury? What does a town that's been through hell and back know about the finer things in life? Well, I'll tell you. More than most. You see, it's the hottest fires that make the hardest steel. Add hard work and conviction. And a know-how that runs generations deep in every last one of us. That's who we are. That's our story. Now it's probably not the one you've been reading in the papers. The one being written by folks who have never even been here. Don't know what we're capable of. Because when it comes to luxury, it's as much about where it's from as who it's for.

Although less directly about handcrafting than is the Cherokee ad, "Imported from Detroit" is all about workmanship. It's about the redemption of a quintessentially American industry and the people that built it—people with "a know-how that runs generations deep." Luxury may be for the self-indulgent tech bros of Silicon Valley, the spot seems to suggest, but it can only be made by the hardworking laborers who may have been to hell and back but are tough enough to rise again. If the redemption narrative isn't clear by now, the spot concludes with the car pulling up to the beautiful Fox Theater as the staccato guitar riff of Eminem's own anthem of self-determination, "Lose Yourself," begins. As he makes his way into the empty theater, a black gospel choir raises its voice in majestic harmony. As he joins them on stage, Eminem directs his solemn gaze to the camera and says, "This is the Motor City. And this is what we do."

Crafted (2016)

Taking a page out of the Chrysler playbook, Mazda debuted its 2016 CX-9 SUV with a campaign steeped in the rhetoric and imagery of craftsmanship. One commercial, introducing the new CX-9, simply called "Crafted," begins with a minimalist piano melody playing over close-up images of a woodworker's hands gripping a hand plane, curlicues of rosewood falling away as he skillfully transforms the rough plank into a velvety board. "Can a car be crafted instead of produced?" inquires a narrator (actor Aaron Paul of *Breaking Bad* [2008–13] fame). Cut to another set of hands carefully smoothing out a supple piece of leather, another hand stitching that leather onto a steering wheel with needle and black thread, and still another gently hand sanding the rosewood into the curved edge of a car console. The narrator continues: "Designed with attention and care, to give a feeling that stays with you? At Mazda, every detail matters."

However, looking at Mazda's larger Driving Matters campaign of which the "Crafted" spot is one example, one sees it's not the working-class heroes of Detroit lovingly crafting the interior that will make drivers fall in love with the new CX-9. Mazda evokes the lineage of the Japanese masters who it claims inspire the company's approach to the "car as art." At the center of the car as art form, according to Mazda's messaging, is the inextricable relationship between objects and human emotion. From the company's website: "Mazda Design is obsessed with the ultimate form of beauty—the artistic forms that can only be shaped by the power and precision of human hands."[42] It goes on to explain that Mazda designers use a unique process called "exploratory preparation" in which they create different forms and objects using various materials, such as clay, to "explore how these forms move people's hearts."

Mazda's glossy online magazine, "Inside Mazda," closely resembles those "meet the maker" stories popular among the handcrafting set. One article, entitled "How Can an Ancient Craft Inspire a Modern Design,?" explains how the traditional Japanese art of knife making inspired aluminum trim for the new CX-9:

> For hundreds of years, knife making has been a revered art form in Japan. Embraced for more than their functionality, these classic designs have created an emotional bond with an entire culture. This legendary craftsmanship was the inspiration for the aluminum trim in the all-new Mazda CX-9 Signature. A sweeping single piece of aluminum adorns the dashboard, emphasizing the width of the forward-angled dashboard, as if it was a sharpened knife. Satin and polished finishes also mirror the honing of handmade blades.[43]

Another asks, "Is the best instrument for creating an emotional design the human hand?"

> To truly capture emotion in a design, the best tool is the human hand. Even as a small car company, Mazda uses more clay for hand-crafted models than any other automaker. There's a reason. You can't touch a CAD model. You can't see how daylight casts shadows over vector-based graphics. Despite all its technology, driving is a very human act. That's why the emotional connection you experience with the Mazda CX-9 begins with human hands.[44]

Mazda designers may hand sculpt their models out of clay in their ideation process, but the CX-9 SUV can hardly be called handmade. Indeed, the marketers choose their words carefully; the cars are "inspired" by Japanese craftsmanship. They are "conceived" through a process of sculpting malleable materials. Its cars, Mazda suggests, inherit the traditional values of Japanese craftsmanship even if they aren't directly wrought by it. At the center of the appeal is the human touch that crafting supposedly confers onto objects—the human ability to detect subtle differences between light and shadow, or the ineffable connection between hand and heart.

Is this the crass corporate exploitation of a traditional craft ethos, of the sort exemplified by the likes of sushi master Jiro Ono? Is it merely a deceitful gloss, obscuring the same old problematic production processes? In part, sure. But the rhetoric here tells us something. I'm less interested in busting companies like Mazda and Chrysler for cynically capitalizing on the handmade trend to sell more mass-produced cars than I am in looking at their rhetorical appeals as a symptom or as an attempt to address a larger syndrome affecting life under industrial capitalism—in particular the problem of meaning. Mazda's "Driving Matters" campaign also includes an ad in high rotation that maps a man's journey from adolescence to parenthood through his relationship with Mazda. Although the vehicles (product specimens) may change over the years, the man's relationship to the Mazda brand is imbued with memories, history, and meaning. This biographical nostalgia strategy has also been used by competitors Subaru and Toyota, but none so explicitly link the emotional connections we feel with the car as object to the human hands that went into its creation.

But if Mazda's rhetoric offers symptomatic evidence of mass production's crisis of meaning, it also contributes to a positive discursive thread in the culture encouraging an intensification of the relationship between making and value. Certainly Mazda is in the business of selling cars—the more the better—and it offers us no cure for the toxicity and waste endemic to industrialization. Intentions notwithstanding, Mazda's rhetoric does encourage what I noted earlier as an empathy for objects. Whereas the Chrysler ads foreground the tough spirit and hard-won skill of the American autoworker, Mazda's rhetoric has a distinctly Japanese flavor, focusing on the intricate, almost spiritual processes of the Japanese crafts tradition—a tradition that is the stuff of legends. Ikuo Maeda, head of Mazda's design division, sums up the company's design philosophy: "In Japan, we feel that craftsmen inject life into what they make, so objects that receive the love and caring attention of these craftsmen have a vital force; a soul. . . . As we are a Japanese car company, we believe that a form sincerely and painstakingly made by human hands gets a soul."[45]

Like Marie Kondo's philosophy in her best seller *The Life-Changing Magic of Tidying Up*, Mazda invites us to see inanimate objects as vital, even soulful. Also like Kondo, Mazda's rhetoric offers no obvious mechanism by which we might slow the seemingly endless tide of enchanting objects we purchase and discard as suits our whim. It does, however, cultivate an attention to the making process and an emphasis on emotional connection we may feel with objects. Although Buddhism (another of Asia's exports to the West) may stress an ethic of nonattachment as the healthiest way to move through this material world, it does so because Buddhist teachings assert as a first principle the notion that craving (the fuel of consumer capitalism) is a central cause of suffering. Forging a more intimate connection to objects, in part through an appreciation for the processes of their manufacture, has at least the potential to mitigate the insatiable cravings of consumerism by fostering a deeper commitment to those things we already have.

This rhetorical marriage between handcraft and high-tech automated manufacturing being espoused by the auto industry makes for strange bedfellows. Indeed, as Nick Offerman notes when asked about his opinion of 3-D printers, "I think they're really neat-o. But here at Offerman Woodshop, part of our flavor is that everything is made by hand. I draw the line far beyond a 3-D printer. We won't even use a cutter jig to cut our dovetail joints. Depending on the intelligence of machinery, to me it's a liability factor in wood crafted pieces. Unless you put your hands on every inch of the piece, you don't know if there might be a flaw."[46] Many die-hard crafters, like those in the Arts and Crafts movement before them, see machines impinging on the pleasure and satisfaction that one experiences when making things by hand. Although the differences between making and crafting are not insignificant, their practices have more in common than not.

They are both responding to the same cultural forces, frustrations, and yearnings.

The Maker Movement

The maker movement includes the more conventional craftsmen and -women I described earlier, but it joins those values and practices with the sensibilities of computer hackers and the skill sets of inventors and tinkerers of all things electronic and mechanical. We might think of it as crafting for the digital age. Makers provide a bridge between a traditional commitment to detailed, quality handwork and the open-source ethics of collaboration and democratic access to tools and resources. They are those experimenting with robotics in makerspace workshops, creating objects they design themselves using CAD software and bring to life with 3-D printers. They are innovators imagining new uses for computer electronics, using open hardware microcontrollers like Arduino. Venues such as *Make* magazine and its popular Maker Faires, as well as the maker and hacker spaces that are popping up across the country—open access, DIY, high-tech workshops—provide opportunities for collaboration and the sharing of information, fundamental components of what many are calling a maker culture revolution.

If crafting has its roots in earlier movements like Arts and Crafts, today's maker culture owes much to the sensibilities of the culture that formed around Stewart Brand's *Whole Earth Catalog*, published between 1968 and 1972. *Whole Earth*'s motto was "access to tools," and it combined an ecological ethic with an unabashed embrace of the high-tech computer and electronics of its time. In fact, it was Brand who initiated the campaign for NASA to release its now-famous photo of Earth from space, which became a powerful symbol for the burgeoning environmental movement. It also inspired the name of the catalog and was the image on its first cover. Steve Jobs called the catalog "one of the bibles of my generation," and *Wired*'s Kevin Kelly has acknowledged it as a progenitor of the blogosphere and a prime example of user-generated content.[47] It's an appropriate description, because *Whole Earth* didn't sell products itself. It served as a clearinghouse for information about where to get tools, books, and other items that enabled self-reliance, and it was a central resource for those looking to live in ways more connected to the land and to their communities. The governing politics of *Whole Earth* was to promote a human-scale, participatory, ecologically minded approach to production and consumption. Liberty gained through self-reliance was its foundational principle. It also promoted progressive philosophies and economic theories in the books it promoted in its "understanding whole systems" section. It's not surprising that amid today's global systems, which are anything but human scale, this approach holds much appeal.

Although we live in an age in which information has become increasingly malleable and the potential for customization and niche marketing more pronounced, the actual production of things themselves, of the physical objects that comprise much of our material world, has evolved in a manner that is increasingly removed from our everyday human experience and knowledge. The same holds true for the physical operation of the overwhelming majority of our devices, which are often presented to us as immaculately conceived black boxes, their inner workings encased safely in an exoskeleton of "good design." Cars and smartphones provide perhaps the most striking examples. They're used daily by millions of people, though few know what is happening under the hood, and fewer are encouraged to find out. Perhaps the popularity of television shows like *Dirty Jobs* (2003–12), *MythBusters* (2003–), and *How Do They Do It?* (2006–) is because they offer audiences a chance to look under the hood of the technologies and processes that make modern life possible.

Responding to the pervasiveness of this transformation from commoner as craftsman to commoner as mere consumer, advocates of the broader maker movement often speak and write about the past with a robust sense of romance and a broad feeling of nostalgia. Mark Frauenfelder, editor in chief of *Make* magazine, explains: "If you owned a Model T . . . you were expected to be a mechanic as well as a driver, making repairs as necessary. . . . This wasn't an unreasonable assumption on the part of the Ford Motor Company, because a large

percentage of the people who bought Model Ts had experience main-
taining farm machinery. The only tools you needed to repair a Model T
were a wrench, a hammer, a screwdriver, and pliers. . . . For these
people, do-it-yourself was a way of life."[48] Today's Fords, by contrast,
require far more technical acumen, and far more specialized equipment, than those early Model Ts. This complexity makes them safer,
more responsive to commands, and more fuel efficient, as well as ca-
pable of performing functions undreamt of in the early decades of the
twentieth century. But complexity comes with the opportunity cost of
inscrutability.

Perhaps this would suffice as an explanation for our generalized ignorance about the things we use, but the complexity of the underlying
technology is only part of the story. Manufacturers and salespeople
have coupled this technological complexity with a marketing push that
celebrates simplified user experiences. As a result, these devices and
their advertising often actively persuade users that they need not know
about the nuts and bolts (virtual or otherwise) of the technologies they
use. As Matthew Crawford points out, a sign of luxury cars today is that
their inner workings are hidden from view. Many cars no longer even
have a dipstick so owners can check their own oil levels. Similarly, in
2009, Apple quietly introduced three different proprietary so-called
flower head screws that made it impossible to open up and see inside
some of their ultraportable laptops and handheld devices, thereby
preventing individuals from replacing the batteries in some of the
larger laptop models. Avid hobbyists found a way around this quickly
enough; they used casts made from the screws to reverse engineer new
screwdriver heads. But for the vast majority of the Apple user population, the message was clear: "Enjoy your Apple device—but don't dare
to look inside. If you have a question, take it to the Genius Bar."

This missed opportunity for connection and attachment, this increasing mystification of the things we use, correlates with growing
bureaucracies that help to solidify, culturally, the diminished capacity and responsibility for making. Crawford cites automobile repair
as a compelling case in point: "Consider the case of a man who is

told his car is not worth fixing. He is told this not by a mechanic but by a clipboard-wielding 'service representative' at the dealership. Here is a layer of bureaucracy that makes impossible a conversation about the nitty-gritty of the situation. This man would gladly hover around the mechanic's bay and be educated about his car, but this is not allowed."[49] What is lost in this increased distancing and the level of mediation between ourselves and the things in our lives, say many makers, is the spirit of inquiry and our ability to be self-reliant—our ability to have the information and techne to respond to breakdown or failure. Instead what we have are cars with no dipsticks, public toilets that flush themselves, and mountains of gadgets that must simply be replaced rather than repaired.

"We now like our things not to disturb us," Crawford notes, but in "becoming less obtrusive our devices also become more complicated." As a result, "both as workers and as consumers, we feel we move in channels that have been projected from afar by vast impersonal forces."[50] These impersonal forces of technology, of capitalism, of a society ostensibly comfortable in its lack of basic making know-how, for making advocates violates a fundamental sense of who we are. In the words of one writer: "Human beings are Makers by nature, but our society deprives us of much expression of that role."[51] The refrain that permeates much maker discourse is that making is in our very DNA. It must be exercised or lost to atrophy. Its proponents suggest that its benefits include the personal pleasure that comes through engagement with the external world and the cultivation of self-reliance or self-determination.

Pleasure, Pride, Engagement

Mark Frauenfelder, a well-known tech writer, cofounder of Boing Boing, and former editor of *Make* magazine, is admittedly no DIY expert, but he may well be maker culture's head cheerleader. In *Made by Hand* (2010), Frauenfelder chronicles his own forays into making things—a chicken coop, an elaborate urban vegetable garden, cigar box guitars—with the goal not of telling readers how easy it all is but rather to highlight what can be gained when we dare to tinker with the objects in our lives. Frauenfelder relays a conversation with Mister Jalopy, a legend in maker circles who the *New York Times* calls "the prophet of the movement," describing the important role of mistakes in one's journey into making:

> What I do is the same as cooking or gardening. The difference is the perception of the barrier to entry. People are afraid that they're going to screw something up, that they're going to ruin something. And, unfortunately, it's valid—they will. You will screw stuff up. Things will be broken. But that's the one step to overcome to get on the path of living this richer life of engagement, of having meaningful connections to the objects around you.[52]

Makers often express the inherent joy or satisfaction one gets from working with one's hands. This satisfaction is often the result of a successful product ("it works!"). Frauenfelder writes, "Who knew that making a chicken door could be so beneficial to one's self-esteem?"[53] But more often it's described as the pleasure of immersing oneself in a manual process. To successfully work with material objects, whatever they may be, one has to get outside oneself and give oneself over to the object. What does it need? How might it respond? This process is quite different from the consumptive impulse, in which the thing is there for me.

Robert Grudin, professor of English at the University of Oregon, recounts his experience designing some wooden tables during his financially lean years as a junior scholar with young children. For Grudin, designing those simple tables taught him something: "I had transcended my own inhibiting academic world and briefly explored the material presences of daily life. I had freed my eyes and hands to converse with varieties of shape and substance. I had engaged my little world and changed it. For these reasons, there is something special for me about the practice of design."[54] Similarly, Crawford, of his work with motorcycles, concludes, "I believe the mechanical arts have a special significance for our time because they cultivate not creativity, but the less glamorous virtue of attentiveness."[55]

The value of attentiveness, or absorption in the task at hand, is an oft-repeated benefit to manual work espoused by makers. Richard Sennett notes that "the craftsman represents the special human condition of being engaged."[56] As Frauenfelder puts it, "I wonder if one of the main reasons people garden, or knit, or retire to their garages and basements to tinker, is because they enjoy this unusual state of consciousness. Some people might be able to achieve it by meditating, but using your hands seems to do the trick, too."[57] Nick Offerman echoes this belief in the healing benefits of crafting. He reports that working in his shop is crucial to his mental health, as it gets him out of his head and into the world: "It makes me more calm. It makes me more in control. So, I definitely think making is a form of therapy."[58] Indeed, Herbert Benson, the Harvard cardiologist who in the 1960s pioneered research into the mind–body connection, writes that the methodical focus handwork required creates the conditions for what he dubbed "the relaxation response": "Working with yarn provides stress relief. Like meditation or prayer, knitting allows for the passive release of stray thoughts. The rhythmic and repetitive quality of the stitching, along with the needles clicking resembles a calming mantra. The mind can wander while still focusing on one task."[59]

Other makers describe a kind of mindfulness honed not just by the process of making but also by surrounding yourself by the things you've made. Eric Thomason, who together with his wife, Julia Posey, chronicled their urban homesteading life on their now-defunct blog, Ramshackle Solid, describes his trial-and-error solution to a broken trash can lid that he eventually solved with some galvanized metal, hoops, and a finishing nail. Thomason's solution took longer than if he had just gone to Home Depot for a hinge. "But that wouldn't be as interesting as what I have now," he says. "And I also have the history that evolves with it. Every time I open that trash can now, I have a little sense of satisfaction over how it opens. I never noticed the trash can opening before."[60]

This noticing, this intimate engagement with the material world around us, is a compelling rejoinder to the distractedness encouraged by commercial culture. Consumerism depends precisely on our not being mindful but instead acting from a place of hunger, preoccupation, and reactivity. Making has the potential to at least serve as an antidote or counterbalance to precisely those things that many scholars bemoan about what consumerism has wrought on modern culture. The world becomes more knowable and recognizable. It also offers an important source of attachment to those things we made ourselves: the IKEA effect in overdrive.

Resilience/Self-reliance

The subtitle of Cory Doctorow's 2009 novel *Makers* is "a novel of the whirlwind changes to come." Doctorow is a successful science fiction writer, a founding editor (with Frauenfelder) of Boing Boing, a fellow at the Electronic Frontier Foundation, and a leading open-source activist. Doctorow envisions in *Makers* a near future in which two genius trash hackers, Lester and Perry, blaze a new trail through the rubble of the old economy, where huge corporations are a thing of the past and small, indie start-ups populate abandoned strip malls and big box warehouses. Our heroes are scrappy DIY geeks with creativity to spare. Lester and Perry face several economic crises that are the undoing of larger operations, but they continually manage to marshal their resources, their skills, and their community in order to survive. Although the plot of *Makers* gets pretty complicated, Doctorow's central theme is clear: In the not-so-distant future, the colossal and increasingly brittle systems we currently deem too big to fail inevitably will. The skills needed for success in the future, as Doctorow conceives it, are adaptability, flexibility, creativity, and technical know-how.

In psychological parlance, the term for this ability to respond to crisis is "resilience," but it's a concept that is increasingly used by ecologists, economists, and systems designers as well. Resilience, explains Jamais Cascio of the Institute for the Future, means the ability of a person, institution, or system to "withstand sudden, unexpected

shocks" and to "recover quickly afterwards." He notes, following the stock market debacle of 2008, that "resilience implies both
strength and flexibility; a resilient structure would bend, but would
be hard to break."[61] One seed of resilience may be germinating in the
makers movement, that loose confederation of tinkerers, hackers, do-
it-yourselfers, crafters, and tech geeks who are experimenting with
both old and novel approaches to the material world. As John Robb,
military strategist and author of *Brave New War* (2007), puts it:

> In almost every resilience scenario I can imagine, there seems to be
> an intense need for people that can fix, repurpose, replicate, or build
> from scratch machines, systems, and tools. . . . If you don't have people
> in your community, group, gang, or tribe that can do this, you only have
> two options: either a bare bones existence (hardscrabble) or a preda-
> tory one. The reverse is also true. The better and more innovative your
> hackers are, the wealthier and safer your community will be.[62]

If we can call the makers movement a movement at all, it is not a typical
one. Although makers' discourse does protest the black-box technology of our consumer goods as well as the "vast and impersonal" system
that controls their life cycle, this critique is merely a jumping-off point
for the real focus of their work. Dissent or negation of the status quo
accounts for little of the motivating rhetoric of the community. Maker
culture is about doing it yourself or doing it with others. In its loftiest
rhetorical moments, it highlights values of openness, collaboration,
and flexibility; it champions human-scale technology. It is animated
by a karma system or reputation economy, in which makers are more
interested in making a contribution than making a profit. That said,
profits are being made by maker businesses. Makerbot Industries,
which makes 3-D printers you can assemble yourself, was bought in
2013 by Stratasys. Subscription-based hacker and maker spaces are
doing a brisk business in many major cities. The 2018 Creative Toy of
the Year award was given to littleBits, which sells open-source modular
electronics the size of Legos that snap together with magnets, allowing

users to make any manner of customizable gadgets. The company's mission is "put the power of electronics in the hands of everyone, and to break down complex technologies so that anyone can build, proto-type, and invent."[63]

Maker culture, in my observation, is not opposed to capitalism. Rather, it is tinkering under the hood of those engines that make capitalism run, demystifying their inner workings, and experimenting with the possibility of an alternative form of consumption and scale, one that works to make our technologies appropriate, "as if people mattered," to cite E. F. Schumacher's famous phrase.[64] To succeed, this future would have to incorporate technical know-how with big-picture or whole-earth thinking, as Stewart Brand might put it. It remains to be seen what the future of the DIY movement will bring. As Tim O'Reilly, founder of O'Reilly Media, explains, "For the last few decades, we have associated technology with a world that is increasingly virtual. What the makers are telling us is that the *physical world* is the next frontier of technology."[65]

Lest we think maker culture is all bearded guys in Seattle work-shops or tattooed women with cat's-eye glasses knitting sweaters in Brooklyn, let us conclude with a brief look at the next generation of makers. One of the most promising aspects of the maker movement is how evangelical it is about the importance of starting young. Makers, through a variety of fairs, classes, and workshops, are reaching out to kids to share their tools and their know-how. "Maker space" not so long ago may have conjured up the image of a chaotic workshop filled with adults tinkering with power tools, 3-D printers, and laser cutters. Today it's part of the standard curriculum in K–12 classrooms around the United States. After-school maker clubs are common, as are des-ignated tech labs in districts that can afford them, and roving maker space buses that visit schools for the day, letting kids sink their hands into a fun project. Of course, the goal for schools is to deliver STEM through the backdoor, turning science and technology lessons into child's play—not that there's anything wrong with that.

Consider, too, Minecraft, the best-selling video game of all time, in which players are free to explore an open terrain, locate and harvest materials, and build elaborate structures from digital blocks, all while fleeing skeletons and zombies. In 2014, Microsoft purchased Minecraft's publishing company for $2.5 billion. It's striking that countless hours and dollars have been spent on a game that is essentially just a series of blocks—what many people describe as interactive Legos. The educational benefits of playing Minecraft are celebrated by educators, and the game is regularly being used in classroom lessons. Online curricula and articles for teachers about how to use it effectively are everywhere. Multiple books have been published about how to best use Minecraft as a teaching tool. Math teachers are using it to teach ratios and proportions. Science teachers are using it in lessons on quantum mechanics. It's being used in history, geography, and even language arts.

Although Minecraft can be used to teach these traditional subjects, it's the game's nonlinear sandbox quality that provides such abundant opportunities for experiential learning as kids creatively explore the world, try things out, fail, try something else, and so on. This type of open-ended play encourages divergent thinking, in which a given problem has multiple possible solutions, forcing players to open their minds to new possibilities, within specific constraints. "Beyond the subject-specific knowledge that they gained," says one fifth grade teacher who used Minecraft in her class, "I was thrilled to see them taking initiative and working collaboratively on the tasks."[66] Because Minecraft isn't competitive, it inspires the maker crafting ethic of working together to accomplish something great. Like many modern crafters, they share the worlds they've built and the techniques they used with others, in thousands of online walk-through videos explaining their process. In addition to this sharing spirit, Minecraft offers opportunities to hone other skills that makers and crafters claim make their processes so valuable. It requires problem solving through trial and error. It asks players to consider parameters of the external realities they find themselves in. It demands patience as one works through a larger iterative process. As my teenage daughter, Lainie, put it when I asked her why she likes Minecraft, "It's cool. It takes time, and it's hard."

The making one does in Minecraft is obviously not making things by hand, which, as we've seen, does have its own valuable benefits. But many of the cognitive skills it cultivates are clearly transferable as kids move from the world of bits to the world of atoms. Coupled with the dramatic increase in recent years of hands-on, maker space–influenced educational environments, this pedagogical trend toward experiential learning offers a refreshing alternative to the "teach to the test" strategy that has dominated education in recent decades. The choice is between passing on to young people a mode of engaging objects dominated by a narrow sense of consumption, of getting it right, and one in which they are active participants experimenting with a creative, iterative process in which failure is a feature, not a bug.

Conclusion

Expanding and Intensifying the Value(s) of Objects

The way we attach to objects, how we assign them value, has evolved as capitalism has evolved. Marx was focused primarily on systems of production and the relationship between labor and capital. Objects were central to his analysis, but more because he was outlining the structure that allowed them, in their commodity form, to obscure the realities of the laborer and the social relations of life under industrialization. Under earlier modes of capitalist production, the use value that objects provided their producer shifted to the exchange value they could fetch from a consumer in the marketplace. To the extent that consumers were of interest to Marx, it was in their role as buyers who remained ignorant of the secret formula that gave commodities their worth, and the reality that exchange value had come to supplant use value.

Today things have grown more complex. Addressing the political and environmental implications of consumerism is more challenging than merely alerting consumers to the hidden world of labor and production behind the products they buy—if it was ever that straightforward. Since Marx's writings in the latter half of the nineteenth century, those theorizing the triumphs and pitfalls of human agency in relation to the marketplace have grappled with the changing role and character of objects. Marx's labor theory of value, astute as it was in his time, no longer explains the multitude of ways capitalism generates value. In the twentieth century, theorists turned their attention to the social, communicative role of objects. Writing at the dawn of the last century, social economist Thorstein Veblen, for example, theorizes about the cultural capital generated through practices such as conspicuous consumption and the emergence of luxury goods that were valuable primarily for the class status they demonstrated. Decades later, Jean Baudrillard's work on the rise of consumerism in *The System of Objects* (1968) and *The Consumer Society* (1970), together with similar projects by others such as Guy Debord, Pierre Bourdieu, and Georges Bataille, who theorized the different ways we consume and what they might mean, were vital augmentations to a Marxist approach concerned primarily with use and exchange. These thinkers signaled a crucial turn by calling our attention to the social functions of luxury, excess, and the emerging cultural practices devised to deal with capital's surpluses.

Rather than a simple formula to be tinkered with or updated, today value is better understood as a network or a constellation of aspects—material, political, affective, and symbolic—that we must consider carefully if we hope to intervene in the current system that produces waste nearly as fast as it produces products. As foundational as the early scholarship on the consumer society has been, capitalism continues to evolve and adapt, to carve out new forms of value and produce new desires. Today, surplus consumption, as Gernot Böhme points out, is no longer the purview of elites only: "Our period might be regarded as a new Baroque," he writes. "Surplus consumption is seldom referred to today as *luxury* or *extravagance*, because it is no longer bound up with certain privileges or limited to certain classes, but is now taken for granted as a universal standard of living."[1] Consider, for example, the number of toys children in the industrialized world own. According to one British study of three thousand families, the average child owned 238 toys but played regularly with only twelve. Even though child psychologists insist that having too many toys actually hinders children's creativity, their desire to collaborate with others, and the pleasure they derive from individual playthings, toy sales continue to escalate year after year. Punctuating Böhme's point, child development scholar David Elkind observes that in the past fifty years or so, mass production has made it a reality that "even low-income children today have more toys than children of earlier generations. Once given to celebrate birthdays and Christmas, toys are now routinely purchased all year long."[2] Economic privilege may allow some kids to have more expensive stuff than other kids, but they don't necessarily have more. Indeed, in many parts of the world, scarcity isn't the problem that needs to be resolved; abundance is.

As I have suggested throughout this book, understanding the plight of objects in an age of aesthetic capitalism requires a reimagining of objects beyond their function as tools for our use, as units of exchange, or as signs that afford us prestige or cool by way of the representational efforts of marketers. There was a time not so long ago when people consumed largely based on need; they disposed of objects only when they had been fully consumed, often after various repairs. Earlier forms of capitalist economics were, as Marx and Hegel before him would argue, about a system of needs, but since then, as Böhme observes, they have been increasingly transformed into desires. Today's capitalism depends on this cultural shift from need to desire if it is to continue to grow, as its systems of production and distribution have evolved to such a degree it can offer more things than we could ever need. But for consumption to continue to surpass mere needs, we must endlessly want. This is achieved through an aesthetic logic that permeates every aspect of daily life, from those stylish staplers, toilet bowl brushes, and vegetable peelers on offer at Target, as well as the endless deluge of objects that seemingly serve no purpose whatsoever, other than to stimulate desire. Importantly, however, unlike need, desire is, by nature, insatiable. "This is because desires cannot be permanently satisfied, but only temporarily appeased," Böhme writes, "since they are actually intensified by being fulfilled. . . . The importance of these forms of surplus consumption should not be underestimated."[3] Consumer culture scholar Arthur Asa Berger concurs that this insatiability is a necessary precondition for consumer capitalism's survival: "We need people to be relatively happy with their purchases, but not so happy that they don't continually explore new avenues of self-fulfillment through consumption. Consumer culture always leaves them wanting that little bit more, that indefinable something that will lead to genuine happiness."[4]

This incessant manipulation and ratcheting up of consumer desire is a significant contributor to the speed with which objects are flowing through the system. If factories can produce things more efficiently and cheaply than ever before, and if complex distribution systems can deliver them across the globe in a matter of days, then designers and marketers are tasked with cultivating surfaces and stories that both intensify their attractiveness and accelerate the waxing and waning of their cachet. Unfortunately, when these things no longer spark joy or adequately arouse desire, they most often become trash, the accursed share, discarded into our already full landfills and oceans.

Today we're seeing new forms of value emerge as objects open up, allowing us to experience more directly their biographies, processes of manufacture, and potential uses and connections. In the previous chapters, we have seen the work of some designers who are grappling, at a material level, with some of the same issues critical theorists have been addressing philosophically. Recall Korean designer Hyerim Shin's "Be My Mother" project, in which she creates household objects that expect something of us, call attention to their own needs, and, in a crafty violation of norms, demand that we do their bidding. Or consider again the work of those engaging in emotionally durable design who marry form and substance in such a way that objects become authors of their own autobiographies, absorbing, rearticulating, and expressing their use patterns, their interactions, and their shared existence with their human and nonhuman interlocutors. On their own, such projects may be insufficient to upend the human hubris Jane Bennett rightly condemns, but as explorations into the subtle ways objects may invite a shift in perception, they offer compelling and, importantly, accessible, case studies in the agency of objects.

Other environmentally oriented designers and engineers are working to reimagine the agency of objects in ways related to but outside the scope of this study. Designers deploying methods of biomimicry, for example, use the natural world's expert capacity to adapt processes and objects to suit specific needs and conditions as models for a more sustainable approach to problem solving. Others are designing modular objects for things like homes and electronics. Modularity can reduce waste during the production process, but it can also extend the use value of objects; broken or outdated parts can be swapped for new ones without having to discard the whole unit.

Regenerative design, better known as cradle-to-cradle (C2C) design, offers a powerful rethinking of the traditionally linear cradle-to-grave trajectory of most objects. Instead of merely slowing the demise of objects through reuse or recycling, C2C advocates William McDonough and Michael Braungart suggest that we can design objects (at a formal and material level) with their future end state in mind. A central premise is that consideration of the end of an object's usefulness must be written into its design from the beginning, and its components should be understood as either technical nutrients (which can be fed back into the industrial cycle) or biological nutrients (which can safely be fed back into the environment). Much ecodesign, known as downcycling, intervenes in the middle of an object's life cycle and so has little control over its overall environmental impact. For example, designing rugs woven from used plastic water bottles may usefully repurpose items that would otherwise be discarded, but this intervention does nothing to address the fact that the cheap plastic source material continues to off-gas in one's living room.[5] By considering the impacts of objects at all their various stages, C2C attempts to create the conditions for upcycling in which the material components of objects may become fodder for future iterations.

Further, economists and policy makers are reimagining the life cycle of objects as one remedy to the environmental crises in which we find ourselves. Although this important work is outside the scope of this study on consumers' relationships to objects, readers with a policy bent will be interested in the creative work being done, for example, by those advocating for a circular economy, which encourages designing out waste and pollution, keeping existing products and materials in use, and regenerating natural systems.[6] Other like-minded projects include industrial ecology and natural capitalism, popularized by the books and ideas of Paul Hawken and Amory and Hunter Lovins. In addition to these systems-level approaches, many manufacturers on the ground are increasingly enacting product stewardship programs, in which the designers and producers of durable goods take responsibility for not just the environmental impacts of the production and distribution processes but also for the end-of-life management of the goods they sell. The nonprofit Product Stewardship Institute, among others, promotes product stewardship legislation that will hold manufacturers' feet to the fire and require them to take greater responsibility for the impacts of the things they produce. Retailers in a variety of categories, including electronics (Best Buy, Costco) and apparel (Madewell, Eileen Fisher), have instituted their own take-back programs in which they accept and recycle used goods purchased in their stores.

These various projects—which represent only some of the productive ways people in different fields are attempting to repattern the life cycle of objects—represent a wide array of efforts invested in understanding the philosophical and practical contributors to material waste. This book has focused less on judging or adjudicating the value of any of those aforementioned efforts and more in facilitating those projects by enriching our understanding of how objects and subjects interact in the process of attachment, and the various modes and moments in which attachment obtains. By doing so, we can better consider how our ambivalence about the meaning of objects is exacerbating the waste epidemic, and it will also help us identify how different modes of attachment can open up and disclose the larger story of their life cycle, thereby revealing, extending, and deepening opportunities for connecting with the manufactured world around us.

Multiplying the Value of Objects

The cases in this book highlight different moments and modes of engagement between humans and the objects we make and use—and, it might be said, that make and use us. These modes of engagement offer opportunities for intensifying our attachment to these objects, to see them from slightly different angles, and to value them in varying and nuanced ways. The goal is not, I hope it goes without saying, to attach to such a degree that we never get rid of anything. Instead, it is to look for those practices that might encourage a deeper or different form of attachment, emerging as an outgrowth of a sense of our connectedness to their past and responsibility for their future. Attachments are not necessarily permanent, nor should they be. Attachment simply connotes connection. Taking advantage of these opportunities to connect subject and object, to define each by way of the other, may help open objects up, revealing to us their larger stories, surfaces, and substances.

No doubt for some scholars deep in thing theories, new materialisms, object-oriented ontologies, and similar attempts to rethink the object, this focus on attachment may seem overly anthropocentric. From my perspective, as a scholar of rhetoric, I approach any analysis of the mutual plight of objects and humans through the pragmatic and practical tradition of a field of study that is, at the end of the day, primarily focused on how meaning-making practices affect human emotions, beliefs, and behaviors. Objects have a rhetorical agency, as do the human subjects who design, craft, and consume them. For a solution or new approach to consumer waste to be of any value at all, it needs to side not with one set or the other but with the intersection of the two.

To that end, I'd like to return to what I have outlined in this book as a kind of taxonomy of the variety of ways we determine or co-constitute value in objects within the current era of aesthetic capitalism. This taxonomy is certainly not exhaustive; nor are all its categories novel. But it is worth stepping back and taking stock of some of the different ways we might attach to (and detach from) objects in different contexts and at different stages in their life cycle. Doing so may allow us to identify rhetorical and material blockages as well as offer new avenues to pursue if we are to develop a consumer culture that doesn't continue to produce unfathomable mountains and tsunamis of waste.

A More Complicated Object Form

Once we dive deeper into the role of objects in consumer capitalism, new details and nuances complicate the Marxist definition of commodities and commodity fetishism grounded in a dialectic of use value and exchange value. Both are alive and well, to be sure, but capitalism is nothing if not a value-generating machine, and new and identifiable values have emerged, reconfiguring objects as a form, much as exchange value reshaped objects into commodities. These basic units of use and exchange have not just been joined by new values; they themselves have changed through a number of overlaps and amplifications. Exchange value is likely still king, even if few economists use the term these days. Indeed, the other values we've explored—sign, ritual, project, staging—are most often deployed for no other purpose than to increase exchange value, or what we today simply call price. Given that most of these other values trade primarily in aesthetics and emotions, no simple equation can identify their worth relative to other commodity objects.

Use value has evolved as well. As Marx points out, under capitalism, use values are put to work in the service of exchange "because, and in so far as, they are the material substratum, the depositories of exchange-value." But use value is not as instrumental as its name might suggest. Usefulness certainly refers to an object's ability to help you get something done—the potato is peeled, the nail hammered. But it is also the pleasure you might take from it on purely sensual or sentimental grounds. The ballerina figurine that makes you smile every time you see it is useful. As it conjoins with other values, use value continues to generate capital in ways that would likely be both familiar and strange to Marx. For example, rituals of use invoke commodities in practices that give them new meanings through, say, repetition. I like to use the same coffee cup every day, for example, even though I own several. Although I got it at Target and it has no sentimental value to speak of, it has a nice heft and a handle that suits me. Filling it each morning and taking it back to bed with me as I ease into the day feels like a small ceremony—a ceremony of my own making in which the cup is a crucial part.

A related mode of use value is regularly touted by advertisers, who for years now have been collectively enthusing, "Nowadays, it's all about brand experience!" Experiential marketing, as it's called, is exploring the rhetorical power of embodied experience (use) over traditional branding. As Morris Holbrook of the Columbia Business School puts it, "Value resides *not* in the product purchased, *not* in the brand chosen, *not* in the object possessed, but *rather* in the *consumption experience(s)* derived therefrom."[7] Corporate brands' shifting their emphasis from signs to experiences coincides with the popularity of online networks for collaborative consumption and for-profit subscription services for things typically owned, allowing members to borrow from online libraries of stock, such as Rent the Runway for designer gowns or Board Game eXchange for tabletop games. These services are still about actual things, of course, but they shift value to the usefulness or aesthetics that is experienced rather than acquired. The notion, popularized by *Wired*'s Kevin Kelly, that access is the new ownership is the central thesis of the sharing economy, and it is just part of a larger, growing cultural sensibility that is giving rise to new practices of use, attachment, and meaning.

Jean Baudrillard was one of the first to attempt to augment Marx's formulation with the addition of sign value—the idea that much of an object's value comes from what it symbolizes relative to the other objects available for consumption. As such, each object is a part of a larger system of objects, just as each word is part of a larger system of language. Understanding sign value remains hugely important, as it is the governing logic of branding, which is a prodigious generator of capital (and waste). As such, sign value has a powerful degree of influence in many of our consumer choices, and because it can be so fleeting and fickle, it may be the most pernicious of the values we place on objects. This is likely why sign value is a common target for environmental activists, who often launch campaigns intended to tarnish or reinterpret what they see as harmful corporate brand messages. Although sometimes successful, as I have argued elsewhere, these campaigns are not always the most productive rhetorical strategy in the face of the seductive powers of the advertising industry.[8]

Sign value contributes, in its most common manifestation, to a closing down of an object. When a shoe bears the symbolic Nike swoosh or a car the curved Lexus "L," that brand identity stands in for a variety of processes. It serves to situate the shoe or car relative to other manufacturers or distributors of shoes and cars, and in so doing it masks the absent reality of labor. But sign value is not coterminous with branding. A vintage good—where "vintage" is just a euphemism for the anachronistic charm some objects acquire with the passage of time—is also a sign of the object's place within the larger system of objects. The meaning many people attach to LPs, for example, may have less to do with their use than with vinyl's symbolic status as analog in a world increasingly defined by the ubiquity of digital streaming services like iTunes and Spotify. In other words, sign value represents the constitutive affirmation of a symbolic relationship between objects. If this has predominantly been used to facilitate the production of desire or to accelerate the logic of exchange, this is because of its application to this point, not necessarily its essential character as a value by which we attach meaning to an object.

Indeed, as we saw with crafting, the visible imperfections of handmade objects produce a sign value that positions the handmade in relation to the readymade, the artisanal to the mass produced. In doing so, the crafted object communicates or symbolizes that this object is the product of a development process and a history that distinguishes it from most consumer objects. Instead of mass production, instead of machines and/or machine learning, instead of the inaccessible genius of an industrial or fashion designer, these objects are the result of the practical, decidedly human know-how of craft. This includes the subjective selection of materials, the cultivation of technique, and the careful work of skilled hands. In effect, what craft symbolizes is an opening up, an explicit recognition of those moments in the life cycle of an object that proceed its acquisition or use. The crafted object may be valued for multiple reasons, but their signifying function as a document of the maker's process is often one of the most powerful. This admixture of project value and sign value offers a potent tonic to the ceaseless flow of fast design.

As Böhme has suggested, today's aesthetic capitalism depends on surplus consumption if it is to continue to advance. This means that intensifying our collective desire, for ever more luxury and extravagance, becomes its central project. For Böhme, the rhetorical strategy in service of this project is to generate desire by way of the display of commodities—what he calls staging value. The commercial exploitation of these displays is lucrative indeed, as "there are no natural limits to presentation, glamour and visibility. Each level, once reached, demands instead its further intensification."[9] Perhaps it makes sense that people like Donald Trump and Kim Kardashian and reality shows like Bravo's *Million Dollar Listing New York* (2012–; in which rich people haggle with other rich people over whether a Tribeca townhouse is worth $12 million or $13 million), command such rapt attention. They theatrically perform a heavily staged version of surplus consumption, coveted by some, renounced by others, but perpetually raising the extravagance bar nonetheless.

However, whereas for Böhme the term "staging value" serves as the central way of understanding the new value form for commodities under aesthetic capitalism, I suggest that although a rhetoric of exhibition and theatricality is no doubt important, we need to be careful not to afford staging status as the all-encompassing source of value, influencing both use and exchange. As I argue in chapter 2, the putting to use of an object, of the auratic quality it bestows, within a larger network of meanings and assumptions is better understood as something more akin to ritual than theatricality. Toward this end, it makes sense to restrict staging value to the increasingly sophisticated ways merchandisers are designing and displaying commodities as objects for our desire.

Take, for example, the gleaming stage of the Apple store. Upon entry, one feels immediately immersed in the atmosphere of the brand. Apple has attended to every detail to produce that sense of immersion, even adjusting the tilt of the Macbooks to precisely the same angle. One might think this is just for looks, explains a writer for *Forbes*: "That's partly true. The tables are uncluttered and the products are clean. But the main reason notebook computers screens are slightly angled is to encourage customers to adjust the screen to their ideal viewing angle—in other words, to touch the computer!"[10] The Macbooks are staged to invite interaction and to provide a multisensory experience, so we will begin to imagine them as our own. We see staging value at work in those carefully crafted seasonal endcaps at box stores, filled with Easter-themed hand towels and oven mitts, or the dining room table in the furniture showroom, complete with linens, flatware, and wineglasses, as if laid out in preparation for a trendy dinner party. It is at work in the ubiquitous sponsored content on blogs and Instagram feeds, in which the latest lines in fashion, tech, and home goods are staged within an endless stream of personal images of garden parties, bathroom refreshes, or guys' nights out. It's the signature scents being piped through mall stores like Abercrombie & Fitch, engaging shoppers at another sensory level.

The sophistication with which commodities are staged for our purchase is staggering, but it cannot fully account for the unpredictable uses, rituals, and projects in which those objects participate after their purchase. As we saw in chapter 4, staging value can be generated to other ends, those not necessarily in the service of capitalist expansion, thereby redirecting, rebooting, or extending the worth of objects. As Joshua Glenn and Rob Walker's clever Significant Objects project demonstrates, the sign value afforded by branding might be combined with the staging value of story or other modes of display, breathing new life into secondhand objects that otherwise might be seen as meaningless and utterly disposable. Similarly, although the thrift shop industry is countercyclical (that is, business gets brisker when times are tough),[11] many owners are finding novel ways of staging and restaging value, such as those in the United Kingdom and Japan using QR codes and handwritten notes from sellers to share an anecdote about an item's former life. Some use the age-old flea market strategy of purposefully leaving things a bit messy, staging the field in which bargain shoppers can enjoy the thrill of the hunt. Others offer elaborate and quirky themed displays, such as Old Hollywood Glamour or 1980s Horror Films. A friend of mine who in the early 2000s owned a beautiful vintage clothing store in State College, Pennsylvania, told me that after Brad Pitt wore them so well in *Fight Club*, those polyester butterfly-collared shirts from the disco era, previously of interest only at Halloween, started flying off the racks. She capitalized on the trend with a Tyler Durden–inspired mannequin.

Perhaps this is all just Merchandising 101, but generating desire for objects that already exist, objects someone else no longer wants, is worth our collective creativity. Imagine if we began looking for occasions to increase staging value at other points in the life cycle of an object, deploying the powerful rhetoric of presentation beyond point of purchase. We could grow accustomed to shopping our own garages and attics for long-forgotten items to enlist in new displays, or better yet, we could shop our neighborhoods at block parties organized for neighbors to meet and trade unwanted stuff. As these new forms of sign and staging value are shared across the vast social media networks, trends can potentially be driven in more productive directions, creating new meanings and values for things that help slow down the cycles that typically carry them to their graves with greater and greater rapidity. Staging value can certainly be blamed for much of the consumer waste we see, but it can also offer other possible points of connection in the relationship between people and stuff.

Walter Benjamin observes the ritualistic use of cult objects; their kind of ritual value perpetuates class distinctions that are based on access. In our current mode of aesthetic capitalism, an age in which technological reproduction is the modus operandi, ritual value is not just the privilege of the few. Even though (or more likely because) ritual value is no longer rooted in scarcity of access, consumers of all stripes use mass-produced objects in a variety of highly ritualized ways—as intimate collaborators in practices of self-expression and group affiliation, for example. This is not to mention all the rituals for sharing those practices publicly on the many social media platforms designed to do just that. Ritual value may often merely perpetuate staging value, picking up at home the work of merchandisers. Objects are, as Böhme suggests, given a particular look—in the enticing in-store display, HGTV makeover, or pictorial in *Country Living* that made them so tempting in the first place. Although staging is often an element of these new practices, it is not only or necessarily so. As consumers bring the staged object home, put it a new context, and embed it in one's own habits, the object participates in new rituals of display and meaning. Ritual value may often work in tandem with sign value or staging value, but as a concept and a value, it is not subsumed by them.

Collectibles, for example, provide their owners with a rich source of ritual value. Years ago, after high school, I worked in a small toy store that specialized in, among other things, Madame Alexander dolls. Before getting the job, I had never heard of Madame Alexander, a nearly hundred-year-old company that makes baby dolls, but also highly sought eight-inch miniatures, released in limited-edition series depicting famous movie actresses, literary characters, and American first ladies. Our Madame Alexander customers, mostly middle-aged white women, would arrive eagerly at the store on the days we received a new shipment. They would gently open the cornflower blue boxes, gingerly remove the layers of pink tissue, and inspect each doll carefully for defects before making their choice. Completing each set is often a powerful moment in the ritual, a closing ceremony of sorts—finally acquiring Glinda the Good Witch, the final installment in the Wizard of Oz series, for example. Of course, new series are initiated each year, which means there are always more limited editions to covet. One customer proudly showed me pictures of her dolls displayed in her home, in a curio cabinet her husband had built just for the collection. This was in the days before eBay, so I suspect the ritual of collecting Madame Alexander dolls has changed in the ways markets for all collectables have changed. Many of our Madame Alexander customers knew each other, mainly through our store, where the owner would occasionally host release parties, but I doubt many of them still purchase the dolls in brick-and-mortar environments. That said, new rituals and venues for acquisition, community, and display have emerged online. Now we have blogs, unboxing and haul videos, and Instagram feeds, where consumers document for followers the things they purchase, how they arrange them in their homes, how they display them on their bodies, and so on.

The rituals of collection that structure the consumption practices such as those of the Madame Alexander devotee keep these branded objects tightly held to the meanings promoted by the manufacturer. It is a version of ritual in which objects are encouraged to remain in their commodity form, and in which acquisition is often the central pleasure. But as with all these aesthetic values, the role of ritual value in the expansion of capital is not necessarily its only function. Those modular electronics I talked about earlier? They have real potential to expand the ways we view objects through a ritual of use encouraged by the objects themselves. By allowing users to swap faulty or outdated components for new ones instead of chucking the whole kit and caboodle onto the e-waste scrap pile, these rituals prolong the viability of objects and also undermine our tendency to see them as discrete and formally stable. Part of the ritual value they afford is augmented by the pleasures (and, yes, frustrations) of the assembly process. This is ritual value overlapping with project value, or what we might think of as the cultivation of a material literacy.

This literacy, refined through ritual, has the potential to recalibrate, however slightly, our engagement with things. It's practical to be able to swap out a broken or outdated component for a new one. But it may also habitualize a set of practices in which new modes of desire and attachment emerge by encouraging an opening up of objects, making it apparent that any given instantiation is just that—a moment in a larger process of change. I wonder if Western European countries recycle nearly twice the waste as the United States not because they've made recycling simpler but because it's much more complicated. One must make an investment to participate. The Swiss, for example, have elaborate rituals for the recycling of consumer waste. On established days of the week, the average citizen in Zurich, for example, takes her glass recycling to the sidewalk, where there are clearly marked blue bins designated for brown glass, green glass, and clear glass. On another day, she stacks and bundles wastepaper, binds it with twine, and leaves it out in neat piles for pickup. On still another day, she bundles her cardboard; another day, metals; and so on. Plastics, as it happens, are returned to the grocery store, where there are sorting bins. For each piece, one must consider its material components and the appropriate way to discard it.[12] These elaborate sorting rituals may not necessarily be pleasurable for those who participate in them. But they do facilitate a potential source of meaning; they insert people into a practice in which the transitory nature of the objects they consume is experienced directly.

In chapter 3, we looked at the ways the IKEA business model—the efficient use of flat packs, outsourcing assembly to consumers—serves to interpellate consumers into the process of bringing mass-produced objects into being. This produces a form of attachment that is an outgrowth of what is now popularly known as the IKEA effect. People attach to an object they put together themselves because it becomes something of a document, a memento of one's own effort. Such objects have what I term project value, because their owners report experiencing a palpable sense of investment for having played a modest yet crucial role in the thing-making (and meaning-making) process. Further, as evidenced by the creative interventions of IKEA hackers, because consumers encounter IKEA furniture in its inchoate state—slabs of particleboard and hardware—opportunities arise for them to be imagined differently, in ways that produce both utility and pleasure. Project value may produce meaning, but it also produces a certain know-how. Granted, putting together a KALLAX shelving unit is hardly rocket science. Still, seeing objects emerge from a set of modular components, through one's own labor, does open up new opportunities for participation. The point is not to say that IKEA itself offers anything resembling a realistic path to waste reduction; it is simply to suggest that any opportunity to relate differently to objects creates possibilities for new points of intervention to emerge.

More significantly, the project value we see produced in the crafting and making process, explored in chapter 5, encourages a dynamic connection between people and objects. These practices may begin with simply admiring the work of a master crafter, which may lead to a trip to the lumber store or registering for a knitting class at a local yarn shop to give it a go oneself. Although these materials—lumber, yarn—are themselves products of industrial capitalism, our engagement with them is altered as we conceive our project and source its components. We begin thinking of them from an angle different from that of simply a consumer. It's possible the synthetic yarn one buys at Michael's to knit a scarf was made in a factory in China. Some might say that following a pattern found online to turn that yarn into a scarf is no more making something than putting together an IKEA chair, that it's just the assembly of mass-produced goods. However, as more and more millennials have gotten into knitting, for example, there's been an increased interest in related skills, relevant earlier in the material life cycle, such as dyeing and spinning wool fleece, even raising sheep, and a growing popularity in buying and making textile arts of all kinds.

Values as Modes of Engagement

As I hope the above taxonomy of values demonstrates, the value that inheres in the act of consumption is more nuanced and multifaceted in today's aesthetic capitalism than it was when Marx issued the first systemic critique of the capitalist system and the commodity form. Some capitalize on our participatory impulses, some elicit the sheer pleasure of a smooth surface or elegant interface, and others weave objects into compelling stories that imbue them with aspiration or nostalgia. If anything, objects are getting better at doing these things—at least in one part, the power of design. The simple reality is that corporate attempts to perpetually intensify our desire for the products of industry are becoming more sophisticated, pervasive, and corporeal. Many of them operate beneath our radar or, alternatively, have so ostentatiously saturated our everyday lives they're essentially invisible. But approaching these various forms of value as merely the secret machinations of capital that must be critiqued and exposed for what they really are is not our only or best choice if we wish to respond to them in a useful way. It's also true that every value, every evocation of desire, is also a prospective source of attachment and a point of connection. Desire is a funny thing. It's a powerful energy, what Gilles Deleuze famously calls a "productive force" that cannot always be predicted or controlled. It's difficult to confront it by way of the negative case.

There is both a rhetorical and material dimension to our relationship with objects, and they are not easily separated. Although they may have always been connected to some degree, in today's aesthetic capitalism, the rhetoric of form and function as well as the interplay of the symbolic and the material are intimately intertwined. If I am a designer, how I conceive my project symbolically—for example, my argument about how best to solve a problem, or my advocacy for a particular practice or habit, or my desire simply to amuse people with a subtle yet clever violation of their expectations—will influence the choices I make materially: about its form, the appropriate source materials, its function. Yet design—giving objects a particular form for a particular function—also influences our symbolic apperception of it. And on it goes.

I have attempted to outline the ways in which objects might be seen as a constellation of values. These values are not mutually exclusive. Sometimes ritual intensifies use. Other times, investing oneself in a project generates a new form of sign value. These values overlap and augment each other, and they affect our esteem for them in the process. In order to understand the meanings of objects and the conditions that induce attachment to objects in aesthetic capitalism, we must experiment with the possibilities these various values afford. They are not under the control of CEOs and marketers alone. Everyday consumers participate regularly in processes of design, influence, making, and attachment. The important question to ask throughout this process is whether a particular form of attachment will contribute to or ameliorate waste. It is, as I have suggested before, an issue of inheritance—of what we choose to inherit through the acts of design and consumption. When we consume objects, what type of material and symbolic systems do we wish to inherit? Those that close objects down and bind them in their commodity form? Or those that open objects up, revealing new possibilities for sustainable consumption?

There are at least two versions of design that offer different approaches to the phenomena I have explored in this book: meaning, attachment, and value. One version of design, and the one most predominant in our current consumer culture, appears to be an attempt to close things down, to suture the breach between symbolic and material reality so tightly that an object can only mean one thing and can only be valued in one way. The value of a Coach handbag, for example, comes from the sign value of the Coach brand, a value in which Coach has invested dearly for decades. Brands can and do inspire long-term loyalty, of course. Sign value can be lasting, even for generations, especially for heritage or prestige brands. But the engine behind the sign power of brands is their ability to create attraction and desire at point of purchase, that crucial moment about midlife for many objects, when they sit beckoning us from the store shelf or the showroom floor. People can and do mess with the signifying power of corporate brands, with varying degrees of success, and doing so is sometimes the most appropriate way to intervene. But in today's immersive, somatic, affective world of design, a rhetorical strategy that asserts itself on only the semiotic plane cedes crucial terrain and neglects fertile ground for change.

Instead of treating design as a stylistic add-on, further binding objects to their role as signs, there is another version in which design is constitutive of objects themselves. This has potential to open objects up, to showcase and intensify the ways that they, and we, are incomplete, unstable, and susceptible to change—and perhaps even to illustrate that this is where our collective power lies. This approach encourages our participation, our influence, and our ability to effect change, even if no one of us can step outside this networked system of objects and order that change as if by fiat. It may invite consumers to begin seeing the subject–object relationship as one instantiation, one transitory moment that we may come to recognize as part of a larger web of meaning and matter that connects us all. This approach operates in both the symbolic and material dimension of objects, and it must be the domain of both designers and consumers. It would be far too simplistic to assume one approach to designing and consuming objects is the answer to the problem of consumption and environmental degradation. Minimalism, emotional durability, crafting, and 3-D printing, for example all offer interesting ways to experience objects in productive ways. But none of them alone solves for the waste epidemic—nor should we expect them to. The point here is to identify the rhetorical and material blockages to waste reduction, and to locate and explore alternate paths. It's not just thinking differently about objects but also about recognizing that there are choices that designers, advertisers, politicians, corporate executives, and consumers make about how we negotiate this symbolic and material network of which we and objects are a part—about how we produce the possibility of value, and with it attachment.

We need to put a thumb on the side of the scale that envisions a more robust mode of design and that offers us new and more thoughtful ways to value objects. The first step is not to call for less consumption (although that may be an important later step). It is to understand better what and how we consume, and what inheritance we commit to when we purchase a particular object. The way we talk about things has real material effects, and the way we design things has real rhetorical effects. It goes both ways. This is a clarion call to scholars, designers, activists, makers, and consumers to think about focusing on an approach to design that opens up the object as an entity with its own life cycle—extraction, design, manufacture, marketing, distribution, acquisition, use, reuse, discardment or dissasemblage, and so on. The more we understand the larger story of the lives of objects, even if we only experience a part of that life, the better we can make decisions about how we use and relate to them.

One of the ways we can open things up is by thinking through where the various object values I have discussed throughout this book get instantiated within the life cycle of the objects. The chart on the next page maps the stages in the life cycle of objects in which, both presently and hypothetically, different object values might adhere. I offer this beginning sketch of a heuristic that may help us—scholars, designers, consumers, makers—think about opportunities for attachment and meaning. By focusing on attachment and meaning, we don't so much resist the temptations of consumer goods as see where else they might lead. The point is not necessarily to take back control but rather to explore ways our practices might intensify our connections with objects and ameliorate some of the problems of waste.

By considering different moments where value might be cultivated and attachment fostered, we can begin to explore possibilities for intervention, for extending or otherwise reimagining objects. What else might they be, beyond their current commodity formation? How might things be improved if we can see them as more than mere units of exchange, symbols, or objects of desire? As Georges Bataille demonstrates with his analysis of the accursed share, how we dispense of our excesses matters. It is a defining characteristic of the system we've created. Today we simply excise objects once their perceived value is gone. Because the vast majority of value and attachment is manifest at the point of sale, the most effective way to manage the remainder in this model has been to discard—out of sight, out of mind—so we can go buy yet more stuff. If we can instead imagine attaching and assigning value to our objects at different stages of their life cycle, managing the disposal differently, then we are potentially seeing objects in new ways. Scientist Barry Commoner, the "Paul Revere of ecology"[13] whom many consider the father of the modern

	Ideation/Design	Production	Distribution	Point of Sale	Use	Reuse	Discard
Use	X				X	X	?
Exchange	X	X		X			?
Sign			X	X	X	X	?
Stage	X			X	X	X	?
Project							?
Ritual		X		X	X		?

Charting opportunities for attaching value to objects.

environmental movement, in 1970 declared as the first law of ecology: "Everything is connected to everything else."[14] This book has been about understanding one particular connection that, however ephemerally, binds people and objects together in the act of attachment. In a world in which everything is connected, each ecosystem to the other, each object to a system of objects, each subject to its objects and vice versa, the only way *out of* our current accursed share might be *through*—not by discarding attachment but by engaging it, deconstructing it in order to construct it anew, and perhaps creating a different world with a different sense of waste and want.

Notes

Introduction

1. For a detailed compilation of Internet data on Kondo's popularity, see Molly McHugh, "How Netflix's 'Tidying Up with Marie Kondo' Cluttered the Internet," January 15, 2019, https://www.theringer.com/.

2. Kevin Rutherford, "Marie Kondo Re-enters Top TV Personalities Social Media Ranking Following Oscars Attendance," *Hollywood Reporter*, March 2, 2019, https://www.hollywoodreporter.com/.

3. Molly Young, "Gurus: Marie Kondo Will Change Your Life," The Cut, February 10, 2015, https://www.thecut.com/.

4. Jura Koncius, "The Tidying Tide: Marie Kondo Effect Hits Sock Drawers and Consignment Stores," *Washington Post*, January 11, 2019, https://www.washingtonpost.com/.

5. Cederström cited in interview with Marie Kondo, "What Marie Kondo Says about Our New Era of Self-Help," conducted by Claire Turrell, *Guardian*, February 22, 2019, https://www.theguardian.com/.

6. Christine Cole, "China Bans Foreign Waste—But What Will Happen to the World's Recycling?," *Scientific American*, October 21, 2017, https://www.scientificamerican.com/.

7. Daniel Hoornweg and Perinaz Bhada-Tata, *What a Waste: A Global Review of Solid Waste Management* (Washington, D.C.: World Bank,

2014), https://siteresources.worldbank.org/INTURBANDEVELOP
MENT/Resources/336387-1334852610766/What_a_Waste2012_
Final.pdf.

8. Joseph Stromberg, "Trashing the Earth: We'll Soon Make 11 Million
Tons of Solid Waste a Day," *Washington Post*, November 18, 2013,
https://www.washingtonpost.com/.

9. Laura Parker, "A Whopping 91% of Plastic Isn't Recycled," *National
Geographic*, December 20, 2018, https://www.nationalgeographic
.com/.

10. Laurent Lebreton et al., "Evidence That the Great Pacific Garbage
Patch Is Rapidly Accumulating Plastic," *Scientific Reports*, March 22,
2018, https://www.nature.com/.

11. Parker, "Whopping 91%."

12. World Economic Forum, "The New Plastics Economy: Rethinking the
Future of Plastics," January 2016, http://www3.weforum.org/docs/
WEF_The_New_Plastics_Economy.pdf.

13. "Apollo 8: Earthrise," NASA, June 25, 2013, https://www.nasa.gov/.

14. The United States, under President Donald Trump in 2017, pulled out
of the agreement, presumably to protect American jobs.

15. Peter Sloterdijk, *Critique of Cynical Reason*, trans. Michael Eldred (1983;
Minneapolis: University of Minnesota Press, 1988).

16. *Waste Land*, dir. Lucy Walker, 2010. The trailer may be viewed at Lucy
Walker, "*Waste Land*—Official Trailer," YouTube, October 12, 2016,
https://www.youtube.com/.

17. Chris Jordan, "Turning Powerful Stats into Art," TED, February 2008,
https://www.ted.com/.

18. Chris Jordan, "Albatrosses Are Full of Our Plastic: An Interview with
the Directors of *Midway*," interview conducted by Whitney Mallett,
Motherboard Blog, September 12, 2013, https://motherboard.vice
.com/.

19. Eugene Rosa, "Review of Chris Jordan's Photographic and Computer
Image Exhibition: Running the Numbers," *Organization and Environment* 22 (2009): 327–33.

20. *Waste Land*.

21. Jane Bennett, *Vibrant Matter: A Political Ecology of Things* (Durham, N.C.: Duke University Press, 2010), xi.

22. Ian Bogost, "Materialisms: The Stuff of Things Is Many," Ian Bogost (blog), February 21, 2010, http://bogost.com/.

23. Levi Bryant, *The Democracy of Objects* (London: Open Humanities Press, 2011).

24. Diana Coole and Samantha Frost, *New Materialisms: Ontology, Agency, and Politics* (Durham, N.C.: Duke University Press, 2006), 6.

25. Coole and Frost, *New Materialisms*, 34.

26. Jane Bennett, *Vibrant Matter* (Durham, N.C.: Duke University Press, 2010), 6.

27. Bennett, *Vibrant Matter*, ix.

28. Bennett, *Vibrant Matter*, xii.

29. Bennett, *Vibrant Matter*, vii.

30. Jeffrey T. Nealon, *Post-Postmodernism, or The Logic of Just-in-Time Capitalism* (Palo Alto, Calif.: Stanford University Press, 2012).

31. Gernot Böhme, *Critique of Aesthetic Capitalism*, trans. Edmund Jephcott (Berlin: Mimesis International, 2017).

32. See excerpts from Shaviro's work in progress, "The Age of Aesthetics," at his blog, Pinocchio Theory, http://www.shaviro.com/Blog/.

33. Ferdinand de Saussure, *Course in General Lignuistics* (London: Open Court Classics, 1972).

34. Sherry Turkle, ed., *Evocative Objects: Things We Think With* (Cambridge, Mass.: MIT Press, 2011), 5.

35. Karl Marx, *Capital: A Critique of Political Economy*, trans. Ben Fowkes (1867; London: Penguin, 1992), 1:163.

36. Marx, *Capital*, 1:163.

37. Marx, *Capital*, 1:165.

38. I. I. Rubin, *Essays on Marx's Theory of Value* (New Delhi: Aakar Books, 2007), 5.

39. Georg Lukács, *History of Class Consciousness* (1923), section on reification, in *György Lukács, History and Class Consciousness: Studies in Marxist Dialectics*, trans. Rodney Livingstone (Cambridge, Mass.: MIT Press, 1971), 85.

40. Lukács, *History of Class Consciousness*, 86.
41. Martin Jay, *Marxism and Totality: The Adventures of a Concept from Lukács to Habermas* (Berkeley: University of California Press, 1984), 109.
42. Jean Baudrillard, *The Consumer Society: Myths and Structures* (London: Sage, 1998).
43. Guy Debord, *The Society of the Spectacle*, trans. Ken Knabb (Detroit, Mich.: Black and Red Press, 2002).
44. Jean Baudrillard, *For a Critique of the Political Economy of the Sign* (St. Louis, Mo.: Telos Press, 1981), 139.
45. Jean Baudrillard, *Ecstasy of Communication*, trans. Bernard Schütze and Caroline Schütze (Los Angeles: Semiotext(e), 2012), 80.
46. Jennifer Abel, "Too Much Stuff? The Self-Storage Industry Keeps on Growing," *Consumer Affairs*, December 2, 2014, https://www.consumer affairs.com/.
47. David Ferrell, "Self-Storage Industry Keeps on Keeping," *Orange County Register*, February 8, 2013, https://www.ocregister.com/.
48. Jon Mooallem, "The Self-Storage Self," *New York Times*, September 2, 2009, https://www.nytimes.com/.
49. Shaunacy Ferro, "The Scientific Reason You Won't Throw Your Stuff Away," *Popular Science*, April 30, 2013, https://www.popsci.com/.
50. "Clean for a Day," season 7, episode 12 of *Modern Family* (ABC, February 10, 2016).
51. Rob Walker, "Fun Stuff," *New York Times Magazine*, February 11, 2011, https://www.nytimes.com/.
52. Sarah Kessler, "Decluttering Your Life Is Not Just a Trend—It's Big Business," *Fast Company*, September 2, 2015, https://www.fastcompany .com/.
53. Barry Schwartz, *The Paradox of Choice: Why More Is Less* (New York: Harper Perennial, 2004).
54. Interview with Katie Kilroy-Marac, "Hoarding: Our Relationship with Stuff," American Psychological Association, YouTube, August 7, 2015, https://www.youtube.com/.
55. Dave Bruno, *The 100 Thing Challenge: How I Got Rid of Almost Everything, Remade My Life, and Regained My Soul* (New York: William Morrow, 2010).

56. "About Josh and Ryan," Minimalists (blog), https://www.theminima
lists.com/.

57. Ken Miguel, "Minimalists Find Happiness Living with Less," ABC
News, April 17, 2014, http://abc7news.com/.

58. Taryn Plumb, "Like Henry David Thoreau, but with Wi-Fi," *Boston
Globe*, December 19, 2012, https://www.bostonglobe.com/.

59. Joshua Fields Millburn and Ryan Nicodemus, "Less, Less, Less, Less,
Less, Less . . . ," Minimalists (blog), https://www.theminimalists.com/.

60. Jacoba Urist, "When the Gospel of Minimalism Collides with Daily
Life," *New York Times*, April 29, 2017, https://www.nytimes.com/.

61. Kyle Chayka, "The Oppressive Gospel of Minimalism," *New York Times
Magazine*, July 26, 2016, https://www.nytimes.com/.

62. Quoted in Urist, "When the Gospel."

63. Steve Kroeter, "Observations and the Aims of Design," Design 101,
n.d., https://web.archive.org/web/20110322050019/http://www
.design101.com/observations.pdf.

64. Bruce Mau, *Massive Change* (London, New York: Phaidon Press, 2004).

ONE The Dreams Stuff Is Made Of

1. Ruth Mugge, Jan P. L. Schoormans, and Hendrik N. J. Schifferstein,
"Product Attachment: Design Strategies to Stimulate the Emotional
Bonding to Products," in *Product Experience*, ed. Hendrik N. J. Schiffer-
stein and Paul Hekkert (Amsterdam: Elsevier Science, 2007), 425–40.

2. "Attachment," Lexico, https://www.lexico.com/.

3. Ruth Mugge, Hendrik Schifferstein, and Jan Schoormans, "A Longi-
tudinal Study of Product Attachment and Its Determinants," *European
Advances in Consumer Research* 7 (2006): 641–47, 430.

4. Seth Goden, *Tribes: We Need You to Lead Us* (New York: Portfolio, 2008).

5. Hendrik N. J. Schifferstein and Elly P.H. Zwartkruis-Pelgrim,
"Consumer–Product Attachment: Measurement and Design Implications," *International Journal of Design* 2.3 (2008).

6. Susan Schultz Kleine and Stacey Mentzel Baker, "An Integrative
Review of Material Possession Attachment," *Academy of Marketing
Science* 2004, no. 1, https://www.uwyo.edu/mgtmkt/faculty-staff/

faculty-pages/docs/baker/material%20possession%20attachment
.pdf.

7. Kleine and Baker, "Integrative Review."

8. Mugge, Schoormans, and Schifferstein, "Product Attachment," 436.

9. Jonathan Chapman, *Emotionally Durable Design: Objects, Experiences, and Empathy* (New York: Routledge, 2005), 24.

10. Susan Lepselter, "The Disorder of Things: Hoarding Narratives in Popular Media," *Anthropological Quarterly* 84, no. 4 (2011): 920.

11. Kilroy-Marac, "Hoarding."

12. David F. Tolin, et al., "Neural Mechanisms of Decision Making in Hoarding Disorder," *Archives of General Psychiatry 69 (8)* 833. The *Diagnostic and Statistical Manual of Mental Disorders*, 5th ed. (Washington, D.C.: American Psychiatric Association, 2013), defines "hoarding" thus: "The persistent difficulty discarding or parting with possessions, regardless of the value others may attribute to these possessions.... For individuals who hoard, the quantity of their collected items sets them apart from people with normal collecting behaviors. They accumulate a large number of possessions that often fill up or clutter active living areas of the home or workplace to the extent that their intended use is no longer possible." Quoted in PsychCentral.com, "DSM-V Changes: Obsessive-Compulsive and Related Disorders," May 29, 2013.

13. Bonnie Tsui, "Why Do You Hoard?," *Pacific Standard*, April 29, 2013, updated June 14, 2017, https://psmag.com/.

14. Randy O. Frost and Gail Steketee, *Stuff: Compulsive Hoarding and the Meaning of Things* (Boston: Houghton Mifflin Harcourt, 2011), 9.

15. David F. Tolin et al., "Neural Mechanisms of Decision Making in Hoarding Disorder," *Archives of General Psychiatry* 69, no. 8 (2012): 832.

16. Frost and Steketee, *Stuff*, 12–13, emphasis in original.

17. Frost and Steketee, *Stuff*, 67.

18. Frost and Steketee, *Stuff*, 70.

19. Frost and Steketee, *Stuff*, 70.

20. A. Whitton, Julie D. Henry, Jessica R. Grisham, and Peter G. Rendell, "Hoarding, Excessive Responsibility and Pathological Guilt: Symptoms

of Empathy in Overdrive?," *International Journal of Psychophysiology* 85 (2012): 321.

21. Gillian Ragsdale, "Hoarding and Empathy," *Psychology Today*, November 7, 2012, https://www.psychologytoday.com/.

22. Frost and Steketee, *Stuff*, 20.

23. Frost and Steketee, *Stuff*, 15.

24. Frost and Steketee, *Stuff*, 15.

25. "Why People Hoard," Understanding Hoarding, n.d., http://under standing_ocd.tripod.com/hoarding1_why1.html.

26. Frost and Steketee, *Stuff*, 105.

27. Hélène Cherrier and Tresa Ponnor, "A Study of Hoarding Behavior and Attachment to Material Possessions," *Qualitative Market Research* 13, no. 1 (2010): 19.

28. Interview with Kimberly Rae Miller, "'Coming Clean' about Growing Up in a Hoarding Household," NPR, July 29, 2013, https://www.npr .org/.

29. Frost and Steketee, *Stuff*, 101.

30. Lorraine (2010).

31. "Why People Hoard."

32. "Why People Hoard."

33. Frost and Steketee, *Stuff*, 137.

34. "Why People Hoard."

35. Frost and Steketee, *Stuff*, 101.

36. See, e.g., Christopher Harding, "Marie Kondo and the Life-Changing Magic of Japanese Soft Power," *New York Times*, January 18, 2019, https://www.nytimes.com/.

37. Muqing Zhang, "The Not-So-Subtle Racism behind the Marie Kondo Criticism," Paper, January 18, 2019, https://www.papermag.com/.

38. Marie Kondo, *The Life-Changing Magic of Tidying Up: The Japanese Art of Decluttering and Organizing* (New York: Penguin Random House, 2014), 41.

39. William Morris, *Prose and Poetry (1856–1870)* (Oxford: Oxford University Press, 1913).

40. Kondo, *Life-Changing Magic*, 160.

41. Kondo, *Life-Changing Magic*, 153.

42. Kondo, *Life-Changing Magic*, 81.

43. Kondo, *Life-Changing Magic*, 73

44. Kondo, *Life-Changing Magic*, 190.

45. Kondo, *Life-Changing Magic*, 130.

46. Kondo, *Life-Changing Magic*, 131.

47. Kondo, *Life-Changing Magic*, 61.

48. Kondo, *Life-Changing Magic*, 60.

49. Angelika Kretschmer, "Mortuary Rites for Inanimate Objects: The Case of Hari Kuyō," *Japanese Journal of Religious Studies* 27 (2000): 380.

50. Stewart Guthrie, *Faces in the Clouds: A New Theory of Religion* (Oxford: Oxford University Press, 1995), 3.

51. Lyall Watson, *The Nature of Things: The Secret Life of Inanimate Objects* (Merrimac, Mass.: Destiny Books, 1992), 12.

52. Tim Harford, "Why More and More Means Less," *Financial Times*, January 2, 2015, https://www.ft.com/.

53. Kondo, *Life-Changing Magic*, 38.

54. Katie Kilroy-Marac, "A Magical Reorientation of the Modern: Professional Organizers and Thingly Care in Contemporary North America," *Cultural Anthropology* 31, no. 3 (2016): 446.

55. Kilroy-Marac, "Magical Reorientation," 446.

56. Marie Kondo, *Life-Changing Magic—A Journal: Spark Joy Every Day* (Berkeley, Calif.: Ten Speed Press, 2015).

57. Rubin posted on her blog on May 31, 2016, "7 Reasons I Disagree with Marie Kondo's *The Life-Changing Magic of Tidying Up*" (https://gretchen rubin.com/). In short, it's too one size fits all. Her alternative? "Know yourself."

58. Kondo, *Life-Changing Magic*, 15.

59. Kondo, *Life-Changing Magic*, 5.

60. Kondo, *Life-Changing Magic*, 45.

61. Kondo, *Life-Changing Magic*, 114.

62. Kondo, *Life-Changing Magic*, 116.

63. Kondo, *Life-Changing Magic*, 47–48.

64. Kondo, *Life-Changing Magic*, 123.

65. Kondo, *Life-Changing Magic*, 123.

66. Bourree Lam, "The Economics of Tidying Up," *Atlantic*, May 13, 2015, https://www.theatlantic.com/.

67. Roland Barthes, *Camera Lucida: Reflections on Photography* (New York: Hill & Wang, 2010), 76.

68. Frost and Steketee, *Stuff*, 97.

69. Kondo, *Life-Changing Magic*, 114.

70. Frost and Steketee, *Stuff*, 134.

71. Kondo, *Life-Changing Magic*, 32.

72. Kondo, *Life-Changing Magic*, 41.

73. "A Spark of Spirit in Everything," CBC Radio, February 26, 2016, https://www.cbc.ca/.

74. "From Students to Improvements," season 1, episode 5 of *Tidying Up with Marie Kondo* (Netflix, 2019).

75. Kondo, *Life-Changing Magic*, 79.

76. Benjamin Noys, *Georges Bataille: A Critical Introduction* (London: Pluto Press, 2000), 103.

77. Georges Bataille, *The Accursed Share, Volume 1: Consumption* (New York: Zone Books, 1988), 49.

78. Bataille, *Accursed Share*, 55.

79. Bataille, *Accursed Share*, 66.

80. Noys, *Georges Bataille*, 108.

81. Kondo, *Life-Changing Magic*, 57.

82. Kondo, *Life-Changing Magic*, 26, 28, and 29.

83. Kondo, *Life-Changing Magic*, 29.

84. Kondo, *Life-Changing Magic*, 64.

85. Bataille, *Accursed Share*, 58.

86. For examples, see Kondo, *Life-Changing Magic*, 48, 60, 61, 69, and 70.

87. Kondo, *Life-Changing Magic*, 111.

88. Rob Walker, "Stuffed," *New York Times Magazine*, December 17, 2009, https://www.nytimes.com/.

89. Walker, "Stuffed."

90. Kilroy-Marac, "Hoarding."

91. Kilroy-Marac, "Magical Reorientation," 442.

92. Ian Hacking, *Mad Travelers: Reflections on the Reality of Transient Mental Illnesses* (Charlottesville: University Press of Virginia, 1998).

93. Interview with Gail Steketee, "When Stuff Takes Over," conducted by Vicky Waltz, *Bostonia* (Boston University alumni magazine), Summer 2010, http://www.bu.edu/.

94. Jane Bennett, "Powers of the Hoard: Further Notes on Material Agency," in *Animal, Vegetable, Mineral: Ethics and Objects*, ed. Jeffrey Jerome Cohen (Washington, D.C.: Oliphaunt Books, 2012), 237–69.

95. "Empathy," Merriam-Webster, https://www.merriam-webster.com/.

TWO   On Target

1. Jean Baudrillard, *The System of Objects* (London: Verso, 2005).

2. Bill Brown, "Thing Theory," in *Things* (Chicago: University of Chicago Press, 2004), 5.

3. Fredric Jameson, *Postmodernism, or The Cultural Logic of Late Capitalism* (Durham, N.C.: Duke University Press, 1991).

4. Rick Gomez, quoted in "Behind the Scenes of the Target Campaign that Serves Up New Brands and So Much More," Target Corporate, September 8, 2017, https://corporate.target.com/.

5. "Behind the Scenes," Target Corporate.

6. A writer for *Adweek*, for example, gushes that the issue is "the smartest and most exciting example of branded entertainment I've ever seen" and that "the iconography of the city is captured cleverly without a cliché in site [*sic*]." Barbara Lippert, "Hitting the Bull's-Eye," *Adweek*, August 22, 2005, https://www.adweek.com/.

7. Lewis Lazare, for example, calls the issue "the most jaw-dropping collapse of the so-called sacred wall between editorial and advertising in modern magazine history." Lazare, "Target, *New Yorker* Cross Line," *Chicago Sun-Times*, August 19, 2005.

8. Blogger Carrie Frye rightly notes that Target is often painted as a brute "with its dirty paws all over the lily-white, virginal *New Yorker* (with the related school of thought that *The New Yorker* is a bit of a whore to let it happen)." "A Few Notes on the Target Issue of the *New Yorker*," Tingle Alley (blog), August 20, 2005, https://www.tinglealley.com/. Indeed,

another writer, in a post on a popular New York media blog, writes only half-jokingly: "Oh, my darling *New Yorker*, sexy as can be. . . . I can't look at you. You have sold yourself utterly to Target and now as I turn your pages all I can see are its smeary fingerprints, branding you, carelessly claiming you for its own." Rachel Sklar, "My Blood Runs Cold: My Sexy *New Yorker*, Despoiled by Target," MediaBistro.com's FishbowlNY, August 16, 2005, https://web.archive.org/web/20060301143318/ www.mediabistro.com/fishbowlny/magazines/my_blood_runs_cold_ my_sexy_new_yorker_despoiled_by_target_24704.asp.

9. For a firsthand account of the *New Yorker*'s controversial embrace (under Tina Brown's editorship) of mainstream American popular culture, see John Seabrook, *Nobrow: The Culture of Marketing, the Marketing of Culture* (London: Methuen, 2000).

10. Quoted in Laura Rowley, *On Target: How the World's Hottest Retailer Hit a Bull's-Eye* (New York: Wiley, 2003), 58.

11. I refer to the slogan for Mizrahi's women's clothing line for Target: "Where Fifth Avenue meets Main Street, USA." Lynn Yaeger, "Target Audience," *Village Voice*, September 23, 2003, https://www.village voice.com/.

12. Virginia Postrel, *The Substance of Style: How the Rise of Aesthetic Value Is Remaking Commerce, Culture, and Consciousness* (New York: Harper Perennial, 2004), 5.

13. Target, "Our Focus on Design," n.d., https://web.archive.org/web/ 20120905041306/https://sites.target.com/site/en/company/page .jsp?contentId=WCMP04-031760.

14. Shaviro, "Try Another World," Pinocchio Theory (blog), June 4, 2006, http://www.shaviro.com/Blog/.

15. Target, "Our Focus on Design."

16. Gomez, quoted in "Behind the Scenes," Target Corporate.

17. Quoted in Edward Relph, *The Modern Urban Landscape* (Baltimore, Md.: Johns Hopkins University Press, 1987), 107.

18. Sarah Vowell, "From Bauhaus to Tract House," Salon, February 11, 1999, https://www.salon.com/.

19. Quoted in Vowell, "From Bauhaus to Tract House."

20. Daniel J. Naegele, "We Dig Graves—All Sizes," in *Commodification and Spectacle in Architecture: A Harvard Design Magazine Reader*, ed. William S. Saunders (Minneapolis: University of Minnesota Press, 2005), 100–102.

21. "Target's New Home Brand Elevates Everyday Items, without Breaking the Bank," Target Corporate, June 6, 2018, https://corporate.target .com/.

22. Quoted in Pallavi Gogoi, "How Target Found Its Grooviness," *Business-Week*, October 3, 2005, https://www.bloomberg.com/businessweek.

23. Peter-Paul Verbeek, *What Things Do: Philosophical Reflections on Technology, Agency, and Design* (University Park: Pennsylvania State University Press, 2005), 2.

24. Verbeek, *What Things Do*, 1.

25. Verbeek, *What Things Do*, 2.

26. Brown makes the point thus: "The story of objects asserting themselves as things, then, is the story of how the thing really names less an object than a particular subject–object relation." Brown, "Thing Theory," 4.

27. Donald A. Norman, *Emotional Design: Why We Love (or Hate) Everyday Things* (New York: Basic Books, 2004), 26.

28. Norman, *Emotional Design*, 10.

29. I want to acknowledge that this supposed depth may itself be the effect of a layering or folding of available surfaces, but I leave this discussion to the more adept Deleuzeans among us.

30. Nealon, *Post-Postmodernism*.

31. Shaviro, "The New," Pinocchio Theory (blog), June 10, 2006, http:// www.shaviro.com/Blog/.

32. Walter Benjamin, "The Work of Art in the Age of Its Technological Reproducibility" (1935), in *Selected Writings*, ed. Howard Eiland and Michael W. Jennings, trans. Edmund Jephcott et al. (Cambridge, Mass.: Belknap Press of Harvard University Press, 2002), 3:105.

33. Benjamin, "Work of Art," 3:105.

34. Mark Dery, *Culture Jamming: Hacking, Slashing, and Sniping in the Empire of Signs* (New York: Open Magazine Pamphlet Series, 1993).

35. Böhme, *Critique*, 46.

36. Nigel Thrift, "Re-inventing Invention: New Tendencies in Capitalist Commodification," *Economy and Society* 35 (2006): 281.

37. Brian Massumi, "Notes on the Translation and Acknowledgments," in *A Thousand Plateaus* (1980), by Gilles Deleuze and Félix Guattari, trans. Brian Massumi (Minneapolis: University of Minnesota Press, 1987), xvii.

38. Norman, *Emotional Design*, 11.

39. Natacha Lorena Poggio, "Making Sense with Design: A Taxonomy of Designed Experiences" (MFA thesis, University of Texas at Austin, 2006), 42.

40. Poggio, "Making Sense with Design," 42–43.

41. Quoted in Phil Patton, "For the Mall Rats, a New Piper," *New York Times*, January 14, 1999, https://www.nytimes.com/.

42. Channing Hargrove, "The Target Brand to Reach $1 Billion in One Year," Refinery29, November 6, 2018, https://www.refinery29.com/.

43. Quoted in Elizabeth Holmes, "Target Rejiggers Brands to Lure Shoppers," *Wall Street Journal*, July 1, 2017, https://www.wsj.com/.

44. Quoted in interview with Ellen Lupton, "Speaking Graphically with Ellen Lupton," conducted by Elizabeth Evitts Dickinson, Metropolis, March 20, 2006, https://www.metropolismag.com/.

THREE Some Assembly Required

1. Matthew Crawford, *Shop Class as Soulcraft: An Inquiry into the Value of Work* (New York: Penguin, 2009), 7

2. Susan Marks, *Finding Betty Crocker: The Secret Life of America's First Lady of Food* (Minneapolis: University of Minnesota Press, 2007), 168.

3. Harry Brignull, "'Just Add an Egg'—Usability, User Experience and Dramaturgy," 90% of Everything (blog), October 20, 2009, https://www.90percentofeverything.com/.

4. Dan Ariely, *The Upside of Irrationality: The Unexpected Benefits of Defying Logic* (New York: Harper Perennial, 2011), 84.

5. Michael I. Norton, Daniel Mochon, and Dan Ariely, "The IKEA Effect: When Labor Leads to Love," *Journal of Consumer Psychology* 22 (2012): 455.

6. GQ, "Ryan Reynolds Tries to Build an IKEA Crib," YouTube, September 21, 2015, https://www.youtube.com/.

7. Corinne Purtill and Quartz, "Why IKEA Causes So Much Relationship Tension," *Atlantic*, September 20, 2015, https://www.theatlantic.com/.

8. Quoted in John Pavlus, "How IKEA Designs Its (In)famous Instruction Manuals," *Fast Company*, October 28, 2015, https://www.fastcompany.com/.

9. John Durham Peters, *Speaking into the Air: A History of the Idea of Communication* (Chicago: University of Chicago Press, 2001), 118.

10. Peters, *Speaking into the Air*, 124.

11. "About," IKEA Hackers (blog), https://www.ikeahackers.net/.

12. "Hacking IKEA," episode 128 of the *99% Invisible* podcast, August 19, 2013, https://99percentinvisible.org/.

13. "Hacking IKEA."

14. "Hacking IKEA."

15. "Hacking IKEA."

16. Kelsey Campbell-Dollaghan, "Why IKEA Shutting Down Its Most Popular Fan Site Is a Giant Mistake," Gizmodo, June 17, 2014, https://www.gizmodo.com.au/.

17. Jules Yap, "Trip Update Part 1: Museums and Meatballs," IKEA Hackers (blog), September 25, 2014, http://jules.ikeahackers.net/.

18. Kenneth Burke, *A Rhetoric of Motives* (Berkeley: University of California Press, 1969), 55.

19. *Fight Club*, dir. David Fincher, screenplay by Jim Uhls (Los Angeles: 20th Century Fox, 1999).

20. The font was until recently a customized version of Futura that the company had used for over fifty years and was a key component of the IKEA brand. In 2009, it switched to Verdana, causing an uproar among IKEA purists and graphic designers. For more, see Lisa Abend, "The Font War: IKEA Fans Fume Over Verdana," *Time*, August 28, 2009, http://content.time.com/.

21. Martin Zwilling, "It's Time to Design Human Experiences, Not Just Products," *Forbes*, December 24, 2015, https://www.forbes.com/.

22. Mimi Hayton, "Some Assembly Required: Memorable Customer Experiences," Customer Think, June 4, 2013, http://customerthink .com/.

23. Slavoj Žižek, *The Sublime Object of Ideology* (New York: Verso, 2008), 28.

24. Žižek, *Sublime Object*, 29.

25. The "Gruen effect" is named after Austrian architect Victor Gruen, who pioneered the modern shopping mall. Gruen later disavowed such manipulative techniques.

26. Alan Penn, "The Complexity of the Elementary Interface: Shopping Space," paper presented at the Fifth International Space Syntax Symposium, Delft, Netherlands, http://spacesyntax.tudelft.nl/media/ Long%20papers%20I/alan%20penn.pdf.

27. "Life at Home," IKEA Corporate, https://www.ikea.com/.

28. Maria Pachaki, "The IKEA Experience: A Case Analysis of Experiential Consumption," unpublished manuscript, September 2013, https://www .researchgate.net/publication/256802795_The_IKEA_Experience.

29. Žižek, *Sublime Object*, 32

30. Ian Bogost, "The McRib: Enjoy Your Symptom," *Atlantic*, November 11, 2013, https://www.theatlantic.com/.

31. Lauren Collins, "House Perfect," *New Yorker*, October 3, 2011, https:// www.newyorker.com/.

32. "The Testament of a Furniture Dealer," IKEA, 1976, https://www.ikea .com/ms/fr_FR/media/This_is_IKEA/the-testament-of-a-furniture -dealer-small.pdf.

33. Tom Wolfe, *From Bauhaus to Our House* (New York: Farrar, Straus and Giroux, 1981), 1.

34. Wolfe, *From Bauhaus to Our House*, 1–2.

35. Interview with Ellen Ruppel Shell, "What's the Matter with IKEA: A Dialogue with Ellen Ruppel Shell," conducted by Megan McArdle, *Atlantic*, August 3, 2009, https://www.theatlantic.com/.

36. Cited in Tim Benton et al., *Architecture and Design, 1890–1939: An International Anthology of Original Articles* (New York: Whitney Library of Design, 1975), 149.

37. Walter Gropius, *The New Architecture and the Bauhaus,* trans. P. Morton Shand (Cambridge, Mass.: MIT Press, 1965), 54.

38. Jeff Carter, "Jeff Carter Talks about the Common Citizenship of Forms," talk and exhibition at Illinois Institute of Technology, video recording, June 12, 2011, https://vimeo.com/25292662.

39. Carter, "Jeff Carter Talks."

40. Carter, "Jeff Carter Talks."

41. Art Editor, "Art Break: Bauhaus vs. IKEA," New City Art, June 13, 2011, https://art.newcity.com/.

42. Carter, "Jeff Carter Talks."

43. Ellen Ruppel Shell, *Cheap: The High Cost of Discount Culture* (London: Penguin, 2010), 135.

44. Ruppel Shell, *Cheap*, 147.

45. Ruppel Shell, *Cheap*, 147

46. However, in autumn 2019, Forever 21 filed for bankruptcy, indicating the "fast" trend has its limits. Industry analysts cited the company's overly ambitious growth and e-commerce competition as the causes of its failure. See, for example, Irene Kim and Kaitlyn Wang, "At its peak, Forever 21 made $4.4 billion in revenue," *Business Insider*, September 30, 2019.

47. Collins, "House Perfect."

48. Ruppel Shell, *Cheap*, 142.

49. "Disposability Consciousness," interview with Julia Butterfly Hill, *GlobalOnenessProject*, https://www.globalonenessproject.org/.

50. Ruppel Shell, *Cheap*, 142.

51. Ruppel Shell, *Cheap*, 147–48.

52. Ariely, *Upside*, 84.

FOUR The Value of Story

1. Vance Packard, *The Waste Makers* (New York: Ig, 2011).

2. Caroline Tell, "The Marie Kondo Effect: A Closet's Loss, a Consignor's Gain," *New York Times*, August 4, 2015, https://www.nytimes.com/.

3. Jane MacDonald, "Tales of Things and Electronic Memory: Jane MacDonald at TEDx Bradford," March 30, 2012, at TEDx Talks, YouTube, November 5, 2012, https://www.youtube.com/.

4. Chris Speed, quoted in Rob Walker, "The Back Story," *New York Times Magazine*, September 3, 2010, https://www.nytimes.com/.

5. "About," Tales of Things, n.d., http://talesofthings.com/.

6. Lesley Ciarula Taylor, "Buy Colin Firth's Suit and He'll Tell You All About It," (Toronto) *Star*, August 9, 2011, https://www.pressreader.com/.

7. Frost and Steketee, *Stuff*, 44.

8. Frost and Steketee, *Stuff*, 45.

9. Bruce M. Hood and Paul Bloom, "Children Prefer Certain Individuals over Perfect Duplicates," *Cognition* 106 (2008): 455–62.

10. Nara Shin, "Tokyo's Pass the Baton Adds a Personal Touch to Vintage," Cool Hunting, November 19, 2014, https://coolhunting.com/.

11. Shin, "Tokyo's Pass the Baton."

12. Shin, "Tokyo's Pass the Baton."

13. Shin, "Tokyo's Pass the Baton."

14. Masamichi Toyama, "Interview with Masamichi Toyama Founder of Soup Stock Tokyo and Pass the Baton," Design Boom, December 16, 2015, https://www.designboom.com/.

15. "The Stories We Wear," Worn Wear (Patagonia corporate Tumblr), https://wornwear.tumblr.com/post/139618106460/ol-blue-jason -antin-golden-colorado-dear.

16. Roberta Naas, "Patek Philippe Celebrates 20 Years of Its Iconic Advertising Campaign," *Forbes*, December 9, 2016.

17. Significant Objects, http://significantobjects.com.

18. Joshua Glenn and Rob Walker, eds., *Significant Objects: 100 Extraordinary Stories about Ordinary Things* (Seattle, Wash.: Fantagraphics Books, 2012).

19. Aditya Chakrabortty, "At Christmas, It's the Thought that Counts," *Guardian*, December 21, 2010, https://www.theguardian.com/.

20. After demonstrating the value story could generate, Glenn and Walker curated two more collections of Significant Object stories, donating the proceeds to youth writing programs 826 National and Girls Write Now.

21. Glenn and Walker, *Significant Objects*, appendix.

22. Dorst quoted in Glenn and Walker, *Significant Objects*, 36.

23. Glenn and Walker, introduction to *Significant Objects*.

24. David Scher, "couch arm," in *Taking Things Seriously: 75 Objects with Unexpected Significance*, ed. Joshua Glenn and Carol Hayes (New York: Princeton Architectural Press, 2007), 86.

25. Mugge, Schoormans, and Schifferstein, "Product Attachment," 428.

26. Mugge, Schoormans, and Schifferstein, "Product Attachment," 428.

27. Mugge, Schoormans, and Schifferstein, "Product Attachment," 429.

28. Chapman, *Emotionally Durable Design*, 26.

29. Interview with Jonathan Chapman, "What Is 'Emotionally Durable' Design?," *Today Programme*, BBC Radio 4, February 9, 2013, https://www.bbc.com/.

30. Chapman, *Emotionally Durable Design*, 10.

31. "Product Introspection: Social Sculpture Denim," Visvim, December 14, 2009, https://www.visvim.tv/dissertations/product_introspection_social_sculpture_denim.html.

32. "Product Introspection."

33. Interview with Hiroki Nakamura, "Visvim's Hiroki Nakamura on the Price of His Clothes and 'Future Vintage,'" conducted by Jian Deleon, *GQ*, September 5, 2013, https://www.gq.com/.

34. Interview with Hiroki Nakamura, "How Visvim Creates 'Future Vintage,'" conducted by Xerxes Cook, *SSENSE*, https://www.ssense.com/.

35. Quoted in Douwe Draaisma, *Metaphors of Memory: A History of Ideas about the Mind*, trans. Paul Vincent (Cambridge: Cambridge University Press, 2001), 25.

36. Draaisma, *Metaphors of Memory*, 26.

37. Torafu Architects, "Gold Wedding Ring," Gallery Deux Poissons, n.d., http://www.deuxpoissons.com/.

38. Robyn Griggs Lawrence, *The Wabi-Sabi House: The Japanese Art of Imperfect Beauty* (New York: Clarkson Potter, 2004), 17.

39. Frog, "Aged to Perfection," Design Mind, September 9, 2011, https://designmind.frogdesign.com/.

40. Chappell Ellison, Etsy Journal (blog), https://blog.etsy.com/en/noted-the-aging-of-electronics/.

41. R. L. Rutsky, *High Technē: Art and Technology from the Machine Aesthetic to the Posthuman* (Minneapolis: University of Minnesota Press, 1999).

42. Ani DiFranco, "Pale Purple," *Ani DiFranco* (Righteous Babe Records, 1990).

43. Jonathan Chapman, "Meaningful Stuff: Toward Longer Lasting Product," in *Materials Experience: Fundamentals of Materials and Design*, ed. Elvin Karana, Valentina Rognoli, and Owain Pedgley (Oxford: Butterworth-Heinemann, 2013), 141.

44. Adrienne LaFrance, "Why eBay Tells Chinese Manufacturers What You're Searching For," *Quartz*, August 6, 2014, https://qz.com/.

45. "Men's Star Wars® Tie Fighter T-Shirt," Target, n.d., https://www.target.com/.

46. Dan Medeiros, "Distressed: Replicas, 'Vintage' Items, and New Old Stock," Dan Medeiros (blog), April 13, 2011, http://www.dan-medeiros.com/.

47. Quoted in Medeiros, "Distressed."

48. Quoted in Travis M. Andrews, "Nordstrom's Is Selling Jeans Caked in Fake Dirt for Hundreds of Dollars," *Washington Post*, April 26, 2017, https://www.washingtonpost.com/.

49. Mike Rowe, "This morning, for your consideration . . . ," Facebook post, April 24, 2017, https://www.facebook.com/TheRealMikeRowe/.

50. Kirsty Major, "Please, in the Name of All That Is Holey: Do Not Buy Pre-ripped Jeans," Vagenda Magazine, July 3, 2015, https://web.archive.org/web/20150708021908/http://vagendamagazine.com/2015/07/please-in-the-name-of-all-that-is-holey-do-not-buy-pre-ripped-jeans/.

51. Major, "Please."

52. Thomas Frank and Matt Weiland, eds., *Commodify Your Dissent: Salvos from the Baffler* (New York: Norton, 1997).

53. Jacob Brogan, "Stop Wearing Pre-distressed Denim Jeans Already," *Washington Post*, September 9, 2014, https://www.washingtonpost.com/.

54. Dominique Muller, "Breathless for Blue Jeans: Health Hazards in China's Denim Factories," IHLO, SACOM, Clean Clothes Campaign, and War on Want, June 2013, http://www.setem.org/media/pdfs/Breathless.pdf.

55. Muller, "Breathless."

56. Medeiros, "Distressed."

57. Hyerim Shin, "Be My Mother: Playful Home Appliance Robots," video, Hyerim Shin (blog), n.d., http://hyerimshin.com/.

FIVE The Handmade Tale

1. Roger Ebert, "Jiro Dreams of Sushi," Rogerebert.com, April 4, 2012, https://www.rogerebert.com/.

2. Silvia Killingsworth, "Perfect Sushi," *New Yorker*, March 9, 2012, https://www.newyorker.com/.

3. Jiro began making sushi at age nine.

4. Hammer in Hand Productions, "About the Show," Craftsman's Legacy, n.d., http://www.craftsmanslegacy.com/.

5. Etsy, "Handmade Portraits: Susan Gibbs, yarn harvester," YouTube video, 6 min. 31 sec., July 10, 2008.

6. "Colin the Chicken," season 1, episode 1 of *Portlandia* (IFC, January 11, 2011).

7. Other funny spoofs: Lauren Kodiak, "Watch This Hilarious Parody of Artisanal Food Makers," August 10, 2015, https://www.thekitchn .com/; Tim Nudd, "If You're Sick and Tired of Hipstery 'Maker' Culture, Watch This Hilarious Video Now," *Adweek*, February 18, 2016, https://www.adweek.com/.

8. David Sax, *The Revenge of Analogue: Real Things and Why They Matter* (New York: PublicAffairs Books, 2016), xiii.

9. Marcel Duchamp, "The Richard Mutt Case," letter to *Blind Man*, no. 2 (1917), rpt. in Charles Harrison and Paul Wood, eds., *Art in Theory, 1900– 2000: An Anthology of Changing Ideas* (New York: Wiley, 2002), 252.

10. ReadyMade online media kit, n.d., https://web.archive.org/web/ 20100328154031/http://www.readymade.com/mediakit.php.

11. Janelle Brown, "Do It Yourself," Salon.com, May 21, 2001, https:// archive.salon.com/mwt/style/2001/05/21/handmade/index.html.

12. Quoted in Brown, "Do It Yourself."

13. Quoted in Robert Gavin, "Everyday Hackers," *Boston Globe*, April 19, 2004.

14. Quoted in Gavin, "Everyday Hackers."

15. The Franklin Institute, "Benjamin Franklin's Glass Armonica," https://www.fi.edu/history-resources/franklins-glass-armonica.

16. Benjamin Franklin, *Autobiography of Benjamin Franklin* (Philadelphia: J. B. Lipponcott & Co., 1869), 274.

17. Richard Sennett, *The Craftsman* (New Haven, Conn.: Yale University Press, 2009), 268.

18. Dale Dougherty, *Free to Make: How the Makers Movement Is Changing Our Schools, Our Jobs, and Our Minds* (Berkeley, Calif.: North Atlantic Books, 2016), 162–63.

19. Dougherty, *Free to Make*, 162.

20. Guild of St. George, https://www.guildofstgeorge.org.uk/.

21. William Morris, *On Art and Socialism* (1884; reprint, New York: Dover, 1999), 129.

22. "William Morris (1834–1896)," Arty Factory, n.d., https://www.artyfactory.com/.

23. Fiona MacCarthy, "William Morris," *Oxford Dictionary of National Biography*, https://www.oxforddnb.com/.

24. William Morris, "Art for All," *Selections from the Prose Works of William Morris* (Cambridge University Press, 1931), 169.

25. Karl Marx and Frederick Engels, *Economic and Philosophic Manuscripts of 1844* (1932; Amherst, N.Y.: Prometheus, 1988), 72.

26. How to Make Everything, "Kyle the Leatherworker: Meet the Makers," YouTube, October 27, 2016, https://www.youtube.com/.

27. Joel Bukiewicz, "Made by Hand No. 2: The Knife Maker," Vimeo, https://vimeo.com/.

28. Bukiewicz, "Made by Hand No. 2."

29. Diana Budds, "6 Designers Explain Why Craft Still Matters in a Digital World," *Fast Company*, May 31, 2017, https://www.fastcompany.com/.

30. Peter Korn, *Why We Make Things, and Why It Matters: The Education of a Craftsman* (Dublin, N.H.: Godine, 2013), 30.

31. Korn, *Why We Make Things*, 29.

32. Crawford, *Shop Class*, 60.

33. Interview with Nick Offerman, "Nick Offerman on Why We Should Build Stuff," conducted by Jennifer Bogo, *Popular Science*, May 6, 2014, https://www.popsci.com/.

34. Interview with Larry Katz, "Get a Liberal Arts BA, Not a Business BA, for the Coming Artisan Economy," conducted by Paul Solman, PBS News Hour, July 15, 2014, https://www.pbs.org/.

35. Crawford, *Shop Class*, 29.

36. Press release, "Williams-Sonoma Expands Its Renowned 'Artisans Market' Program," Business Wire, January 15, 2016, https://www.businesswire.com/.

37. Press release, "Target and Designer Todd Snyder Celebrate Local Pride with a Series of Exclusive Collections," Target Corporate, July 15, 2015, https://corporate.target.com/.

38. The Italian automaker Fiat, the name sometimes derisively taken to be an acronym for "Fix It Again, Tony," has long been regarded by many as making stylish but poor-quality sports cars.

39. The song, recorded in 2003, was released posthumously on *American V: A Hundred Highways*. A quite different version of the folk traditional was recorded under the title "Run On" by Moby on his 1999 smash album *Play*.

40. Naomi Klein, *No Logo: Taking Aim at the Brand Bullies* (New York: Picador, 2000), 346.

41. Klein, *No Logo*, 346.

42. "Mazda Design: Car as Art," Inside Mazda, n.d., https://insidemazda.mazdausa.com/car-as-art/.

43. "How Can an Ancient Craft Inspire a Modern Design?," Inside Mazda, n.d., https://insidemazda.mazdausa.com/the-mazda-way/design/aluminum-trim/.

44. "Is the Best Instrument for Creating an Emotional Design, Human?," Inside Mazda, n.d., https://insidemazda.mazdausa.com/the-mazda-way/design/modeling-clay/.

45. "Artful Design Breathes Life into Every Detail," Mazda Feel Alive, https://www.mazdafeelalive.com/artful-design-breathes-life-into-every-detail/.

46. Offerman, "Nick Offerman on Why We Should Build Stuff."

47. Quoted in Carole Cadwalladr, Stewart Brand's Whole Earth Catalog, the Book that Changed the World," *Guardian*, May 4, 2013, https://www.guardian.com.

48. Mark Frauenfelder, *Made by Hand: Searching for Meaning in a Throwaway World* (New York: Portfolio, 2010), 25.

49. Crawford, *Shop Class*, 54.

50. Crawford, *Shop Class*, 7.

51. Gilbert.

52. Frauenfelder, *Made by Hand: Searching for Meaning*, 23.

53. Frauenfelder, *Made by Hand: Searching for Meaning*, 118.

54. Robert Grudin, "The Bakers Table," Design Observer, August 8, 2010, https://web.archive.org/web/20100816152143/http://observatory.designobserver.com/entry.html?entry=14218.

55. Crawford, *Shop Class*, 82.

56. Sennett, *Craftsman*, 20.

57. Mark Frauenfelder, *Made By Hand: My Adventures in the World of Do-It-Yourself* (New York: Portfolio/Penguin, 2011), 103.

58. Nick Offerman, "#Why I Make: Nick Offerman," Infosys Foundation USA, YouTube, June 19, 2017, https://www.youtube.com/.

59. Quoted by Sara Gottfried, "Knitting as Mantra," Dr. Sara Gottfried MD (blog), December 29, 2013, https://www.saragottfriedmd.com/.

60. Frauenfelder, *Made by Hand*, 57–58.

61. Jamais Cascio, "Resilience in the Face of Crisis," *Fast Company*, April 2, 2009, https://www.fastcompany.com/.

62. John Robb, "Are Hackers Essential to Resilience?," *Global Guerrillas*, November 4, 2009.

63. littleBits Electronics, https://en.wikipedia.org/wiki/LittleBits.

64. E. F. Schumacher, *Small Is Beautiful: Economics As If People Mattered* (New York: Harper Perennial, 2010).

65. Tim O'Reilly, "Maker Movement Gaining Recognition," O'Reilly Radar, January 11, 2008, https://www.oreilly.com/.

66. Saima Zaidi, "Minecraft in the Classroom," Teach Magazine, March/April 2016, http://teachmag.com/.

Conclusion

1. Böhme, *Critique*, 2.
2. David Elkind, *The Power of Play: Learning What Comes Naturally* (Philadelphia, Pa.: De Capo, 2007), 15.
3. Böhme, *Critique*, 11.
4. Arthur Asa Berger, *The Objects of Affection: Semiotics and Consumer Culture* (Amsterdam: Springer Nature, 2010), 100.
5. I borrow this example from my UW colleague, designer Kristine Matthews.
6. "Concept: What Is a Circular Economy?," Ellen MacArthur Foundation, n.d., https://www.ellenmacarthurfoundation.org/ circular-economy/overview/concept.
7. Morris Holbrook, *Consumer Value: An Analysis for Analysis and Research* (London: Routledge, 2002), 9, emphasis in original.
8. Christine Harold, *OurSpace: Resisting the Corporate Control of Culture* (Minneapolis: University of Minnesota Press, 2007).
9. Böhme, *Critique*.
10. Carmine Gallo, "How the Apple Store Seduces You with the Tilt of Its Laptops," *Forbes*, June 14, 2012, https://www.forbes.com/.
11. "Thrift Stores: Market Research Report," IBIS World, January 2017, https://web.archive.org/web/20170808210343/https://www.ibis world.com/industry-trends/specialized-market-research-reports/ consumer-goods-services/apparel-accessories-stores/thrift-stores .html.
12. For a detailed video demonstration, see Karflooie, "Bizarre Swiss Recycling Rituals," YouTube, May 17, 2012, https://www.youtube.com/.
13. "Environment: Paul Revere of Ecology," *Time Magazine*, February 2, 1970.
14. Barry Commoner, *The Closing Circle: Nature, Man, and Technology* (New York: Random House, 1971).

Index

Bergdof Goodman, 152

Berger, Asa, 214

Berger, Shoshana, 177–78

Berkus, Nate, 83, 95, 134

Bertelsen, Karen, 34

Besta media console, 117

Best Buy, 216

Better than Before (Kondo), 60

Betty Crocker, 100, 114, 126

Beuys, Joseph, 151

Beyoncé, 2, 160

Billy bookcases, 107, 128, 129, 130, 179

bingeing, 2, 3, 71, 72

Birkenstocks, 157

BJURSTA dining table, 121

Bloom, Paul, 137

Board Game eXchange, 219

Bogost, Ian, 16, 119

Böhme, Gernot, 20, 213, 224; staging value and, 93, 145, 221; surplus consumption and, 212

Boing Boing, 110, 202, 205

bonds, 41, 52, 110; emotional, 42, 43, 129, 135; human–object, 138

Boston Globe, 33

Bourdieu, Pierre, 25, 92, 212

boutiques, neighborhood, 191

Brand, Stewart, 199, 207

branding, 20, 36, 88, 93, 134, 144, 145, 222; logic of, 219–20; personality-driven, 95

Brando, Marlon, 163

brands, 33, 118, 141, 142, 186; clothing, 96; corporate, 219, 220, 229; exposure to, 7; heritage, 143; mass-appeal, 96; popular, 100; prestige, 229

Brave Little Toaster, The (film), 127

Brave New War (Robb), 206

Bravo, 221

Breaking Bad, 195

Brignull, Harry, 101

British Museum, 139

Brogan, Jacob, 163

Brown, Bill, 77

Brown, Janelle, 177

Brown, Tina, 243n9, 244n26

Bruno, Dave, 32

Bryant, Levi, 16

Bukiewicz, Joel, 185

Burke, Kenneth, 111, 112

Buying In: What We Buy and Who We Are (Walker), 143

CAD models, 196, 199

Callon, Michel, 15

Canon cameras, 155

capital: expansion of, 225; labor and, 211

Capital (Marx), 21

capitalism, 27, 35, 77, 202, 207, 212, 222; abstract system of, 90; aesthetic, 18, 20, 74, 91, 93, 213, 217, 221, 224, 227; consumer, 2, 3, 18, 73, 75, 162, 198; cultural life and, 20, 213; evolution of,

214, 218, 229; environment and, 12; fantasy of, 112; language/imagery of, 36; mass-produced, 74; modern, 135

consumer goods, 45, 73, 206

consumerism, 78, 140, 188, 198, 205, 209; cookie-cutter, 177; environmental effects of, 18; excesses of, 71; excessive, 32; rhetoric of, 36; rise of, 212

consumers, 15, 106–7, 133, 165, 188, 202, 227, 230; design and, 98; designers and, 96; imagination of, 2; marketplace and, 176, 211; objects and, 88, 96, 166; participation by, 101

Consumer Society, The (Baudrillard), 212

consumption, 6–7, 11, 14, 19, 25, 31, 38, 67, 70, 74, 167, 175, 176, 186, 207, 209, 213, 219; acts of, 229; collaborative, 219; conspicuous, 7, 177; craft, 190; environmental degradation and, 151, 230; inheritance and, 29; luxury, 190; mass, 17, 77, 140; model of, 95; obsession with, 13; production and, 25–28, 87, 150, 200; surplus, 212, 221; sustainable, 17, 150

Consumption and Its Consequences, 15

Container Store, 31

Coole, Diana, 16

Cooper-Hewitt National Design Museum, 88, 121

Costco, 29, 216

"Couch Arm" (Scher), 147–48

Country Living, 224

cradle-to-cradle (C2C) design, 215

craft, 192; art and, 182; as critique, 180–84; design and, 178–80; human and, 184–89; traditional, 176

Craft Corner Deathmatch, 171

"Crafted" (campaign), 195–99

crafters, 206, 227; corporate, 189–92

crafting, 180, 197; making and, 176, 198; practice/consumption of, 175; technology and, 189

crafting and making process, 167, 177, 227, 230

Craft Lab, 171

craftsmanship, 87, 125, 128, 170, 172, 174, 192, 193–94; handmade, 152; Japanese, 196–97; obsolescence and, 129

Craftsman's Legacy, A (American Public Television), 172

craftsmen, 181, 182, 186, 187, 190, 191, 198; skilled, 173; worker-citizen, 87

Craft Wars, 171

Crate and Barrel, 164, 190

Crawford, Matthew, 100, 133, 187, 190, 201

creativity, 97, 130, 172, 189, 205, 223

critical theory, 16, 21, 27

cultural theory, 15, 88, 90

INDEX

empathy and, 50–51; hidden, 51–52; as mental disorder, 49; as pathology, 47; shame/secrecy of, 47; struggling with, 62, 63; understanding, 75–76

Hoarding: Behind Closed Doors (Discovery Life), 46

Hoarding: Buried Alive (TLC), 46, 74

Holbrook, Morris: on value, 219

Hollywood, 2, 127, 158, 223

Home Depot, 204

Hood, Bruce, 137

Hoornweg, Daniel, 5

Horchow Collection, 113

"How Can an Ancient Craft Inspire a Modern Design?" ("Inside Mazda"), 196

How Do They Do It?, 200

How to Make Everything (YouTube), 184

Hulk, 160

Hunger Games, 72

identity, 43, 94, 110–12; brand, 83, 87, 93, 141, 193, 220; craft, 37; cultural, 157; as fluctuating phenomenon, 158; memory and, 44; unique, 91, 92; veneer of, 113

ideology, 16, 24, 115

IKEA, 28, 86, 97, 98, 101, 106, 114, 142, 145, 159, 188, 227; Bauhaus and, 123, 124; boxes, 102, 130; brand, 115, 134; cartoon about, 104 (fig.); catalog, 112, 120;

commercial from, 126–27; criticism of, 128, 129–30; customers, 107, 116, 120; design by, 120–22, 125; disposability and, 125–32; durability/cost and, 124; effect studies and, 130, 134, 166, 205, 226; fantasy of, 118, 120; fetishization and, 115; identification with, 110–11; imagery of, 119; as lying facade, 122–25; mass production and, 179; materials used by, 109, 124, 128; message from, 126; modularity of, 108; nesting instinct and, 113; objects by, 123, 134, 179; PAX system of, 108; self-assembly and, 167; shopping at, 116–17, 131; slogan from, 121; thesis of, 130; waste generation by, 129

IKEAFans.com, 109

IKEA furniture, 102, 103–4, 109, 124, 127–28, 132, 134; assembling, 104, 107, 118; experiencing, 111; imagining, 226–27

IKEA hackers, 106–11, 130, 176, 178, 199, 206, 226

Illinois Institute of Technology, 123, 248n38

iMac computers, 87

imagination, 2, 45, 111, 119, 147, 172, 183

"Imported from Detroit," 194–95

industrialization, 4, 58, 119, 182, 197, 211

266

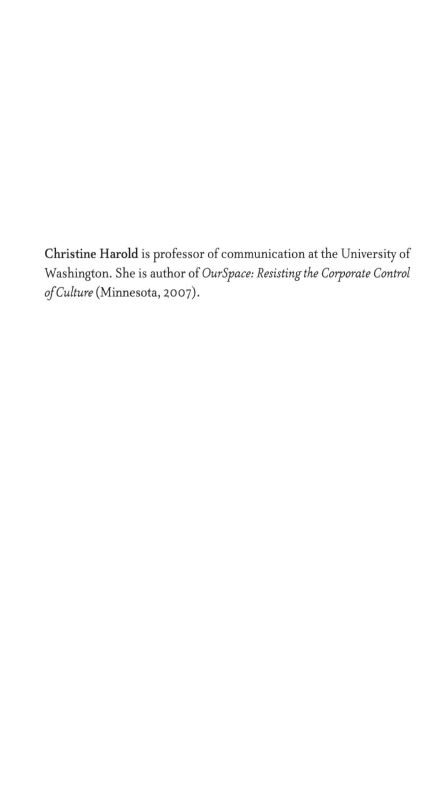

Christine Harold is professor of communication at the University of Washington. She is author of *OurSpace: Resisting the Corporate Control of Culture* (Minnesota, 2007).

CPSIA information can be obtained
at www.ICGtesting.com
Printed in the USA
BVHW071500230620
581832BV00009B/138